Developmental Macroeconomics

T0384430

Developmental Macroeconomics: New developmentalism as a growth strategy offers a new approach to development economics and macroeconomics. It is a Keynesian–structuralist approach to economics applied to middle income countries that emphasizes the strategic role of demand in creating investment opportunities that are essential to economic development. It also explores crucial links between short-term full employment and financial stability with medium-term growth.

While this book emphasizes the central role played by the exchange rate, it does not ignore other macroeconomic prices (the interest rate, the inflation rate, and the profit rate). It develops a group of concepts and models and blends them together in the model of the tendency to the cyclical overvaluation of the exchange rate in developing countries. According to this model, the exchange rate tends to be chronically overvalued. Insofar as this is true the exchange rate ceases to be just a short-term problem to be treated by macroeconomics and becomes central to development economics. It should be crucially oriented to manage the exchange rate and keep it competitive at the industrial equilibrium level.

The book closes with the presentation of new developmentalism – a national development strategy based on the system of models previously discussed that is both an alternative to old national-developmentalism and to liberal orthodoxy or the Washington consensus.

Luiz Carlos Bresser-Pereira is Emeritus Professor of Getulio Vargas Foundation, Brazil.

José Luís Oreiro is Associate Professor at Universidade Federal do Rio de Janeiro, Brazil.

Nelson Marconi is Associate Professor and Head of Research Center for Structuralist Development Macroeconomics at Sao Paulo School of Economics, Brazil.

Routledge Studies in Development Economics

Developmental Macroeconomics

New developmentalism as a growth strategy

Luiz Carlos Bresser-Pereira, José Luís Oreiro, and Nelson Marconi

Routledge
Taylor & Francis Group

LONDON AND NEW YORK

First published 2015 by Routledge

2 Park Square, Milton Park, Abingdon, Oxfordshire OX14 4RN
52 Vanderbilt Avenue, New York, NY 10017

Routledge is an imprint of the Taylor & Francis Group, an informa business

First issued in paperback 2018

British Library Cataloguing in Publication Data
A catalogue record for this book is available from the British Library

Library of Congress Cataloging-in-Publication Data
Developmental macroeconomics : new developmentalism as a growth strategy /
    edited by Luiz Carlos Bresser-Pereira, José Luís Oreiro and Nelson Marconi.
        pages cm
    Includes bibliographical references and index.
  1. Development economics. 2. Macroeconomics. 3. Foreign exchange
rates—Developing countries. 4. Economic development—Developing
countries. I. Pereira, Luiz Carlos Bresser. II. Oreiro, José Luís.
III. Marconi, Nelson.
    HD75.D4987 2014
    339.509172'4—dc23
    2014008579

ISBN: 978-0-415-81778-3 (hbk)
ISBN: 978-0-367-17879-6 (pbk)

Typeset in Times New Roman
by Apex CoVantage, LLC

Contents

Figures

Tables

Preface

This book is an attempt to illicit a new way of thinking. New not only in relation to neoclassical thinking, but also in relation to Keynesian thinking – although the authors are part of this school of thought. New, essentially, because it views as the main macroeconomic variables the exchange rate and the current account deficits, instead of the interest rate and the budget deficits. New because we argue, counter-intuitively, that in most of the time developing countries should portray current account surpluses instead of current account deficits. New because it argues it is not enough to guarantee effective demand; that, additionally, is necessary to assure *access* to it. This is a theory book, but the historical models that constitute it are or intend to be the representation of how developing countries – particularly middle-income countries – grow with financial and price stability.

Economic theory seeks to understand how capitalist economic systems work and which policies should be used to make them perform better. It aims to improve the standards of living and make the national systems more stable and less inequalitarian. An economic system is *stable* when it is approaches full employment, when inflation is low, and when the threat of financial crises is remote. It *develops* when productivity and per capita income increase in a sustained way, wages increase, and standards of living improve. It is reasonably *fair* when economic inequalities are moderate. In this book, our goal is to set out simple and consistent developmental macroeconomics and the associated policies designed to achieve these objectives. It discusses how developing countries, particularly middle-income countries, use the two fundamental institutions at their disposal – the state or the government[1] (the legal system and the organization that sustains it) and the market – to achieve economic growth with stability and converge to the levels of per capita income of rich countries.

Our approach is Keynesian and developmental, and our method, historical–deductive, not hypothetic–deductive. Keynesian macroeconomics began in 1936 with the publication of the *General Theory.* Development economics (which we will call in this book "developmental economics" to emphasize its historical–deductive character and to distinguish it from the neoclassical economics of models of growth) was conceived between the 1940s and the 1960s, in the context of the great optimism in the aftermath of World War II. The structuralist pioneers of development economics framed a theory and a development strategy that criticized neoclassical economics and economic liberalism, and showed that developing countries depended on state intervention in order to carry out their industrial revolution.[2] Developmental economics as well as Keynesian macroeconomics prevailed between the 1940s and the 1960s, largely as a result of the crash of 1929 and of the Great Depression of the 1930s, which caused the collapse of economic liberalism and of the neoclassical theory that legitimized it. The postwar era was the time of the Bretton Woods regulation of international finance, of the World Bank as a developmental institution, and of the Golden Years of Capitalism. Several developing countries profited from developmental theories and strategies by industrializing and transforming themselves into middle-income countries.

However, in the 1970s the economic slowdown that occurred in the U.S. and British economies resulted, towards the end of that decade, in a crisis in Keynesian and structuralist ideas. This crisis which made it possible for neoliberal ideology and neoclassical economics to become once again hegemonic or *mainstream* in the universities. In 1981 Albert Hirschman composed the obituary of developmental economics. Whereas the huge financial crisis that was the foreign debt crisis of the 1980s debilitated the Latin American countries and led them to surrender to the liberal orthodoxy, the fast-growing Asian countries suffered less; their elites proved to be less dependent, and remained more faithful to the structuralist ideas. Yet some of them were not as resistant to the Washington Consensus as they should have been – which explains the major financial crisis that four of them experienced in 1997 – but eventually they were able to change from the old developmentalism to the new during the 1980s.

In Latin America some economists, including the three authors of this book, were unhappy with the hegemony of neoclassical ideas in the 1990s, with a "policy regime" so dominant that governments adopted dominance of a set of policies regardless of whether the political coalition in power was conservative or social democratic (Przeworski, 2001). Well before the 2008 Global Financial Crisis, we realized that a succession of financial crises had demonstrated the failure of neoliberal policies and reforms. They achieved some price stability but did not guarantee financial stability, or growth, or a reasonable income distribution. At that time, as of the early 2000s, one of the authors of this book revived the idea of developmentalism – of a "new developmentalism" – and designed the first models that would constitute developmental macroeconomics, for the first time fully developed in this book.

Developmental macroeconomics is the theory and new developmentalism is the economic strategy that developing countries should use to achieve accelerated economic development with macroeconomic stability. A structuralist macroeconomics was already a concern for the pioneers of economic development and gained a more specific and formal quality thanks to the work of Lance Taylor (1983, 2004). In the Latin American countries, the failure of the neoclassical tradition and of the liberal orthodoxy in promoting development with stability, or, in other words, the succession of financial crises, phases of low growth, and exacerbation of economic inequalities that characterized the neoliberal years, opened the way for developmental political leaders and for new ideas – for a revival of structuralism and Keynesianism. The new developmentalism is associated with this revival and with a review of the previous developmental ideas, which on one hand had become exhausted insofar as countries had reached a new stage of development, and on the other hand had been hindered by populist practices in the context of the foreign debt crisis of the 1980s.

The new ideas originated in a paper by Bresser-Pereira and Nakano, "Economic growth cum foreign savings?" (2003) and a paper by Bresser-Pereira, "The new developmentalism and conventional orthodoxy" (2006). Also in 2006, Luiz Fernando de Paula published "Rethinking developmentalism" (2006), and Paulo Gala concluded his PhD dissertation: "Foreign exchange policy and the macroeconomics of development" (2006). In 2007 Bresser-Pereira published a book on the Brazilian economy, *Developing Brazil: Overcoming the Failure of the Washington Consensus,* where he applied the new models to the Brazilian economy. In 2008, in the paper "The Dutch disease and its neutralization: a Ricardian approach", he introduced the concept of "industrial equilibrium exchange rate". In 2009, José Luis Oreiro and Luiz Fernando de Paula circulated the paper "New developmentalism and the agenda of macroeconomic reforms for sustained development with prices stability and social equity", in which they argued that "the new macroeconomic model for Brazil should be based on these pillars: a flexible inflation target regime, a fiscal regime based on the generation of current account surpluses, and foreign exchange rate management". All these ideas came together in Bresser-Pereira's *Globalization and Competition* (2009) where the thesis of the tendency to the cyclical and chronic overvaluation of the exchange rate first appeared. Robert Boyer, writing the Introduction to the French edition of this book, suggested that a new school of thought was emerging in Brazil. Actually, a significant group of development economists were working together to rebuild developmental economics that was now evolving towards a developmental macroeconomics or structuralist development macroeconomics. In the United States, Lance Taylor was a pioneer in that matter. In Geneva, this rebirth was evident in the *Trade and Development Reports* of UNCTAD, first under the coordination of Yilmaz Ayuz and Jan Kregel, and later of Heiner Flassback, which provided development economics with a more solid macroeconomic foundation; in Paris, Michel Aglietta and Robert Boyer oriented the Regulation School to the study of financial crises; in Cambridge, Ha-Joon Chang organized the Caporde – Cambridge Advanced Program on Rethinking Macro and Development Economics – a program that revived the structuralist approach to economic growth with the participation, among others, of Gabriel Palma and José Antonio Ocampo; in Brazil, Luiz Gonzaga Belluzzo and Luciano Coutinho, in Unicamp, elaborated the critique of financialization; and, in Argentina, Roberto Frenkel and his group of economists at CEDES promoted the study of the relations between finance and macroeconomics. In May 2010, with support from the Ford Foundation, an international workshop was held in São Paulo on the *Ten Theses on New Developmentalism* – a clear alternative to the Washington Consensus.[3] Approved and underwritten in the months that followed by a large number of world-renowned economists and political scientists, the document now has its own website and the *Ten Theses* are published in various languages. In this way, new developmentalism, which is a development strategy, has become an institution. And, the large number of economists who fell attracted by the new ideas, some people are referring to New Developmental School. This book benefits from all these contributions.

Throughout the book, we try to keep the language at the level of the citizen-reader. It is true that, at certain points, we also made use of mathematics, but in a relatively simple way. And, whenever possible, we prefer graphic explanations to mathematical ones. We are persuaded that basic economics can and should be known to all individuals with a higher education insofar as it serves as a basis for policies that have a direct and lasting effect on the lives of us all.

This book is a collective product in which we benefited from the contributions of many economists and political scientists who, on several points, helped us to develop our ideas: Adam Przeworski, Aldo Ferrer, Amit Bhaduri, Antonio Barros de Castro, Arturo Guillén R., Arturo O'Connell, C.P. Chandreskar, Carlos Aguiar de Medeiros, Cícero Araujo, Deepak Nayar, Edwin Le Heron, Fernando Cardim de Carvalho, Fernando Ferrari Filho, Francisco Eduardo Pires de Souza, Franklin Serrano, Gabriel Palma, Gerald Epstein, Ha-Joon Chang, Heiner Flassback, James Galbraith, Jan Kregel, Jan Priewe, Jayati Ghosh, Kwame Sundaran Jomo, Lance Taylor, Lauro Gonzalez, Lauro Matei, Luiz Antônio Oliveira Lima, Luiz Fernando de Paula, Luiz Gonzaga Belluzzo, Martin Rapetti, Mathias Vernengo, Nelson Barbosa, Osvaldo Sunkel, Pascal Petit, Paulo Gala, Pedro Paulo Zaluth Bastos, Philip Arestis, Pierre Salama, Ricardo Bielschowsky, Ricardo Carneiro, Robert Boyer, Robert Guttmann, Roberto Frenkel, Thomas I. Palley, Vera Cepeda, and Yoshiaki Nakano.

Notes

1 By "state" we understand the sovereign institution in each country: the legal system and the organization that guarantees it. We observe the convention in economics of treating the words "government" and "state" as synonyms, although we sometimes use "government" to mean the governing process.
2 We refer to economists such as Rosenstein-Rodan, Ragnar Nurkse, Gunnar Myrdal, Raul Prebisch, Hans Singer, Celso Furtado, and Albert Hirschman.
3 The participants in this conference were Amit Bhaduri, Antonio Barros de Castro, C.P. Chandreskar, Daniela Prates, David Kupfer, Edwin Le Heron, Fernando Cardim de Carvalho, Fernando Ferrari, Franklin Serrano, Gabriel Palma, Heiner Flassback, Jan Kregel, Jayati Ghosh, Jose Antonio Ocampo, José Luis Oreiro, Leonardo Burlamaqui, Luiz Carlos Bresser-Pereira, Luiz Fernando de Paula, Nelson Barbosa, Nelson Marconi, Miguel Bruno, Osvaldo Sunkel, Paulo Gala, Philippe Faucher, Ricardo Bielschowsky, Ricardo Carneiro, Robert Boyer, Roberto Frenkel, Rogério Sobreira, Thomas Palley, and Yoshiaki Nakano. We thank them all.

Part I
Growth and constraints

1 Theoretical traditions and the method

Macroeconomics and development economics are usually studied separately, as if it were one thing to study the stability of economic systems, and another to understand the long-term process of economic growth. In this book, we systematically integrate these two perspectives. After all, the long term is the sum of macroeconomic short terms; investment is strategic in achieving sustainable demand as well as economic growth; and full employment is associated with growth. Therefore, it is more reasonable to integrate macroeconomics and development economics under the designation of development macroeconomics. Yet, our approach is not associated with economic liberalism, but with developmentalism – a form of organizing capitalism and achieving the growth and stability that combines reasonably free markets with a moderate intervention of the state. Thus, ours is a Keynesian and structuralist development macroeconomics – or, to be short, a developmental macroeconomics. Our political assumption – which is not discussed in this book, but is discussed at length in Atul Kohli's (2004) *State-Directed Development* – is that the more the state is integrated with the business sector, or the more cohesive the ruling class coalition is oriented to growth, the more developmental the state will be, and the more successful industrialization will be in catching up.

Developmental macroeconomics is a theory applied to developing countries, particularly to middle-income countries where markets are already reasonably efficient in allocating economic resources in the competitive industries. But, as Keynes argued, markets are unable to keep the macroeconomic aggregates balanced. Given the chronic insufficiency of demand in capitalist economies, the expected profit rate tended to be unsatisfactory, and so the rate of investment fell below the level that full employment required. In our developmental macroeconomics, the key macroeconomic variables (besides the investment rate) are composed of the current account deficit and the exchange rate – the less studied of the five macroeconomic prices. Imports, exports, the investment rate, the savings rate, and inflation depend on the exchange rate. Investments depend on it: We may think of the exchange rate as the light switch that connects or disconnects the efficient business enterprises existing in a country from foreign markets and their own domestic markets. We will argue also that the main problem facing developing countries is the tendency towards cyclical and chronic overvaluation of the exchange rate. If this tendency is not dully neutralized, the macroeconomic prices will be out of equilibrium: The exchange rate will be overvalued, the wage rate and all other revenues will be artificially high, the expected profit rate will be depressed, the interest rate will tend to be high, and, if the depreciation of the national currency is still taking place (meaning it didn't level out), the inflation rate will fall. Thus, while the rentier capitalist will be happy with a high real interest rate, the business entrepreneurs – the men and woman who really accumulate capital and innovation – will only invest to keep their plants technologically competitive. Thus, in this book, we will argue for an active exchange rate policy – which, together with the interest rate policy and the fiscal policy, will keep the macroeconomic prices right, and the economy growing with price and *financial* stability.

The tendency to the cyclical and chronic overvaluation of the exchange rate – plus the fact that developing countries are financed with foreign money (money that they cannot issue) – means that developing countries are prone to currency or balance of payment crises, which are seldom observed in rich countries whose governments become indebted in their own money. That is the reason why the typical financial crisis in rich countries is a banking crisis. On the other hand, we will see that developing countries (including middle-income countries) tend to suffer from the Dutch disease – the structural cause of the overvaluation. Other causes include policy (particularly the growth cum foreign savings policy), the use of the exchange rate as an anchor against inflation, and exchange rate populism. Thus, to avoid such overvaluation – which fuels consumption, dampens investments, and exposes countries to cyclical financial crises – developmental macroeconomics shows, counterintuitively, that developing countries should have their current accounts balanced or showing moderate surpluses. Only in special occasions it is true that capital-rich countries should transfer their capitals to capital-poor countries.

Not neoclassical

Our approach is not neoclassical. The distinction between developmental macroeconomics and neoclassical macroeconomics does not require an extended discussion. Developmental macroeconomics adopts a different method. There are two major methodological currents of economic thought: the historical tradition and the hypothetical–deductive tradition. The historical tradition uses the empirical, or historical–deductive, method in order to make generalizations from observations of reality – of the regularities and tendencies that characterize this changing reality. The neoclassical tradition, however, defines its core theories (the general equilibrium and rational–expectations macroeconomics theories) using the hypothetic–deductive method, which is suitable for the methodological sciences – such as mathematics, econometrics, and economic decision-making theory – but unsuitable for the social sciences, which are substantive sciences aiming to explain how social systems are coordinated and change through time.

The two theoretical traditions correspond to two ways of organizing national economic systems, policymaking styles, and associated ideologies. The neoclassical tradition is associated with economic liberalism; the historical tradition, with new developmentalism. New developmentalism – as a growth strategy and as a school of thought – has been associated in the past with mercantilist thought, and today is associated with Keynesian, structuralist, and historical–institutionalist thought.

Economists such as William Petty, Adam Smith, Karl Marx, Thorsten Veblen, John M. Keynes, and Joseph Schumpeter – and developmental structuralists like Gunnar Myrdal and Arthur Lewis – belong to the historical tradition. The authors of this book are likewise associated with it. Within the hypothetical–deductive tradition, the greatest economist was Alfred Marshall. His major contribution to economic thought, however, was not to explain how economic systems operate, but to found a complementary to economic theory and highly relevant autonomous science: the theory of decision-making in markets, or economic decision theory, later completed by game theory. For this discipline, the hypothetical–deductive method, based as it is on axioms, is appropriate because it is a methodological science, not a substantive science such as economics, which deals with a concrete social and economic reality.

The neoclassical school and economic liberalism maintain that it is enough to guarantee property rights and contracts and to keep the public budget in balance; then the market will take care of coordinating the economic system in an optimal way that will generate growth, stability, and a satisfactory distribution of income. In contrast, according to new developmentalism, the government has additional macroeconomic roles. Besides guaranteeing property rights, conducting a responsible fiscal policy (which keeps the budget deficit under control), and implementing a competent monetary policy (which keeps the inflation under control), the government is supposed to have an active exchange policy to keep the current account under control and the exchange rate in equilibrium.

Whereas neoclassical economists develop complex mathematical models from a hypothetical–deductive method that assumes the rationality of economic agents, historical economists observe the behaviour of economic aggregates, search for possible regularities and tendencies, and formulate from them simple economic models. Whereas the hypothetic–deductive method authorizes neoclassical economists to formulate highly mathematized and "precise" models, the historical–deductive method allows for less mathematical and more modest models, which are constantly reviewed as technologies, types of property, power relations, and institutions change, or as econometric studies falsify them. Whereas orthodox economists work with the false certainty of their core models, and uncertainty is something that for them depends not on theoretical castles in the air but on their individual capacity to think, historical economists know from the start that economic agents always make decisions under conditions of uncertainty, and that, therefore, economic policymakers also deal with uncertainty daily.

The neoclassical tradition prevailed in the universities between the end of the nineteenth century and 1929, and between 1979 and 2008. Even though it has proven to be essentially misguided (because it uses an unsuitable method for a substantive science such as economic theory), and also damaging (because it inspires an economic liberalism that assumes that markets are self-regulated and always efficient), it continues to dominate graduate programs in the leading universities. Therefore, it continues to inspire misguided economic policies. There are excellent economists with a neoclassical formation, but their real contributions are made when they forgive their core neoclassical models, and use *general economics* (the economics that all economists are supposed to know) and their privileged intelligence.

Differences from Keynesian and development economics

Our approach is Keynesian and structuralist. It is *Keynesian* because, first, we are persuaded that the obstacles to economic development are on the demand side rather than on the supply side, despite the significance of development factors on the supply side – particularly education and, consequently, technology, innovation, and productivity. Second, because it is not the interest rate that determines savings, and savings that determine investment (as neoclassical theory assumes), but the other way around: It is investment that determines savings, provided that there is credit available to entrepreneurs. In other words, developmental macroeconomics is based on Keynesian and Kaleckian macroeconomics.

But there are substantial differences between developmental and Keynesian macroeconomics, besides the fact that the former focuses on explaining unemployment and discussing how to achieve full employment, whereas developmental macroeconomics is focused in growth with stability – growth that produces catching up. First, in Keynesian macroeconomics there is the tendency to the insufficiency of demand, whereas for developmental macroeconomics there is additionally the tendency to the insufficiency of *access* to demand. Therefore, the core Keynesian argument is that investment depends on the existence of effective demand, whereas for developmental macroeconomics, guaranteeing effective demand is not enough: Governments must also formulate an active exchange rate policy, which assures business enterprises the *access* to demand that an overvalued national currency denies.

Second, given the existence of five macroeconomic prices (the rate of profit, the exchange rate, the interest rate, the wage rate, and the rate of inflation), for Keynesian macroeconomics the *wrong price* is the interest rate, which will be too high in severe recessions due to the liquidity trap. For developmental macroeconomics, besides the interest rate in recessions, there are three chronically wrong macroeconomic prices: the exchange rate, which will tend to be overvalued, the expected profit rate, which will tend to be depressed, and – less clearly – the real interest rate, which will tend to be high (the liquidity trap will have less explicative clout).

Third, whereas for Keynesian (and also neoclassical) macroeconomics, the two *key* macro variables are the budget deficit and the interest rate, for developmental macroeconomics they are the current account deficit (or surplus) and the exchange rate – two variables that are directly interdependent. It is true that, given the twin deficits hypothesis, choice between either one or the other deficit would be indifferent, but such a hypothesis only holds when the exchange rate is in equilibrium, and this does not happen often.

Fourth, whereas for neoclassical and Keynesian macroeconomics, current account deficits are natural, for developmental macroeconomics, they should show a surplus if the country faces the Dutch disease.

Fifth, whereas Keynesian and developmental macroeconomics explain both insufficient savings and financial crises with excessive budget deficits or fiscal populism, developmental macroeconomics also explains them with excessive current account deficits (exchange rate populism).[1]

Sixth, the Keynesian model was originally a closed model, whereas developmental macroeconomics is an open theory from the start.

Seventh, developmental macroeconomics accepts the Keynesian assumption that the exchange rate is highly volatile, but adds that such volatility or such misalignments are not just up-and-down directed, but in developing countries they tend to the overvaluation of the national currency.

Eighth, whereas Keynesian and Minskyan macroeconomics assume that countries become indebted in their own currencies and are prone to banking crises, developmental macroeconomics stresses that developing countries become indebted in foreign currencies (which they can neither issue nor devalue) and, for that reason, are prone to balance of payments or currency crises.

Finally, whereas Keynesian macroeconomics considers only fiscal and interest rate policy, developmental macroeconomics asks for an active exchange rate policy. If the country is able to effectively neutralize the Dutch disease with an export tax on the commodities that originate it, moving the exchange rate to the industrial equilibrium, and if the exchange rate policy is able keep the exchange rate floating around this equilibrium, the developing country will experience not current account deficits, but current account surpluses.

Besides Keynesian, our approach is *structuralist,* meaning it is associated with developmental economics (the theories of Rosenstein-Rodan, Ragnar Nurkse, Gunnar Myrdal, Arthur Lewis, Raul Prebisch, Hans Singer, Albert Hirschman, and Celso Furtado),[2] which was dominant from the mid-1930s to the mid-1970s, together with Keynesian macroeconomics, and were instrumental in the Bretton Woods regulation of the international financial system. Development economics came to a crisis along with Keynesian macroeconomics in the late 1970s, when neoclassical economics once again became mainstream economics. Developmental macroeconomics is structuralist because it sees economic growth as a structural process of technological sophistication. It shares with structuralist economics the historical method, the understanding of economics as political economy, the assumption that the state and the market (regulated by the state) are the two main institutions coordinating capitalist societies, and the understanding of economic growth as a structural process involving the three aspects of a society: the economic, the institutional, and the ideological (or cultural).

But developmental macroeconomics differs from classical structuralism on several accounts. First, developmental economics assumed that developing countries were making their transition to capitalism, and their markets were poorly formed, unable to perform their role of resource allocation in the same way as developed countries. Developmental macroeconomics applies to countries in a different *stage* of growth – to middle-income countries, which are already fully capitalist countries competing in a global economy. The key difference that middle-income countries have in relation to rich countries is not the "traditional" character of their economy and society, but the fact that they get indebted in foreign currency, not in their own currency.

Second, in violation of neoclassical economics, the pioneers of development focused on legitimizing *industrialization,* industrial policy, and economic planning. Their main models, based on the assumption that developing countries had not yet industrialized, were (*a*) the big push model, which is the thesis that new manufacturing business enterprises in preindustrial countries depend on positive economic externalities that originate in other business enterprises investing at the same time in the search for profit – a condition that only a government-managed "big push" could provide; (*b*) the tendency towards the deterioration of the terms of trade, which demonstrated that productivity increases in rich countries were not automatically transferred to developing countries, as neoclassical economics supposes; and (*c*) the infant manufacturing industry argument, which was a well-established argument in favour of the protection of manufacturing industry in the early stages of development since the time of Alexander Hamilton and Friedrich List. Developmental macroeconomics assumes the validity of these criticisms, but downplays their significance because middle-income countries have modernized their economic structure and converged to the market system of advanced capitalist countries.

Third, developmental economics attached great importance to the foreign constraint argument, which showed that in developing countries the income elasticity of demand for imported manufacturing goods was greater than 1, while in rich countries the income elasticity of demand for primary goods exported by developing countries was relatively inelastic, or less than 1. Given the foreign constraint, most structuralist economists favour the growth cum foreign savings policy. Developmental macroeconomics acknowledges the existence of the foreign constraint, but maintains that it has lost much of its explanatory power because middle-income countries have become exporters of manufactured goods. On the other hand, it argues that given the Dutch disease and the high rate of substitution of foreign for domestic savings, developing countries are supposed to grow with current account surplus, not a current account deficit. And for that reason, developmental macroeconomics and new developmentalism are critical of the policy of growth with foreign indebtedness. They don't reject foreign direct investment, but don't welcome multinational enterprises whose aim is just to occupy the domestic markets. They require that foreign investments come accompanied with transference of technology and contribute to exports of the country.

Fourth, developmental economics developed the structuralist theory of inflation based on the assumption that in some markets, the supply didn't respond to an increase in demand, and such price inelasticity generated a structural inflation. Developmental macroeconomics argues that today this type of explanation has become marginal insofar as middle-income countries evince well-structured markets.

Fifth, the core policy of developmental economics is industrial policy. When we read major books analyzing the developmental states – such as the books by Chalmers Johnson on Japan (1982), by Alice Amsden on South Korea (1989), and by Robert Wade on Taiwan (1990), or Linda Weiss's (1998) analysis of the three experiences – what we read is essentially a system of successful industrial policies coupled, in the case of the latter, with government–industry cooperation. Developmental economics and new developmentalism are in favour of industrial policy, and strongly emphasize the need of a developmental class coalition, but their core policy is not the set of strategic policies that form an industrial policy: It is exchange rate policy. Industrial policy was only able to successfully promote the growth of these countries because they were adopted within a macroeconomic environment in which the interest rate and the exchange rate were not wrong, but right prices. Developmental macroeconomics does not confound industrial policy with exchange rate policy, as structuralist economists did when they neutralized the Dutch disease with the use of high import taxes and export subsidies and interpreted that policy as "industrial policy", whereas neoclassical critics viewed it as "protectionism". For developmental macroeconomics and new developmentalism, exchange rate policy, not industrial policy, is the key macroeconomic policy, together with monetary and fiscal policy. This explains why growth with financial stability requires, besides fiscal responsibility (in Keynesian terms), exchange rate responsibility.

Sixth, developmental economics argued for economic planning; development macroeconomics and new developmentalism favour economic planning but only to the non-competitive sector of the economy. It claims that, in middle-income economies, the market is the best institution to allocate the factors of production within its competitive sector, but a modern economy has a large non-competitive sector – particularly the infrastructure industry and some basic industries – in which the coordination by the market is by definition absent, regulatory agencies have a limited role, and the government must coordinate the required investments and make a part of them.

Given its Keynesian and structuralist approach, would developmental macroeconomics and new developmentalism also be *institutionalist?* Yes and no. Yes, because the institutions are the fundamental form of coordinating societies, but the problem with them is that they are present in the three structural "instances" of society (the economic, the political or normative, and the ideological), but particularly in the political instance, where the key institution is the state or the government (the two expressions are equivalent).[3] When we think of structures, we must also think of institutions, because they are the norms that directly affect and modify behaviours. Structuralism and institutionalism were the outcome of nineteenth-century German thought – of Marxism and of the German Historical School, including Max Weber. Institutions are the fundamental norms that coordinate societies. Social change happens when change occurs in any of these instances; change in one instance propagates to the others. In some cases changes in the economic and social structures precede changes in institutions; in other cases, institutions change first. They are embodied in the relations of production or the forms of property that exist in the economic instance, in the political instance, and also in the ideological instance.

When we don't have a clear notion that institutions are part of society's infrastructure we may easily make the mistake of believing that we can change institutions, that we can promote "reforms", without taking into consideration the country's structural stage of development. By being just institutionalist (not asserting the structural character of growth) we may incur the mistake of believing that a country needs only to protect property rights and contracts to experience growth. Instead, for us, development's primary institution is the set of informal agreements, understandings, goals, laws, and public policies that constitute a "national development strategy", creating investment opportunities for business enterprises. We also understand economic development as a process of structural change that happens, historically, within each country. Finally, we understand that development amounts to industrialization, or, more broadly, to *productive sophistication,* meaning the continuous transfer of labour from low to high per capita value-added industries with diversification of the productive structure. Thus, we may say that we are institutionalist, but our institutionalism is historical, not just hypothetical–deductive.

The method

Our method is *historical* in several senses. First, because the main models that we will develop are historical models; they are generalizations based on the regularities and tendencies that we observe in the real world, rather than mathematical deductions from axioms. Second, because actual middle-income countries are our reference group – countries with developed capitalist markets, relatively capable governments, competent business enterprises, and a large middle class. However, unlike rich countries, they don't get indebted in their own currency, but in foreign currencies that they cannot issue. The historical models that we develop intend to be the generalization of the actual behaviour of economic agents, instead of hypothetic models deduced from *homo economicus* and associated with general equilibrium. Historical models are not precise (because economic regularities are never full regularities), but from them we can deduce policy. In developing our historical models, we often qualify our generalizations with adverbs such as "usually" or "often" to underline their provisional, or *modest,* character. Third, in building our models, we take into consideration the behaviour of economic agents and also the behaviour of policymakers. Or, in other words, we assign a major role to what we call in this book "conventional policies" or "conventional policymaking". To the extent that these policies are conventionally adopted, it is possible to predict how, in the medium-term, economic systems will evolve.

Historical models should not be confused with what we call "economic syllogisms", which start from a conditional premise to achieve to a conclusion. Economic syllogism can be useful when attempting to understand certain economic relations, but either they are false if the premise is false, or they are dangerous if policymakers derive directly policy from them. The more general example of false economic syllogism is "given that man is rational, we can deduce from that the core models of economics". Examples of useful but dangerous syllogisms are the law of comparative advantages,[4] the Marx-inspired identity relating the capital-output rate with the profit rate and the functional distribution of income,[5] the Marshall-Lerner condition, or Thirlwall's law. They are logical, but their premises are conditional, and, for that reason, we cannot derive policy from them. When

Schumpeter called "Ricardian vice" the practice of deducing policies from theories, he was probably thinking in economic syllogisms, not in historical models.

Summary

In short, developmental macroeconomics is a Keynesian and structuralist system of thought. It innovates in several accounts to have explanatory power in a changed world where middle-income countries compete. To do that, developmental macroeconomics and new developmentalism benefit from a historical–deductive method, which is less "precise", or less mathematical, than the core of neoclassical economics, but has more explicative and predictive power, and leads good policymakers to make less and less serious policy mistakes.

Developmental macroeconomics asserts that the growth rate will be a function of the rate of capital accumulation. This rate depends on the expected rate of profit (and the interest rate) – which, in turn, depends on the existence of demand and on the *access* to it, which is only assured when the exchange rate is floating around its competitive equilibrium. In this book, we call this "industrial equilibrium exchange rate" – the exchange rate that makes competitive the business enterprises that use state-of-the-art technologies independently of protectionist policies. The purpose of development is to increase wages and the standards of living. But, a caveat: This goal cannot be achieved if liberal, as well as developmental, policymakers display a high preference for immediate consumption by keeping the exchange rate chronically overvalued. Keynes didn't abolish scarcity or condemn frugality; he only showed that in moments of insufficiency of demand, to increase expending instead of saving is the best conduct. When countries incur chronic budget deficits – and, mainly, when they accept the current account deficit and the matching overvalued currency – they are choosing consumption, not growth.

Notes

1 Whereas vulgar liberal orthodoxy resolves all problems with reducing government expenditures, vulgar Keynesians do the same by increasing government expenditures.
2 These were some of the "pioneers of development". They built development economics. Although only the Latin-American branch of development economics called their theory "structuralist", we understand that all were structuralists.
3 We will use the two expressions interchangeably. When we, in Portuguese, refer to "governo" to indicate the sum of politicians and bureaucrats that governs, we will use the expression "the administration" or "the government authorities".
4 The "law of comparative advantage" is a perfect syllogism that shows the advantages of international trade, but not as a historical model. We cannot predict that countries that frame their trade policy accordingly will experience faster growth rates than those that ignore it. In the early stages of development we observe precisely the opposite.
5 The equation that Marx used to argue on the falling tendency of the rate of profit was $K/W = K/Y \, / \, W/Y$, where K/W is the organic composition of capital. Adapting it to the capital–output ratio, we have the identity relating the productivity of capital, capital–output rate, with the profit rate and the functional distribution of income between profits and wages, $K/Y = K/R \, / \, Y/R$.

2 Some definitions and productive sophistication

Historically, economic development is a process of capital accumulation with systematic incorporation of technical progress, which implies increasing productivity and improvement of the standard of living. It begins when a given people become a nation, build a state, and achieve an industrial revolution.[1] It is only from then on that technical progress gains momentum and business enterprises have no alternative but to reinvest its profits to remain competitive.

In the framework, the strategic role is shared by the state and the business enterprises. Whereas the state, which is the main institution in each society, invests in the infrastructure and in the basic industries, the entrepreneurs invest and innovate in the competitive industries. In the growth process, all institutions are relevant, but the key one for growth is the state or the government, which we understand as being the law system and the sovereign organizations that guarantee it. The state is the main instrument of collective action of each nation; it is the main tool for the achievement of its political goals of security, freedom, welfare, social justice, and protection of the environment. In this respect, the state is the normative institution that, together with the market, coordinates the modern economic systems. Therefore, there is no sense in the opposition between the state and the market. Instead, we need to understand the historical relationship between the two institutions. In the early phase of economic development – in which the original accumulation and the industrial revolution take place – the government has been without exception the main agent of economic development. This is true for England and France, which made their industrial revolution in the framework of the mercantilist system, and of the United States, where trade liberalization began just before World War II. In certain cases, as in Japan, Russia, and China, the state became practically absolute in this role. But once this industrial revolution was over, the government gradually withdrew from productive activities and transferred them to entrepreneurs and private enterprises, except for part of the monopolistic or quasi-monopolistic enterprises that the market is not able to coordinate.[2] From then on, in the competitive sector of each national economy, the economic coordination has been the role of the market, whereas to the government fell the coordination of investments and the close regulation of the monopolistic sectors, particularly infrastructure. For the economy as a whole, it fell to the government to carry out active macroeconomic policy to guarantee financial and price stability, demand, and *access* to demand to the competent business enterprises. The need to manage aggregate demand was demonstrated by Keynes by criticizing Say's Law, according to which supply creates its own demand. The need to guarantee to the business enterprises utilizing world state-of-the-art technology will be demonstrated in this book.

A classification of countries

In this book, we are not just interested in growth, we are interested in catching up. But since economic development entered the agenda of all countries after World War II, many countries developed, but just a few – South Korea, Taiwan, Singapore, and China – were able to show real convergence to the levels of income per capita and standards of living of rich countries. Developmental macroeconomics and new developmentalism are an attempt to understand which national development strategy worked for not only these countries, but also the countries that developed and became a middle-income country but didn't catch up, like Brazil. We also aim to develop a new structuralist development macroeconomics to explain the success and the failures that all these countries experienced in the last 70 years.

According to the classification that we will use in this book, countries are either rich countries or developing countries. The latter may be poor, preindustrial, middle-income, or emerging countries. Capitalist societies that have already realized their industrial revolution are categorized as middle-income countries; countries that are in the process of realizing their industrial revolution are preindustrial; countries that are far from realizing their industrial revolution are poor. This is just a descriptive classification. In order to understand the catching up and underline the national character of economic growth, an alternative classification distinguishes the "original development countries" from the "late development countries". Original development countries are those that achieved their primitive accumulation and their industrial revolution without having to face industrial or modern imperialism. Those countries include Britain, followed by France, Belgium, the Netherlands, and the United States, and later Germany, Italy, the Scandinavian countries, and three countries colonized by Britain besides the United States: Canada, Australia, and New Zealand.[3] All of these countries adopted a developmental strategy in order to achieve their industrial revolutions and didn't have to challenge industrial or modern imperialism in order to develop. They include four countries that belonged to the British Empire because Britain's colonization did not involve slave mercantile exploitation, as happened in Latin American countries and in the South of the United States, but a colonization by settlement in which the settlers reproduced the type of advanced society that existed in Britain, rather than organizing plantations to export tropical goods or devoting themselves to mining.[4] Original economic development has been studied by a great number of analysts, from renowned economists such as Adam Smith and Karl Marx to celebrated historians such as Alexander Gerschenkron,[5] Fernand Braudel, and David Landes. Germany and the Scandinavian countries, whose development took place in the second half of the nineteenth century, are included in this category.

The first late development country was Japan, who made the Meiji Restoration (1868) to challenge the foreign domination and industrialize. All middle-income countries today are latecomers that had to face the rich imperial countries' practice of "kicking away the ladder" to get involved in productive sophistication and grow.[6] Among middle-income countries it is possible to distinguish between those that have achieved full national autonomy, have a national developmental strategy and, therefore, grow fast and achieve catching up, and those that continue to face the contradictions that characterize what we call "national-dependent" development – an oxymoron that well describes the ambiguity of their elites – and grow more slowly. The first group includes, among others, South Korea, India, and China; the second group, countries like Mexico and Brazil, which have not been able to achieve full national autonomy; in the 1970s they became highly indebted in foreign currencies, in the 1980s they experienced a major financial crisis, which their ambivalent elites were unable to resolve, and, around 1990, submitted to the neoliberal consensus.

Productive sophistication and wages

Economic development is a process of capital accumulation with the incorporation of technical progress, resulting in an increase in productivity, wages, and the population's standard of living. This increase in productivity is associated with industrialization or, more precisely, with "productive sophistication": the transfer of labour to sectors with higher value added per capita. This association of economic growth with technological sophistication was already known in the distant year of 1336, when the English King Edward III prohibited exports of raw wool; he wanted the production of wool to be completed by the production of fabric in order to increase the value added by English workers to the product. From this perspective, the increase in productivity, or in efficiency in production, happens not only in the same goods and services produced (a microeconomic approach), but also in the transfer of labour to technologically more sophisticated goods and services, which pays higher wages and implies a higher value added per capita (a developmental approach).

Of the two forms of technical progress or of productivity increase – one taking place in the same products, the other occurring with the transfer of labour to industries with higher value added per capita – the latter is more important in promoting catching up. If a country produces both a simple product such as a commodity, and a complex product such as a cell phone, it will be easier for this country to increase productivity by transferring labour to the production of the phone than by continuing to produce the commodity.

Economic development makes sense only if it implies an increase in actual wages and an improvement in standards of living. In the short run, wages fluctuate according to the supply and demand of labour, reflecting workers' skills and negotiating power. This power, in turn, depends on the unemployment rate and on institutional factors that affect labour relations. In the long run, wages are determined foremost by the cost of reproduction of the workforce as long as there is an unlimited supply of labour, which, in turn, is determined not merely by biological factors but also by the prevailing social and historical conditions and customs. This is what enabled the classical economists, in their theory of distribution, to consider wages as given and profits as the residue – what remained after the payment of the living wage. And this assumption also enabled the classical economists to formulate the hypothesis of the tendency to a falling profit rate and to economic stagnation in the long run, even though labour productivity continued to increase in their own time. For Ricardo, the stagnation would be caused by the decrease in land productivity due to the cultivation of increasingly less fertile areas; and for Marx it would be caused by the decrease in capital productivity, that is, in the output–capital ratio, caused by a more capital-intensive work processes together with capital-intensive technical progress.[7]

But these hypotheses were not borne out historically. First, there was no decrease in productivity, whether of land or of capital. Second, when the supply of labour ceased to be unlimited in each country, it was noticed that the wages began to increase with the increase in labour productivity. Third, the profit rate did not fall; it continued to fluctuate within the business cycle, but remained constant in the long run. These facts led Bresser-Pereira (1986) to propose a new theory of distribution that inverted the classical theory. Rather than the wages, it is the profit rate that is assumed to remain constant in the long term, and wages are the residuum, growing with productivity if technical progress is neutral. The profit rate fluctuates widely throughout the economic cycle, but in the long run remains at a satisfactory level for entrepreneurs to invest because technical progress is no longer capital-intensive. In particular, it no longer implies replacing labour with capital, and has become neutral (i.e. with a constant output–capital ratio), or even capital-saving, insofar as technical progress in the main ceases to flow from "mechanization" (the replacement of labour with capital) but involves replacing old, less efficient machines with more efficient ones.

Wages rise proportionately to the increase in labour productivity when technical progress is neutral. If technical progress is capital-intensive, the profit rate being the same, wages increase more slowly less productivity. Since wages were at the subsistence level at the time of the classical economists, it was impossible to reduce them in real terms. This is why the classical economists predicted stagnation. Yet when technical progress involves saving capital, wages can grow faster than productivity while leaving the profit margin at a sufficient level to attract investment. This is what seems to have happened in the rich countries after World War II, when for the first time in the history of capitalism the rate of inequality fell consistently for two or three decades. However, as of the mid-1970s real wages in those countries began to grow more slowly than productivity, and income became concentrated again, even though technical progress was no longer characterized by capital-intensive "mechanization" (replacement of labour with capital) but by the capital-saving replacement of less efficient machines with more efficient ones (Bresser-Pereira, 1986). The chief explanation for this change is exogenous to the economic systems of those countries. The fall in wages growth below that of productivity reflected pressure on wages from, first, new competition originating in the developing countries – which, in the 1970s, started to export manufactured goods – and second, migration to rich countries.

In this chapter, our subject is the relationship between wages, development, and industrialization in the developing countries. We begin by analyzing the initial building phase of a capital base, generally through commodity exports that profit from Ricardian rents and, later, the import-substitution industrialization, which benefits from the existence of an unlimited supply of labour. This strategy, however, is necessarily limited and exhausted if wages remain depressed by an excess supply of labour, since the problem arises from lack of demand. The most successful countries solved this problem by exporting manufactured goods and by concentrating income among the upper class and the middle class, while the wage increases for less skilled workers were held below the increase in productivity. Finally, we demonstrate how wages are determined in the process of industrialization. Wages increase as labour becomes technically skilled; however, it is transferred from sectors with low value added per capita to sectors with high value added per capita. Thus, the classical theory of value helps us to understand the increase in wages and economic development as long as the economic sectors with higher value added per capita are technologically sophisticated sectors, which require skilled labour at the technical and administrative levels whose socially acceptable cost of reproduction becomes increasingly higher.

The "Lewis turning point"

Poor and pre-industrial countries have a productive structure in which subsistence (traditional sectors) and modern sectors coexist. They are "dual" societies, in which the traditional sectors, usually concentrated in subsistence agriculture and in services, live side by side with the more advanced sectors, concentrated in manufacturing and service industries. As a result, Arthur Lewis (1954) identified the existence of an unlimited supply of labour in those countries – a supply of workers from the traditional sectors that can be transferred to the modern sectors. Goods produced in traditional sectors require few skills on the part of the workers; therefore, value added per capita, or productivity, is low, and wages are correspondingly low also.

Economic development usually takes place in these countries when local or foreign entrepreneurs take advantage of the availability of abundant and cheap natural resources – and the Ricardian rents that they provide – and are able to produce a commodity according to international standards and export it. However, the average wages paid by this sector are very low and do not increase in direct proportion to productivity because the entrepreneurs profit from the unlimited supply of labour in the traditional sector. Through the production of commodities the country achieves its primitive capital accumulation. The government participates in the formation of this original accumulation by taxing the exports of those commodities and investing the revenue in the country's infrastructure.

From a certain moment on, the country will industrialize (if it is able to neutralize the Dutch disease, which permanently appreciates the exchange rate), profiting from the energy, transportation, and communications infrastructure that the commodity exports financed. The industrial revolution then breaks out, led by the combined investments of the government and industrial entrepreneurs. In a first stage, the problem of demand is solved by the import–substitution strategy because it creates demand for intermediate goods. At the same time, income becomes concentrated, given the existence of an unlimited supply of labour, which remains because, as Furtado (1966) suggests, investments are highly capital-intensive. This import–substitution stage must be brief because it implies that productive efficiency is falling as an increasing number of industries are protected. This stage tends to begin with the protection of manufacturing industries, in which the country can achieve satisfactory productivity, but over time substitution is extended to increasingly sophisticated industries whose production the country is not able to conduct efficiently, and so it requires (harmful) protection.

Once import–substitution industrialization is exhausted, the problem arises of the insufficiency of demand. Entrepreneurs still benefit from low wages but they lack buyers. Growth requires domestic demand, but this demand tends to remain insufficient insofar as there still is an unlimited supply of labour, and wages increase at a lower rate than productivity. Despite this, for a certain period the low incomes of unskilled workers can be offset by the salaries of the techno-bureaucratic middle class, which grow and represent an alternative source of aggregate demand. This class buys luxury consumption goods, especially vehicles. However, this strategy is also short-lived because it implies a still greater income concentration. From then on, the deficiency in demand that results from the tendency of wages to grow more slowly than productivity manifests itself very clearly and becomes a greater obstacle to sustained growth. Growth rates decline and the drive to product diversification loses impetus. In this setting, profit margins are high but the level of the aggregate demand is not enough to encourage entrepreneurs to invest. The country can no longer rely only on protected domestic demand to continue growing and industrializing. It has no alternative but to export the manufactured goods whose technology it has mastered. This is what happened in Brazil and South Korea in the 1960s. In addition, the government can adopt a wage policy of real wage increases in order to guarantee domestic demand, particularly by raising the minimum wage, but this policy is limited by the entrepreneurs' required satisfactory profit rate. And government may increase its investment and social expenditure, which increases wages indirectly. This is more efficient than increasing wages when it comes to improving people's quality of life and of creating demand.

When a country accomplishes this second stage of its industrialization, and engages in the export of manufactured goods, it completes its industrial and capitalist revolution and becomes a medium-income country. For some time its international competitiveness still benefits from the unlimited supply of labour that continues to force down wages. China and India, for instance, present these conditions today. However, as a result of the process of industrialization and urbanization, the birth rate falls, while life expectancy indicators increase, and the government invests in the substantial social services of education, health care, and social security. Around 15–20 years after the fall in the birth rate, the labour supply is affected, and the country attains the "Lewis turning point" – the point at which the unlimited supply of labour runs out. Also, the insufficient growth of domestic demand – due to the tendency of wages to grow at a lower rate than productivity – is no longer an obstacle to development. This, for instance, is what happened in Brazil in the 2000s. From then on, wages grow along with productivity and the domestic market once again plays a decisive role in economic development. However, this does not mean that the country can return to the import–substitution model. The maintenance of growth will depend on the country's ability to continue to export manufactured goods because it will remain infeasible, from an economic standpoint, to reduce the coefficient of imports. Investment will also have to be substantial in order to guarantee a productivity increase in line with the increase in wages caused by the exhaustion of the unlimited supply of labour. This, in turn, strengthens the domestic market and guarantees the necessary profit rate to the entrepreneurs.

Summary

Briefly, economic development is a process of capital accumulation with the incorporation of technical progress and improvement in the standards of living of a country's population. It is a historical process associated with a country's national and industrial revolution, or capitalist revolution. It is only when a nation succeeds in actually forming an autonomous nation–state that it is able to build a domestic market and promote industrialization, which is initially oriented to this domestic market. For backward countries, economic development is a process of catching up in which they are forced to cope with the industrial imperialism of the countries that originally industrialized.

Economic development is a process of increasing the productivity of labour or per capita income that implies industrialization or, more precisely, productive sophistication. There are two ways of increasing productivity. One is to improve the productive processes of a given good or service; the other is to transfer labour from technologically unsophisticated, low-skilled sectors where employees have low skill levels, receive low wages, and represent low value added per capita, to technologically sophisticated sectors that require skilled labour. This second way of increasing productivity is historically more important and expresses itself in industrialization – the transfer of labour from agriculture to manufacturing industry. Today, however, when we also have highly technologically sophisticated services, it is better to identify economic development not with industrialization but with productive sophistication.

Economic development in a backward country often begins with the production of commodities from which the country derives Ricardian rents and, for that reason, can be exported with profit despite low productivity. In a second moment, if the country is able to neutralize the Dutch disease, the country industrializes through import substitution. Yet this kind of growth, based on protected domestic demand, is soon exhausted insofar as the excessively protected manufacturing industry becomes inefficient. After an inevitable economic crisis, the successful country profits from cheap labour by exporting manufactured goods, whereas the existing unlimited supply of labour depresses wages and domestic demand. Eventually, as the birth rate falls, the unlimited supply of labour is also exhausted, and the developing country, which is now a middle-income country, reaches the "Lewis turning point", after which growth, productivity, wages, and exports must grow in a relatively balanced way.

Notes

1 By "people", we mean a group that usually has a common history and a shared destiny; a "nation" is this same group when, in the context of the capitalist revolution, it is able to form a sovereign state.
2 Japanese industrialization in the late nineteenth century was almost completely undertaken by the state; around 1910, however, there was a fast and radical process of privatization. As for Russia and China, the revolutions that pretended to be socialist were in fact national and industrial revolutions; paradoxically, they were part of the capitalist revolution.
3 Australia and New Zealand didn't experience an industrial revolution *sensu stricto*, but developed a manufacturing industry, and their primary sectors adopted sophisticated technologies from the beginning.
4 This distinction between colonization by settlement and colonization by mercantile slave exploitation, drawn in order to explain the backwardness of the countries that adopted the second type of colonization, was classically made by Caio Prado Jr. in the three first chapters of his *História Econômica do Brasil [Economic history of Brazil]* (1945).
5 Alexander Gerschenkron (1962) called Germany and the Scandinavian countries "latecomers", because they were late in realizing their industrial revolution. In our meaning of the expression, they were countries characterized by original development.
6 In 1846, Friedrich List first used the expression "kick away the ladder" to describe Britain's behaviour when it tried to persuade the Germans not to industrialize. Britain used the arguments of classical liberal economics, which Britain did not follow when realizing its industrial revolution. The expression was invoked by Ha-Joon Chang (2002) to describe rich countries' present behaviour toward developing countries.
7 We understand technical progress to consist of the increase in labour productivity. It is capital-using, neutral, or capital-saving, according to the fact that it decreases, maintains, or increases the output–capital ratio or productivity of capital. Countries such as Britain and France, which usually serve as a parameter for long-term analyses, showed neutral technical progress between the mid-nineteenth century and the mid-twentieth century. Surprisingly, in the second half of the twentieth century, technical progress tended to become capital-intensive, even though what prevailed was no longer the replacement of labour with machines (which characterizes the capital-using technical progress), but the replacement of old machines with new, more efficient ones (which characterizes laboursaving progress).

3 Demand-led growth

In a country that has already completed its process of industrialization or its capitalist revolution and become a medium-income country, long-term growth is determined by the aggregate demand. This is because growth does not depend on previous savings or on the availability of the means of production but, contrary to the teachings of orthodox economics, on the existence of lucrative investment opportunities and on the availability of credit. In a mature capitalist economy, albeit at a medium stage of development, the means of production are produced within the system, so that their supply can never be taken for granted. In this setting, the pace of the creation of productive resources is determined by the rate of expansion in aggregate demand. More specifically, it is determined by the expansion in those components of aggregate demand that are autonomous in relation to the level and/or variation in production and in income, since it is this expansion that creates investment opportunities and encourages active capitalists or entrepreneurs to invest.

In a small open economy that lacks a convertible currency,[1] such as is found in medium-development countries, the autonomous component of aggregate demand consists of exports. Therefore, economic development depends essentially on exports. Domestic consumption cannot drive long-term growth unless the share of wages in income persistently increases over time, which is, in principle, incompatible with an expected satisfactory profit rate – unless technical progress is capital-saving,[2] or consumers are taking on debt (which is not sustainable). Therefore, the existence of defined limits on the increase in the participation of wages in income makes it indefinitely impossible to drive output growth by increasing wages faster than labour productivity. The alternative – growth led by public expenditure – is also untenable because, if that expenditure increases without a decrease in entrepreneurs' profits and in workers' wages, it will sooner or later lead to inflation and to a balance-of-payment crisis.

From the Keynesian–structuralist perspective, the potential rate of long-term growth is a function of the rate of investment or the increase in the stock of capital, given the marginal productivity of capital or the output–capital ratio. Investments, in turn, depend on the existence of investment opportunities, particularly export-oriented investments. As long as entrepreneurs in developing countries, in which labour is relatively cheap, start to utilize a technology similar to the one existing in more advanced countries, they obtain credit and invest. Domestic savings consequently increase, the country's growth rate accelerates, and its share in world exports increases.

However, it is usually pointed out that potential growth might not be realized because of "external" (i.e. balance-of-payments) constraint. On the assumption that the developing country exports primary goods and imports manufactured goods (which is usually not the case when it becomes a medium-income country), the income elasticity of the demand for imported goods would be higher than the income elasticity of the demand for primary goods (because most of the latter are essential goods), so that the foreign constraint would soon emerge when income increases. In fact, no country can grow indefinitely with a structural imbalance in its balance of payments. And this is even truer for countries whose currency is non-convertible, such as developing countries. This reasoning, however, presumes that the country still is a mere commodity-exporting country – which is no longer true for middle-income countries. On the other hand, if the exchange rate is balanced, that is, if it is at the "competitive or industrial equilibrium" level (a concept that we explore later in this book), the country is neutralizing its Dutch disease and will tend to present a current account surplus, and therefore would not be subject to any "external" constraint.

Supply-determined growth

Orthodox economics often makes the mistake of confining itself to reproducing common sense, rather than examining how economic variables actually interact in the market. Just as neoclassical economists presume that economic agents first save to invest later, neoclassical growth models, beginning with the Solow model (1956, 1957), presume that the fundamental limit to long-term growth is determined by the economy's supply conditions, so that there is no point in considering whether demand for the goods exists. More specifically, these models consider that the long-term growth of real output is determined by the accumulation rate of the factors of production (capital and labour) and by the rate of growth of labour productivity, made possible by technological progress. Aggregate demand is relevant only to explain the degree of utilization of productive capacity, and has no direct impact on the determination of its pace of expansion. Although Keynes made the definitive criticism of Say's Law in the first chapter of the *General Theory* (1936), it remains valid according to neoclassical theory. Consequently, a mere accounting identity (the output or the sum of aggregate production is equal to the sum of wages, profits, and returns on capital, which is equal to consumption plus investment in a closed economy) is transformed into an economic law incompatible with economic crises: supply (the availability of factors of production) determines aggregate demand.

From the neoclassical perspective, the factors on the supply side of the economy determine the *tendency* for capitalist economies to grow in the long run. Aggregate demand is responsible merely for the fluctuations or "economic cycles" that the economy experiences as it manifest its long-term tendency. Therefore, the essence of the neoclassical approach to long-term growth consists in the belief that the tendency for capitalist economies to grow is *independent* of aggregate demand. The estimation of the long-term tendency is based on so-called "growth accounting", which was originally developed by Robert Solow in an article published in 1957. In that article, Solow tries to quantify the contribution of capital accumulation to North American economic growth in the first half of the twentieth century. For this purpose, Solow presumes the existence of a macroeconomic production function in which the amount produced in a given period of time is a function of the amount of capital and labour employed, so that $Q = A.F(K,L)$, in which Q is the amount of goods and services produced, K is the amount of capital employed, L is the amount of labour employed, and A is a variable that represents the "state of the art" of the economy – that is, the technological level existing in the economy at a given moment. The function $F(.)$ is presumed to be linear homogeneous – that is, the returns to scale are considered constant. Finally, perfect competition prevails in all markets, so that each factor of production is remunerated according to its marginal productivity. It follows that the whole income generated in the economy is fully spent in the remuneration of the factors of production according to their marginal productivities (Sargent, 1987, ch.1). Nothing remains of aggregate income to remunerate the effort to research and develop new technologies. In this setting, technological progress can only be treated as exogenous to the economic system.

In this setting, the growth rate of real output can be broken down, based on its determinants, according to the following equation:

$$\frac{\dot{Q}}{Q} = \frac{\dot{A}}{A} + \alpha_K \frac{\dot{K}}{K} + \alpha_L \frac{\dot{L}}{L} \tag{3.1}$$

where $\frac{\dot{Q}}{Q}$ is the growth rate of the real output, $\frac{\dot{A}}{A}$ is the growth rate of the "total productivity of the factors of production", $\frac{\dot{K}}{K}$ is the growth rate of the stock of capital, $\frac{\dot{L}}{L}$ is the growth rate of the labour force, α_K is the participation of profits in value added, and $\alpha_L = 1 - \alpha_K$ is the share of wages in value added.

Equation (3.1) presents two unknowns; namely, the growth rate of real output and the growth rate of the "total productivity of the factors of production". Therefore, the known variables are not enough to enable an estimation of the potential growth rate.

In the 1957 article, Solow circumvents this problem by making the total productivity of the factors of production a purely residual variable, determined by the difference between the average growth rate of real output observed in the past and real output growth resulting from the accumulation of factors of production – that is, from the sum of the growth rate of the stock of capital (weighted by the share of profits in value added) and the growth rate of labour force (weighted by the share of wages in value added). In other words, "technological progress" in the Solow-inspired growth models is just a "measure of our ignorance", that is, that part of long-term growth that we are unable to explain through the accumulation of the factors of production.[3]

The most serious problem with this procedure is that the economy's past behaviour now determines the estimates of its potential growth. Consequently, if we had slow growth in the recent past, then the "estimate" of the growth rate of the total productivity of the factors of production will be low, thus "signaling" that potential output growth is also reduced. However, if growth accelerated during a long enough period of time (for instance, about 10 years), the growth estimates of the total productivity of the factors of production would be revised up, and, consequently, so would potential output growth. Thus, Solow's formula is unable to provide an estimate of potential output growth that is independent of the recent behaviour of the real output growth rate.

Solow's formula suffers from an obvious issue of logical circularity in the estimate of the potential output growth rate; and we could add another issue arising from the debate that became known as the "capital controversy". In fact, during the 1950s Joan Robinson and Piero Sraffa raised serious questions about the methodology employed by neoclassical theory to measure the stock of capital. Robinson and Sraffa's fundamental argument is that the value of the stock of capital is not independent of the functional distribution of income between wages and profits, so that it is impossible to estimate the value and/or the growth rate of the stock of capital independently of the share of capital in value added.[4] In other words, *there is no methodologically acceptable way of separating the growth rate of the stock of capital from the share of profits in value added.* In this setting, Solow's formula simply cannot be applied due to the impossibility of calculating the contribution of capital to long-term economic growth.

In addition to the theoretical and methodological problems involved in "growth accounting" exercises, the neoclassical approach has lately faced empirical issues. More specifically, the recent developments of time-series econometrics have shown that it is incorrect to break down the behaviour of real output into "tendency" and "cycle". This is because the time series for gross domestic product, of both developed and developing countries, present a "unitroot", so that temporary shocks – whether of demand or supply – have permanent effects on real output.[5] Therefore, the cyclic component of economic activity, traditionally associated with variations in aggregate demand in the short term, affects the tendency for capitalist economies to grow in the long run. In other words, low growth rates during crises are not offset by high rates during booms; after all, growth in the medium term is the sum of growth in short terms. In this setting, the growth tendency becomes dependent on the path that capitalist economies actually described over time. This phenomenon is known in literature as "path dependence".

Path dependence has strong implications for macroeconomic theory and policy. In terms of macroeconomic theory, path dependence shows that we cannot accept the traditional division in macroeconomics between the "short term", in which the issues related to aggregate demand are relevant, and the "long term", in which these issues have no relevance whatsoever (Dutt and Ros, 2007, p. 97). The reason is that what happens in the short term has effects on the long term. In terms of macroeconomic policy, the practice of using highly contractionary policies to deal with exogenous shocks, as seems to be the historical experience of Latin American countries, is not advisable in view of their long-term effects on output and employment. Aggregate demand contractions, if necessary, should be small and reversed as soon as possible in order to mitigate their long-term adverse consequences (Ibid, pp. 97–98).

Growth determined by aggregate demand

The neoclassical theory of growth presumes that the availability of technology and factors of production are independent of aggregate demand. However, we have already seen that path dependence leads us to reject this idea. But there are stronger arguments showing that the economic growth is led by aggregate demand. First, investment depends directly on demand. No entrepreneur will invest if he does not know whether there is demand for the goods and services he intends to produce. Second, investment, of its nature, increases the availability of capital and productive capacity. In fact, both the growth rate of the availability of the factors of production and the pace of technological progress are determined, in the long term, by the rate of expansion in aggregate demand.

Developmental economics emerged when Keynesian thought became dominant worldwide, so that structuralist economists had no doubts about the significance of demand for economic development. Celso Furtado (1966), in particular, was very clear on this issue. Entrepreneurs invest only if they perceive good investment opportunities, which depend on demand.

Nicholas Kaldor (1978, p.157), in his turn, argued that growth is led by demand because the means of production employed in a modern capitalist economy are themselves goods that are produced within the system. Consequently, the "availability" of means of production can never be considered as being independent of their demand. In this setting, the fundamental economic problem is not the allocation of a given amount of resources among a number of available alternatives, as a neoclassical economist would think, but rather the determination of the pace at which these resources are created. In the words of Mark Setterfield (1997, p.50), one of the exponents of this theoretical approach:

> The use of produced means of production implies that the "scarcity of resources" in processing activities cannot be thought of as being independent of the level of activity in the economy. What is chiefly important in processing activities is the dynamic propensity of the economy to create resources (that is, to deepen and/or widen its stock of capital) rather than the static problem of resource allocation.

In order to understand the long-term endogeneity of the availability of factors of production, we should start by analyzing the availability of capital. The existing amount of capital at a given point in time – or rather, the productive capacity existing in the economy – results from past decisions to invest in fixed capital. It follows that the stock of capital is not a constant determined by "nature", but depends on the pace at which entrepreneurs want to expand the stock of capital existing in the economy.

Consequently, the fundamental determinant of the "stock of capital" is the decision to invest. Investment, in turn, depends on two sets of factors: (*a*) the opportunity cost of capital; and (*b*) the profit opportunities perceived by the enterprises conditioned by expectations regarding the future growth of demand for goods and services. In this setting, if entrepreneurs forecast a steady growth of demand for their goods and services – as one could expect in the case of an economy that is showing strong and sustainable growth over time – then they will make large investments in the expansion of their production capacity.

In other words, investment adjusts to the expected growth in demand, provided that a fundamental constraint is satisfied – namely, that the rate of return on capital expected by entrepreneurs must be higher than the cost of the capital paid to rentier capitalists. And the greater this difference is, the larger the investment opportunities, and the higher the rate of investment. When we observe very high investment rates, as occurred during the "Brazilian miracle" of 1968–72, or China's growth since 1980, we can be certain that the interest rate is low and the profit rate is high. Therefore, the "availability of capital" cannot be seen as an obstacle to long-term growth. It is true that in the short and medium terms production cannot increase beyond what the economy's physical production capacity makes possible. In the long term, however, production capacity can be expanded – through investment in physical capital – so as to satisfy the aggregate demand for goods and services.

Orthodox theory opposes the idea of demand-led growth on the grounds that investment depends on "previous savings" – that is, any increase in investment expenditure requires, before its implementation, an increase in the savings rate of the economy. In this setting, orthodox economists argue that the "availability of capital" is limited by the fraction of its income that a society is willing not to consume – that is, by total savings, the sum of private savings (of households and enterprises), government savings, and foreign savings. Thus, instead of assuming a monetary economy where business entrepreneurs have access to credit and acknowledge with Keynes that investment is determined by the investment decisions financed by credit, we are back to the economics of the piggy bank, where children place their savings.

The relationship between savings and investment was the subject of intense debate between neoclassical and Keynesian economists after the publication of Keynes's *The General Theory of Employment, Interest and Money* in 1936,[6] probably because the counterintuitive and innovative assumption that Keynes presented in that book was that investment does not need prior savings to be implemented. In reality, the execution of investment expenditure requires only the availability of credit, which, in turn, depends on the creation of liquidity by the financial system. This is the so-called demand for money arising from the "finance" motive (Carvalho, 1992, pp. 148–153). If the banks are willing to extend their credit lines – albeit short maturity ones – under favourable conditions, it is possible for enterprises to start to implement their investment projects by ordering machines and equipment from producers of capital goods. Once the investment expenditure has been implemented, an aggregate income of equivalent magnitude will have been created. This will stimulate consumption, creating a multiplier effect of the initial investment such that, at the end of the process, aggregate savings will grow due to the income increase, and be adjusted to the new value of the investment in physical capital. Savings thus created may then be used to *fund* enterprises' short-term debts with commercial banks; that is, enterprises will be able – through retained earnings, sales of shares, or placements of securities on the market – to pay out the debt incurred with commercial banks whenever they need liquidity to implement their investment projects. Savings, therefore, always and somehow adjust to the level of investment desired by the entrepreneurs (Davidson, 1986).[7]

Obstacles to the expansion of productive capacity have a financial nature; more specifically, they arise from the possibly excessive cost of capital. As we have observed, enterprises will be willing to adjust the size of their productive capacity to the anticipated growth of demand provided that the expected internal rate of return of the new investment projects are higher than the opportunity cost of capital. Roughly speaking, we can define the cost of capital as equal to the average interest rate that an enterprise must pay for the funds required to finance its investment projects. There are three sources of funds for the financing of investment projects: retained earnings, indebtedness, and stock issue. As such, the cost of capital is an average of the cost of each of those sources of financing weighted by the proportion of each in an enterprise's total liabilities. Whereas entrepreneurs or active capitalists – whose reason for existence is investment or capital accumulation – wish the cost of capital to be as low as possible (which Keynes famously referred to as "euthanasia of the rentier"), rentier capitalists fight for this cost of capital to be as high as possible and the inflation rate as low as possible, so that the real interest rate is high.

What about the availability of labour? Can the amount of labour be seen as an obstacle to the growth of production in the long run? For a number of reasons, limitations on the availability of workers can hardly be seen as an obstacle to growth. First, the number of hours worked, within certain limits, may increase rapidly in response to an increase in the level of production. Second, the rate of participation – defined as the percentage of the economically active population that makes up the workforce – may increase in answer to a strong increase in the demand for labour (Thirlwall, 2002, p. 86). In practice, during periods in which the economy grows fast, the opportunity cost of leisure – measured by the income "lost" by an individual who "choose" not to work (young men, married women, and retirees) – tends to be very high, leading to a strong increase in the rate of participation in the labour force. In this setting, the growth rate of the labour force may accelerate due to the inflow of individuals who, during the previous periods, had decided to remain outside it. Finally, we should stress that the size of the population and the size of the labour force are not fixed from the viewpoint of the national economy. This is because an occasional shortage of labour – even of skilled labour – may be corrected by the immigration of workers from foreign countries. For instance, countries such as Germany and France were able to maintain high growth rates during the 1950s and the 1960s with the immigration of workers from the periphery of Europe (Spain, Portugal, Greece, Turkey, and southern Italy).

Development and technical progress

The last element to be considered is technological progress. Can the pace of innovation or the inventiveness of the economy be considered a constraint on long-term growth? If we consider technological progress to be exogenous, then certainly the pace at which technology expands will limit growth. However, technological progress is not exogenous to the economic system. First, the pace of introduction of innovations by the enterprises is largely determined by the pace of capital accumulation, since most technological innovations are "incorporated" into recently produced machines and equipment. According to this key perspective of developmental economics, particularly in the work of Ragnar Nurkse and Celso Furtado, technical progress is incorporated into the process of capital accumulation. Kaldor (1957) formalized this idea through his "technical progress function", which established the existence of a structural relationship between the rate of output growth per worker and the rate of capital growth per worker. According to Kaldor, it is impossible to distinguish between the productivity growth which results from the incorporation of new technologies and the growth which results from an increase in capital per worker. This is because most of the technological innovations that increase labour productivity demand the utilization of a greater volume of capital per worker because they are incorporated into new machines and equipment. So an acceleration in the rate of capital accumulation – induced, for instance, by a more favourable prospect of increased demand – leads to a faster pace of technological progress and, therefore, of labour productivity growth.

Second, that part of technological progress that was "not incorporated (into capital accumulation)" is caused by "dynamic economies of scale" such as "learning by doing". Consequently, a "structural relationship" is established between the growth rate of labour productivity and the growth rate of production, which is known in economic literature as "Kaldor–Verdoorn law" (León-Ledesma, 2002). In this setting, an increase in aggregate demand, by inducing acceleration in the growth rate of production, eventually accelerates the pace of labour productivity growth.

As a corollary of this whole argument, it follows that the concept of "potential output" or "full employment output level", so important for neoclassical approaches to economic growth, is basically a short-term concept that ignores the fact that the availability of factors of production and the pace of technological progress itself are endogenous variables in the process of economic growth or development.

Investment and technical progress

If the availability of factors of production cannot be seen as the determinant of the economic growth in the long term, what then are the factors that determine growth? In the long run, the basic determinant of output and, therefore, of development is aggregate demand, which encourages investment with the incorporation of technical progress. Therefore, the fundamental issue of development is to know on what the rate of investment depends, or what makes it grows faster. The answer to this question is reasonably consensual. The fundamental motivation of entrepreneurs and enterprises is profit. Therefore, the rate of investment depends on the existence of lucrative investment opportunities, which in turn depend on aggregate demand. If there is demand, enterprises will respond by increasing production and productive capacity, provided that the profit margin is high enough to give entrepreneurs a "satisfactory" rate of return on capital – that is, provided that the expected profit rate is substantially higher than the cost of capital. When capital accumulation occurs, technical progress also occurs, through its incorporation in both capital and labour. This progress is expressed in rising productivity, or a production increase per worker. It is also reflected in capital productivity or the output–capital ratio, which no longer tends to be capital-intensive and becomes neutral or even capital-saving on account of this technical progress.

Investments can be oriented to the domestic or to the foreign market. The former depends on the existence and growth of demand in the domestic market and on the government's decision to invest. Growth in the domestic market, in turn, besides investment, depends on consumption, which is a function of wage growth. Investments oriented to foreign markets depend on external demand, which, in turn, is represented by exports, which, as it is widely known, depend on world economic growth and on the income elasticity of the country's exports.

However, a fundamental assumption of developmental macroeconomics is that, in developing countries, another variable is more important than world economic growth in determining export-oriented investments: the shift of the exchange rate from a situation of chronic overvaluation. It is more important because, when a developmental macroeconomic policy places the exchange rate at the competitive or industrial equilibrium, the whole existing external demand, and not only its growth, becomes accessible to the enterprises using world state-of-the-art technology.

In open economies, there are two autonomous components of the aggregate demand, namely exports and public expenditure.[8] Private investment expenditure is not an autonomous component of the aggregate demand, since the decision to invest in fixed capital is fundamentally determined by business expectations regarding future expansion in the level of production and sales, according to the so-called investment accelerator hypothesis (Harrod, 1939). In other words, investment is not an "exogenous" variable from the standpoint of the growth process, since it is induced by the increase in income and production levels.

Consumption, in turn, depends largely on total wages which, given the distribution of income between wages and profits, is a function of the level of production and employment. Consequently, given the functional distribution of income, consumption is not an autonomous component of aggregate demand, and it cannot push or pull long-term economic growth. This means that a consumption-led growth pattern or regime is possible only in a setting in which the functional income distribution is changing over time in favour of the working class – that is, if there is a persistent increase in the share of wages in income.[9]

From this it follows that, given the functional distribution of income, the long-term growth of income and production is the weighted average of the growth rates of exports and public expenditure.

For a small open economy that lacks a convertible currency, as is the case in the vast majority of the medium-development countries, the exports growth rate is the exogenous variable par excellence. The reason is that, if the growth rate of public expenditure is higher than the exports growth rate, then output and domestic income will grow more than exports. If the income elasticity of imports is higher than 1 (as it usually is in medium-development countries), then imports will grow more than exports, generating a growing trade deficit which will probably be untenable in the long term.

The exports growth rate is equal to the product of the income elasticity of exports (ε) and the income growth rate of the rest of the world (z).[10] Therefore, we may conclude that the potential growth rate of the real output (g_*), in the Keynesian approach of aggregate demand-led growth, is given by:

$$g_* = \varepsilon z \tag{3.2}$$

Summary

In this chapter, we presented the Keynesian–structuralist approach to development, whose fundamental element is the theory of aggregate demand-led growth. We argued that, in a small open economy with a non-convertible currency, long-term growth is determined by the exports growth rate. Consumption may lead to economic growth only temporarily, as long as it is politically and economically possible to induce a redistribution of income in favour of the working class. The existence of defined limits on the increase in the share of wages in national income makes the expansion in exports, in the long run, the agent of economic growth.

Notes

1 On the concept of convertible currency, see Franco (1999).
2 Capital-saving technical progress is the kind of technical progress caused by the decrease in the cost of capital as compared to its ability to increase output – or, in other words, by the increase in the output–capital ratio.
3 Observation: Solow estimated that roughly seven-eighths of North American economic growth in the first half of the twentieth century could not be explained by the increase in the stocks of capital and labour. In other words, seven-eighths of North American economic growth in the first half of the twentieth century has no explanation based on neoclassical economics.

4 A good review of the "capital controversy" may be found in Harcourt (1972).
5 For a study of the existence of a unit-root in the GDP time series of Latin American countries, see Libânio (2009).
6 On the debate between Keynes and the classical economists on the relationship between savings and investment and the determination of the interest rate, see Oreiro (2000).
7 We should note that the determination of savings by investment also happens in an economy that operates in a "full employment" situation. Actually, as argued by Kaldor (1957), in an economy that operates on a path to growth balanced by full employment of the labour force, an increase in the rate of investment will result in an increase in profit margins, thus giving rise to a redistribution of income from workers to the capitalists. Since the capitalists' propensity to save is higher than the workers' propensity to save, this increase in the share of profits in income will result in an increase in the aggregate savings rate.
8 We should make an important distinction here between the government's current consumption expenditure and its investment expenditure. Although both kinds of government expenditure are "autonomous" regarding the level and/or the variation in the current income, investment expenditure gives rise to a positive externality on private investment, partly because its multiplier is larger. For those reasons a growth policy based on fiscal expansion should prioritize an increase in investment expenditure rather than in current consumption expenditure. On the effects of public investments on long-term growth, see Oreiro, Silva, and Fortunato (2008).
9 Modifications in the functional distribution of income between wages and profits may occur only within certain limits, at the risk of making the existence of capitalist economies impossible in the long term. As remarked by Kaldor (1956, 1957), the share of profits in income has a lower limit determined by the need to obtain a minimum profit rate, below which capitalists cease to invest and/or to employ their capital productively. Therefore, it becomes impossible to maintain indefinitely a consumption-led path to growth: At some point, the increase in the share of wages in income will cause the share of profits in income to reach its minimum value. When this happens, consumption will no longer be able to grow autonomously in relation to the growth in the level of production and income.
10 This presumes that the terms of trade remain constant over time.

4 Foreign constraint

We have assumed so far that production adjusts, in the long term, to the increase in autonomous aggregate demand. However, the economy may not present a long-term growth rate equal to the value given by equation (3.1), due to the existence of constraints on the expansion in the level of production at the pace determined by the expansion in exports. These constraints result from factors that prevent the full adjustment of enterprises' productive capacity to the projected increase in their sales, as well as from the need to keep the balance of payments in equilibrium in the long term. In this chapter we analyze these two constraints in detail.

Capacity constraint and distribution of income

In Chapter 3 we argued that the productive capacity is not a constraint on long-term growth, since investment will expand it (and the output–capital ratio may fall). Our argument in this chapter is that, if investment does not occur, due to a low expected profit rate or the high cost of capital, productive capacity becomes a constraint. In order to determine the output growth rate compatible with entrepreneurs' investment plans, we assume that the amount of goods and services produced at a certain point in time is given by:

$$Q = vuK \qquad (4.1)$$

where v is the output–capital ratio (the maximum amount of output that can be obtained from a unit of capital, $\bar{Q}/K$), u is the rate of productive capacity utilization, and K is the stock of capital.

In the long-term equilibrium, the rate of utilization of productive capacity is equal to the normal level of utilization capacity – that is, the level of capacity utilization is the one desired by business enterprises in their competition strategy (Oreiro, 2004, p. 47). If we assume that the output–capital ratio is also constant, we have:

$$\Delta Q = vu\Delta K. \qquad (4.1a)$$

If we assume that the depreciation of the stock of capital is equal to δ, gross investment will be:

$$I = \Delta K + \delta K. \tag{4.2}$$

Substituting (4.2) for (4.1a) and dividing both terms by Q, we obtain the following expression:

$$y^* = \frac{\Delta Q}{Q} = u_n \left(v \frac{I}{Q} - \delta \right) \tag{4.3}$$

where u_n is the normal level of capacity utilization.

Equation (4.3) defines the "warranted rate of growth" – that is, the growth rate which, if obtained, will keep utilization capacity at its long-term normal level (Park, 2000). This concept originates from the seminal model of Roy Harrod (1939). Given the normal rate of capacity utilization (u_n), the output–capital ratio (v) and the rate of depreciation (δ), the warranted growth rate is a function of net investment as a proportion of production, which depends, as we have argued, on the expected profit rate and on the opportunity cost of capital.

The profit rate can be expressed by the following equation:

$$R = \frac{P}{K} = \frac{P}{Q} \frac{Q}{\bar{Q}} \frac{\bar{Q}}{K} = muv \tag{4.4}$$

P is the aggregate profit, $\bar{Q}$ is economy's potential output (that is, the maximum amount of goods and services that may be produced from the existing productive capacity), and m is the share of profits in production (or, broadly speaking, in national income).

In its turn, the profit rate depends critically on the real exchange rate, which defines the condition of access not only to the foreign market but also to the domestic market for business enterprises.[1] Equation (4.4) presupposes either a closed economy or that the exchange rate is always in equilibrium. If we assume, as the developmental macroeconomics being expounded here does, that there is a tendency to the cyclical and chronic overvaluation of the exchange rate in developing countries, we will have to consider that this overvaluation will affect the profit rate negatively, because it implies more competition from abroad and artificially higher real wages. An eventual depreciation will, in the short-term, further reduce the profit rate, because the demand for consumption will decline due to the fall in real wages. However, in the medium-term, the increased competitiveness of business enterprises and their recovered access to domestic and foreign markets will entail a higher expected profit rate and a faster growth rate. This will also allow for an increase in real wages at the pace of the increment in the demand for labour.

Foreign constraint and exchange rate

Another constraint on long-term growth is the foreign constraint. This is an old idea in development theory. In the "big push" model of Rosenstein-Rodan (1943), which is the basis of structuralist development theory, this constraint is assumed. From this perspective, which acquired a theoretical foundation with the idea that the income elasticities of developing countries' imports would be larger than 1 (because these countries import mainly manufactured goods) whereas the income elasticity of the imports of primary goods by rich countries would be lower than 1 (since most of them are necessity goods), developing countries would always face a shortage of hard currency. The "two-gap" model of Hollis Chenery and Michael Bruno (1962) was the most significant formalization of this idea. The economic policy prescription that could be inferred from the foreign constraint was always to advise a developing country to accept a current account deficit and to pursue foreign financing.

Subsequently, in the 1980s, in the context of the crisis of the first structuralism and when post-Keynesian ideas became widespread among heterodox economists, the problem of the foreign constraint on long-term growth came to be associated with the increase in countries' exports, and with the contribution of A. P. Thirlwall to the relationship between exports and growth (1979, 1997, 2001). The concept of a balance-of-payments equilibrium growth rate developed by Thirlwall starts from the observation that the growth models of cumulative causality of Kaldorian inspiration, in which the growth rate of export demand is the fundamental motor of long-term economic growth, are incomplete since they do not include a condition of equilibrium in the balance of payments in their formal analytic structure. In this setting, and based on the assumption of the difference between elasticities, Thirlwall (2001, p. 81–82) stated that a path to growth made possible by the rate of capital accumulation could be untenable from the standpoint of the balance of payments. He argued that a path to accelerated growth led by a strong pace of expansion in exports might generate a growing trade deficit by inducing an untenable increase in imports. In this setting, the feasible growth rate in the long term would be the rate compatible with equilibrium in the balance of payments, in which imports and exports grow at the same rate because, in Thirlwall's words, "deficits cannot be financed forever and debt has to be repaid".

Let us first examine the growth rate of exports $(\dot{x})$. It depends on the growth rate of world demand $(\dot{y}_m)$ and on the income elasticity of the demand for exports (ε).

$$\dot{x} = \dot{y}_m * \varepsilon. \tag{4.5}$$

For instance, if world income is growing at 4 per cent per year, and the income elasticity of exports is 0.9, exports will grow at 3.6 per cent per year. At this point, we are assuming that the country's share of world exports and the real exchange rate are constant.

In order for the current account to remain in balance, imports must grow at the same rate as exports. Demand for imports (m) depends on domestic income (y) and on the income elasticity of imports (π), which is greater than 1 and greater than the income elasticity of exports for developing countries. Continuing to assume that the real exchange rate is constant, we have:

$$\dot{m} = \dot{x} = \pi * \dot{y}. \tag{4.6}$$

Replacing (4.5) with (4.6), we conclude that the rate of growth that guarantees the current account equilibrium depends on the income elasticity of imports and exports, and on the rate of growth of world demand. This is the well-known "Thirlwall law":

$$\dot{y}_{cce} = \frac{\dot{x}}{\pi} = \frac{\varepsilon}{\pi} * \dot{y}_m \qquad (4.7)$$

where $\dot{y}_{cce}$ is the growth rate consistent with the intertemporal equilibrium of the current account.

For instance, if exports are growing at 3.6 per cent a year, and the income elasticity of imports is 1.2, the equilibrium growth rate will be 3 per cent a year. This example shows that if the income elasticity of imports is larger than 1, the growth rate consistent with current account equilibrium will be lower than the growth rate that the current rate of investment and the output–capital ratio would authorize.

In this case, the foreign constraint is "binding" and justifies the adoption of a policy that overcomes it. Which policy? We would have nothing to object to in the formal concept of foreign constraint that we have just presented if it were not accompanied by the inference that the way to overcome this constraint is the economic policy of obtaining foreign savings – that is, the policy of incurring current account deficits and financing them with international loans and direct investments. Although Thirlwall did not make this inference, in practice the concept of foreign constraint and, particularly, the two gaps model is always accompanied by support for this policy. But, as we will see in the following chapters, this policy necessarily implies an exchange rate appreciation that, in most cases, will discourage investment, so provoking a high rate of substitution of foreign for domestic savings that is contrary to the country's interests.

Fall in the equilibrium growth rate

Let us return to the foreign constraint model. Equation (4.7) presumes that international capital mobility is equal to zero, so that countries cannot incur debt to finance current-account deficits. The extension of Thirlwall's model to an economy with capital flows was made by Moreno-Brid (1998–99), among others. In Moreno-Brid's model the existence of international capital flows is admitted, but the dynamics of foreign indebtedness must fulfill the condition of long-term external solvency. In particular, the model developed by this author assumes that the relationship between the current account deficit and domestic income should remain constant in the long term for the country to be solvent in its foreign accounts. In this setting, if we admit that the terms of trade are constant in the long term, the current account equilibrium growth rate is given by the following expression:

$$\dot{y}_{cce} = \frac{\varepsilon\theta}{\pi - (1-\theta)} \qquad (4.8)$$

where θ is the ratio between the initial amount of exports and the initial amount of imports.

We should note that θ might be expressed alternatively as the ratio between the revenue from exports and the sum of the current-account deficit $(M - X)$ and the revenue from exports. Therefore, we have:

$$\theta = \frac{X}{(M-X)+X} = \frac{\left(\dfrac{X}{Q}\right)}{\left(\dfrac{M-X}{Q}\right)+\dfrac{X}{Q}} = \frac{x_Q}{cc + x_Q} \tag{4.9}$$

where x_Q is the share of exports in domestic income and cc is the current-account deficit as a proportion of domestic income.

According to equation (4.9), a current-account deficit decreases the value of θ; consequently, in view of equation (4.8), this deficit reduces the rate of growth consistent with the equilibrium of the current account $(\dot{y}_{cce})$. In other words, the current-account deficit has a *negative*, although negligible, impact on the growth rate compatible with equilibrium in the balance-of-payments (McCombie and Roberts, 2002, p. 95). This is an illuminating model, which shows that foreign indebtedness, when "solving" the foreign constraint problem, does not accelerate but rather reduces the growth rate. However, we must stress that Moreno-Brid underestimates this reduction because he does not take into account either the fact that the external debt increase will lead to a demand for more foreign currency resources to be repaid or a fundamental assumption of this book, namely that a current-account deficit corresponds to an overvalued exchange rate, which, in turn, further reduces the growth rate.

Developmental economics defined the concept of foreign constraint in the 1950s to explain why developing countries at that time faced a chronic "foreign currency shortage" or, more precisely, a lack of hard convertible currencies. There was no lack of investment opportunities at that time, since countries such as Brazil, Mexico, and South Korea were still in the early phase of their industrialization, to which the import–substitution model was appropriate. At that moment the theory of the two elasticities (of exports and imports) emerged, as explained above, which seemed to "explain" the problem. But, first of all, this is not the chief cause of the foreign currency shortage. The key assumption of developmental macroeconomics is that in developing countries the exchange rate tends to be cyclically and chronically overvalued. Therefore, the chronic overvaluation of the exchange rate implies a current account deficit and, therefore, a lack of hard currency. The existence of the two elasticities also plays a role, but certainly a *minor* one as compared to the role of chronic exchange-rate overvaluation. On the other hand, as we have already seen, to try to overcome the constraint by resorting to foreign savings carries the risk of worsening it. Given the tendency to the cyclical and chronic overvaluation of the exchange rate, foreign indebtedness adds little to current investment, as it creates financial obligations for the country in the future in the form of interest or profit to be sent abroad, and places the country under the threat of a currency crisis. There-fore, the essential thing to have is an exchange rate policy, in order to place the exchange rate at the competitive equilibrium – that is, at the industrial equilibrium.

We can demonstrate this conclusion with a second example. We saw that, given the income elasticity of imports and exports, for a country that grows with a bal-anced foreign account, the growth rate of exports must be higher than the growth of GDP. In the following simplified example, the output–capital ratio, v, is 0.25, the rate of capacity utilization is 0.8, and net investment is 25 per cent of GDP. In this case, the equilibrium growth rate, $\dot{y}_e$, will be:

$$\dot{y}_e = u_n \left(v \frac{I}{\overline{\overline{Q}}} - \delta \right)$$

$\dot{y}_e = 0.8 * 0.25 * 0.25 = 0.05$.

But, given an income elasticity of imports, π, of 1.2, and given the desired annual 5 per cent growth rate, the rate of growth of exports, $\dot{x}$, will have to be 6 per cent.

$$\dot{x} = \pi * \dot{y}_e = 6\%$$

But suppose also that exports increase just 5 per cent per year in a country that exports only commodities. In that case, even though its capacity constraint allows for a 5 per cent annual growth rate, its equilibrium growth rate will be 4.16 per cent per year without current account deficits, because the income elas-ticity of imports is 1.2. In a second moment, the investment rate would also fall as a result of the decline in aggregate demand, and the capacity constraint would accordingly also fall. How to grow at the desired 5 per cent? The solution, which seems obvious – and which is usually inferred from the two gap model and the Thirlwall law – is that the country should resort to foreign savings by incurring a current-account deficit. Yet this increased foreign indebtedness has a high cost, because the country will have to pay interest or dividends on the increased debt, and because it will risk incurring a currency or balance-of-payments crisis. Thus, given the high rate of substitution of foreign for domestic savings that we discuss in the following chapters, having recourse to foreign savings to overcome the foreign constraint is a false solution. The real solution is to adopt a set of poli-cies that neutralize the tendency to the cyclical and chronic overvaluation of the exchange rate – that is, to make the exchange rate to float around the competitive equilibrium that we call the industrial equilibrium. As a result, the annual growth of exports will increase to a new equilibrium of around 6 per cent per year, which will be consistent with the 5 per cent annual growth of GDP that the country's investment rate (and output–capital ratio) will allow.

Elasticities as endogenous variables

However, even if we limit ourselves to the problem of the two elasticities, in middle-income countries it is no longer possible to easily presume that the income elasticity of imports is higher than that of exports, insofar as the country is an exporter of manufactured goods. This suggests the hypothesis that the income elasticities of exports and imports are not variables exogenous to the model, determined only by the country's level of technological knowledge, but that they depend on the real exchange rate. The elasticities would therefore be endogenous variables that depend on the exchange rate. As we argue below, when the level of the real exchange rate is chronically overvalued due both to the non-neutralization of the Dutch disease and to uncontrolled and unnecessary capital inflows, the country's productive structure will be affected, inducing a process of perverse specialization in the production of natural resource-intensive goods and causing low growth because of deindustrialization. Alternatively, when the country manages to neutralize the tendency to overvaluation, the industrial-equilibrium exchange rate will pave the way for a process of industrialization in which the country manages to steadily increase the generation of value-added in the productive process. It follows that exchange rate depreciation (or overvaluation) affects the country's productive structure, by increasing or decreasing the share in value-added of tradable goods and services that are not the commodities, which give rise to the Dutch disease. Consequently, the income elasticity of exports and imports increases (or decreases) and the foreign constraint disappears or is strengthened.

This means that each country's productive structure and, therefore, the income elasticities of exports and imports are not immutable constants, but depend on the exchange rate; more precisely on the relationship between the current value of the exchange rate and the industrial-equilibrium exchange rate. When the exchange rate appreciates in value relative to the industrial equilibrium, there begins a process of deindustrialization and re-primarization of the export basket, which acts to reduce the income elasticity of exports and to increase the income elasticity of imports. In this setting, there will be a progressive reduction in the balance-of-payments equilibrium growth rate up to the point where it will be compatible with the structure of a primary-exporting economy. Conversely, if the current value of the exchange rate is at the level of the industrial equilibrium – or a little above it – then there will be a deepening of the country's process of industrialization, which will lead to an increase in the income elasticity of exports and to a decrease in the income elasticity of imports, therefore raising the balance-of-payments equilibrium growth rate.

Thus, the relation between the income elasticity of imports and the income elasticity of exports will depend on the difference between the nominal exchange rate and the industrial-equilibrium exchange rate (also in nominal terms):

$$\Delta\frac{\varepsilon}{\pi} = \beta\left(\frac{e}{e_{ind}}\right) \tag{4.10}$$

where β is a positive constant; e_{ind} is the industrial equilibrium exchange rate; and e is the nominal or market price exchange rate.

In the discussion about equation (4.9) we saw that the growth cum foreign savings policy offers only a temporary solution: the long-term growth rate. But, in

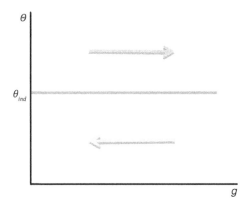

Figure 4.1 Growth dynamics and industrial equilibrium exchange rate

fact, substituting equation (4.10) for (4.7) and considering the variation in growth rate, we arrive at the following equation:

$$\dot{y}_{cce} = \Delta\beta\left(\frac{e}{e_{ind}}\right)\dot{y}_m. \qquad (4.11)$$

And then we realize in the expression (4.11) that the balance-of-payments equilibrium growth rate will be adjusting over time, depending on the relationship between the current value of the exchange rate and the industrial-equilibrium exchange rate. If the exchange rate is overvalued – that is, if the observed exchange rate is below the industrial equilibrium – then the growth rate compatible with the equilibrium in the balance-of-payments will be decreasing over time, thus intensifying the foreign constraint. Analogously, if the exchange rate is undervalued – that is, if the exchange rate is above the industrial equilibrium – then the balance-of-payments equilibrium growth rate will progressively increase over time. From that it follows that any real output growth rate is compatible with equilibrium in the balance of payments when the exchange rate is at the industrial equilibrium level (see Figure 4.1). Consequently, in the long term, we cannot talk about a foreign constraint to growth if the exchange rate is duly aligned – that is, at the level compatible with the industrial equilibrium. Industrialization eliminated the foreign constraint.

Summary

In this chapter, we have discussed the two restrictions on long-term growth led by aggregate demand, namely the capacity constraint and the foreign constraint. The first constraint amounts to stating that a country's growth rate depends fundamentally on the rate of investment, given an endogenous process of productivity increase in capitalist economies. The rate of investment, in turn, depends on lucrative investment opportunities, which finally depend on the neutralization of the tendency to the cyclical and chronic overvaluation of the exchange rate, which is central in developmental macroeconomics.

The foreign constraint, in turn, derives from the existence of two income elasticities: the income elasticity of imports larger than 1 in the developing countries and the income elasticity of imports of primary goods in the rich countries. This constraint was defined in the 1950s in terms of a chronic shortage of dollars that was attributed to the lack of availability of foreign financing at that time, instead of being attributed to the tendency to the cyclical and chronic overvaluation of the exchange rate. This constraint was formalized in the two-gaps model. The problem regarding the foreign constraint does not lie in whether it exists but in how to neutralize it. The usual way, implicit in the two-gaps model, is to resort to savings or to foreign indebtedness. We reject this policy and propose instead a competent exchange rate policy, so that it remains at its competitive equilibrium level: the industrial equilibrium.

Furthermore, we need to stress that the income elasticities of exports and imports are not exogenous variables, but are determined only by the developing country's level of technological development and by its ability, after a brief phase of import substitution, to export manufactured goods to rich countries.

Note

1 Access to the domestic market is constrained because the exchange rate appreciation stimulates imports, thus creating a leakage of potential aggregate demand.

5 Value and price of the exchange rate

The exchange rate plays an essential role in the growth process insofar as investment depends on the expected profit rate, which depends on the exchange rate, and given that developing countries' currencies tend to be overvalued. It is the exchange rate that guarantees competent business enterprises access to markets. A middle-income country is an industrialized country that has a technical capability in some manufacturing industries. Thus, we assume that the business enterprises in those industries have reached world state-of-the-art technology and are able to export. However, if the exchange rate in developing countries is cyclically and chronically overvalued, as we argue that it is, these business enterprises will be disconnected from global demand. Worse, they will be subject domestically to competition from foreign firms whose technology may be equal or even inferior to their own. The exchange rate affects both the expected increase in sales to domestic and foreign markets and the expected profit margin. In fact, it determines the degree of access of domestic business enterprises to these markets. Therefore, the exchange rate is a variable of the utmost importance in the process whereby investment adjusts to the increase in autonomous demand; it is the most strategic macroeconomic price for economic development.

However, economic theory, regardless of the school of thought, generally assumes that the exchange rate is balanced in the long run. This is probably why the exchange rate is not taken into account as a relevant variable in most textbooks on economic development, and receives relatively little attention from economic theory. Orthodox economists assume that the exchange rate oscillates gently around the equilibrium. Keynesian economists, more realistically, know that the exchange rate is volatile, but orthodox and Keynesian economists alike believe that misalignments of the exchange rate are relatively temporary problems. They admit that, depending on the intensity and duration of the misalignment, misalignments may cause currency crises. However, since they do not believe that the exchange rate tends to remain overvalued over long periods, they do not consider it when they discuss economic growth.

Developmental macroeconomics does not share the assumption that deviations from the equilibrium, the high volatility of the exchange rate, and its recurrent misalignment are just short-term problems. As we will see in Chapter 6, its more general assumption is that in developing countries there is a tendency to the cyclical and chronic overvaluation of the exchange rate. Given this tendency, which makes the overvaluation of the exchange rate a long-term problem, we place the exchange rate together with the current account at the centre of economic theory. Of the five macroeconomic prices (the exchange rate, the profit rate, the wage rate, the interest rate, and the inflation rate), the exchange rate is the most strategic. Not only imports and exports depend on it, but so do real wages, the inflation rate, investment opportunities, the investments themselves, and savings.[1]

The exchange rate is the price of the foreign currency; it is how much you need in your national money to buy one unit of foreign money. This is usually the definition of exchange rate in developing countries, but you may define it inversely as rich countries do: The exchange rate is how much you need in each foreign currency to buy one unit of your national money. In this book we use the first definition, but to avoid confusion we avoid saying that the exchange rate "increased" or "decreased"; we say that it "depreciated" or "appreciated". For developing countries the exchange rate is the price of the reserve currencies (usually the dollar) that the country uses in its dealings with foreign countries.

In this chapter, we first make a brief reference to the exchange rate regimes; second, we discuss the existing theories explaining the long-run equilibrium of the exchange rate, particularly purchasing power parity theory (PPP); third, we present the value theory of the exchange rate (Bresser-Pereira, 2013), and, fourth, we discuss three candidates to the long-term equilibrium: the industrial equilibrium, the current equilibrium, and the foreign debt equilibrium.

Exchange-rate regime

The economics literature has long featured the debate about the optimal exchange-rate regime. The options are presented in the binary form of "fixed or floating": fixed, as the exchange rate regime was under the Bretton Woods system, or floating, as it is supposed to be nowadays. In practice, most exchange-rate regimes are managed – policymakers usually define for themselves minimum and maximum values for the exchange rate, which may float within this range. Fully floating regimes are rarely observed, particularly in developing countries, given the high volatility they imply. Fixed-exchange rate regimes existed in the framework of the Bretton Woods Agreement; they made sense in the context of a wide international agreement. Today only a few oil-exporting countries that run huge current account surpluses and accumulate large reserves, such as the United Arab Emirates, maintain this regime.

The radical fix-or-float dichotomy allows no room for an exchange-rate policy. It makes little sense because in practice, as noted above, the exchange rate is never fixed and never really floats; it is always to some extent managed by governments and their central banks. The degree of management varies, and governments always deny having an exchange-rate policy. They also deny intervening in the exchange rate because conventional economics views such intervention unfavorably as "manipulation" of the exchange rate and as a way to "beggar thy neighbor". Yet a clear exchange rate policy, that is, a policy that aims to keep the exchange rate floating around the equilibrium, is crucial for a country pursuing stable development. For the country to grow at high rates and to catch up, it must neutralize the tendency to the cyclical and chronic overvaluation of the exchange rate and keep it at the equilibrium level – that is, at the level that makes its efficient business enterprises competitive.

The consequences of the opening of capital accounts in the 1980s and early 1990s were a brutal increase in the capital inflows and outflows, and an increase of the volatility of the exchange rate. This fact convinced many economists that it was now impossible to predict what will happen to the exchange rate of a country. Indeed, in the short-term, it is very difficult if not impossible. Given the speculative character of international flows into and out of developing countries, speculative bubbles involving foreign credit and the exchange rate market price are rather the rule than the exception, and the volatility turns still stronger despite the adoption of a floating regime. In Chapter 6, we will argue that developing countries are subject to the tendency to the cyclical and chronic overvaluation of the exchange rate, which can only be explained in the context of a floating regime if we assume that the formation of credit bubbles is frequent. Only this explains why it takes time for creditors to lose confidence and stop lending to a country that is already clearly fragile in financial terms. The volatility of the exchange rate comes to a pic in the moment of a balance of payment crisis, when foreign creditors stop refinancing the country, but it is also a consequence of events in the rich countries – major events like the global financial crisis of 2008, or minor but significant changes in monetary policy of rich countries, like what happened in 2013 when the prospect that the U.S. Federal Reserve would suspend "quantitative easing" policy led to strong currency depreciations in developing countries.

In rejecting exchange-rate policy, conventional economists invoke a trilemma – Robert Mundell's "impossible trinity". This economic syllogism states that it is impossible for a government to simultaneously manage the exchange rate, implement an independent monetary policy, and allow free capital flows. Combinations of any two of these policies are possible, but never a combination of all three. In practice, the liberal orthodoxy has interpreted this hypothesis as ruling out exchange-rate policy. Given that free capital flows are "inevitable" and that governments cannot renounce monetary policy, they should not have an exchange-rate policy.

We must, however, consider two issues. First, there is no reason to reject the feasibility of intermediate interventions, such as, for instance, limited capital controls, management of the exchange rate within a price range, and reasonable autonomy for monetary policy. Second, in this trilemma no one questions the need for the government and its central bank to retain their discretion in pursuing the monetary policy, but there is no reason to presume, as neoclassical economics does, that it is impossible to control capital flows. As long as a country's policy regime includes capital controls, the possibility of pursuing an exchange rate policy without undermining freedom in monetary policy remains open – and compromises between the three policies will be the rule.

The long-term equilibrium of the exchange rate

What determines the exchange rate? Economics teaches that the demand for and the supply of foreign money determines the exchange rate in the short run, and, in the long run, the usual explanation is given by the purchasing power parity theory, specifically by the absolute PPP. Instead, we present in this chapter an alternative theory. We distinguish the value of the exchange rate from its market price, and limit the expression "equilibrium" to the concept of the exchange rate in terms of value. In the long term, the market exchange rate floats around the value of the foreign currency, which we define as the exchange rate that covers the "production cost", or, in other words, the rate that allows the country's representative enterprise in the tradable sector to achieve a satisfactory profit rate.[2] The long-term equilibrium of the exchange rate corresponds to its value. We call this long-term equilibrium of the exchange rate "current equilibrium" – the exchange rate that remunerates adequately competent business enterprises producing tradable goods and services and balances intertemporally the current account of the country. In principle, this would be the only value of a currency, but, as we will see in Chapter 6, if the economy suffers from the Dutch disease, there is a second equilibrium in value terms: the "industrial equilibrium exchange rate", which we define as the actual equilibrium, or the competitive equilibrium. In the short term, the market price exchange rate floats around the value determined by the supply of and demand for foreign currency. Supply and demand involve the revenues and expenditures that originate not only in exports and imports, but also in capital flows. If the country accepts relatively permanent current account deficits, because it hopes to grow with foreign savings, and if the net capital inflows that are required to finance these deficits are equal to the growth rate of GDP (or of exports), then the ratio of foreign debt to GDP (or exports) will be constant, and we call the resulting exchange rate the "foreign debt equilibrium exchange rate". The market exchange rate that corresponds to this "equilibrium" is the one that conventional economists usually *recommend* to developing countries, given that they favour a policy of promoting growth cum foreign savings and that they ignore the Dutch disease.

Robert Z. Aliber (1987, vol. 2, p. 210), in the *Palgrave Dictionary of Economics* distinguished five approaches towards explaining the level of the exchange rate and changes in the exchange rate (purchasing power parity, elasticities, portfolio balance, and the asset market approach). We are not going to review these disparate approaches, which signal how poor the existing theories on the exchange rate are. Here we will only discuss the concept of real exchange rate and the purchasing power parity approach. When we say that the exchange rate is a relationship between the prices of tradables and those of non-tradables, wages being the most important price of a non-tradable service, we are thinking of it in terms of value. Sebastian Edwards (1988, p. 3), for instance, understands that "the real exchange rate is defined as the relative price of tradable with respect to non-tradable goods". But here the "real" term does not mean that prices in a series were deflated, but that the depreciation indeed happened; that it was not "eaten" by inflation. In fact, an "actual" depreciation means that the cost of non-tradable services fell in relation to that of tradable goods and services. Actually, the relative prices of tradables with respect to non-tradable goods and services do not tell us which is the equilibrium exchange rate; they are rather the consequence of a depreciation or an appreciation.

Among these five approaches to the long run equilibrium of the exchange rate, the more acceptable alternative to the value theory is the PPP theory. According to it, the "absolute" purchasing power parity is the exchange rate that equates the cost of the same basket of goods in two countries having different currencies.[3] Thus, if the cost of a basket of goods in Brazil, in reais (let us say, R$ 90.00), is equal to its cost in dollars in the United States of the same basket of goods (US$ 30.00), the "absolute" PPP will be R$ 3.00 per dollar.

According to PPP theory, which assumes that goods are homogeneous, the real exchange rate floats around a constant level in the long term, which also, implicitly, guarantees the current account equilibrium of the balance-of-payments. In that setting, what prevails is the "law of one price" produced by the representative business enterprise, according to which homogeneous goods should have the same price in different countries, adjusted by the nominal exchange rate. The obvious problem with PPP theory is its assumption that relative prices in different countries are the same or almost the same. This may make sense in countries with similar levels of development, but does not when considering a developing and a rich country. Even among similar countries, there is the problem of the national tax systems, which may be very different and, so, making relative prices very different in one country in relation to another. On the other hand, there is the problem of which goods and services to include in the basket. In the countries with the Dutch disease, the prices of the commodities will be low in relation to the other tradable goods.

Value and price of foreign currency

Instead of defining the equilibrium exchange rate in terms of the comparative prices of a basket of goods and services, we define it in terms of value; as all goods and services, the foreign money also has a value and a price. Instead of mixing the concepts of real exchange rate with PPP, we distinguish the real exchange rate (which is the price-level adjusted nominal exchange rate) from the equilibrium exchange rate, which we define in value terms. To know if a currency is misaligned throughout time or not we don't use as reference PPP index price-level adjusted. Instead we use an index having as basis the originally defined value of the exchange rate for a given year; the following numbers of the index are not just price-level adjusted, but additionally defined according to the evolution of the unit labour cost in one country compared to another or to a basket of countries.

Whereas demand for and supply of foreign money define in the short-term the market price of the exchange rate, its *value* determines it in the long-term; it is around it that the exchange rate floats. As market prices determined by supply and demand reflect the labour value, or, more simply, the cost plus reasonable profit relative to the production of goods and services generally, in the case of foreign currency the market price likewise reflects its value.

How to define the value of a good, or of a service, or of foreign currency? In strictly theoretical terms, according to the classic doctrines of David Ricardo, value corresponds to the amount of socially necessary labour to produce the good or service; or, more precisely, it corresponds to the value transformed into price through the equalization of the profit rates. In practical terms, it corresponds to the production cost plus a reasonable profit that stimulates competent enterprises to keep producing the good or service. In other words, it is the "necessary price" of the good or service.

Given this second definition of value – the cost of production– we may *define* the value of the exchange rate: it is the value of foreign currency expressed in terms of domestic currency that allows the country's representative business enterprises that participate in foreign trade and guarantee the equilibrium of its current account to obtain a revenue that covers their costs plus a reasonable rate of profit. If we assume the absence of tariff protection, it is the value of the foreign money or "necessary price" that ensures that business enterprises using world state-of-the-art technology are competitive. If we assume current account equilibrium and a decreasing scale of competitiveness, the value of the exchange rate corresponds to the value that covers cost plus a reasonable profit (in domestic currency) of the last or the marginal business enterprise that manages to export.[4] The business enterprises that determine the value of the exchange rate are, therefore, those that are competitive enough to participate in the country's foreign trade. If we take into account business enterprises' different levels of efficiency, the current account equilibrium establishes the threshold for determining those business enterprises that jointly form the representative business enterprise and define the value of the exchange rate.

Therefore, as happens with the other goods and services, the value of the exchange rate or of foreign currency does not depend on variations in the currency's supply and demand, whether they result from international trade or from capital flows. Indeed, it is the market price of the exchange rate that depends on those variations and on its value. The value of the exchange rate depends essentially on the cost of production – that is, on the wages and on the corresponding productivity existing in the country, relative to those of other countries, as expressed by the comparative unit labour cost index. When unit labour costs in a given country rise in relation to those in its trading partners, this means that the value of its exchange rate valorized.[5]

The value of the foreign currency is not constant. It is always changing in response to changes in technology that reflect the ability of business enterprises to keep pace with changes in technology in other countries. And it is always changing as real wages change in relation to wages in other countries. If the unions succeed in forcing up wages in excess of productivity, whereas the same does not happen in other countries, relative unit labour costs will increase, the value of the exchange rate will increase, and the real exchange rate will also appreciate, thus confirming the loss of competitiveness that has taken place in the productive sector of the economy.

In synthesis, the competitiveness of the country and the motivation of companies to invest, therefore, depend, in real terms, on the comparative index of unit labour costs and, in monetary terms, the exchange rate. Given the competition in the market, the exchange rate should fluctuate around this index because that index is determining the value of the exchange rate. Given the evolution of unit labour cost in the country and the average unit labour costs of competing countries, we have the comparative index of unit labour cost, which corresponds to the value of the exchange rate and tells us about which value should floating the exchange rate market. If this ratio grows, the value of foreign currency and the exchange rate market will depreciate correspondent. However the correlation between the value and the price is far from perfect in developing countries due to the cyclical and chronic tendency to the overvaluation of the exchange rate in developing countries. The price of the exchange rate is determined at every moment by supply and demand in currency markets, which include capital flows. Given the high degree of liquidity in financial markets, that is, given the abundance of money in modern global capitalism, the willingness of financial agents in rich countries to lend increased considerably and for a relatively long time. On the other hand, foreign loans are always vulnerable to the formation of bubbles. These two factors enable exchange rate overvaluation to last for a relatively long time, making the exchange rate *chronically* overvalued. Without the assumption of a bubble, the overvaluation of the currency could not last; the exchange rate would be volatile, but not chronically overvalued. When the exchange rate became overvalued, creditors immediately would pull back and the exchange rate would depreciate.

Which of the three equilibriums?

In this chapter we have discussed so far the determination of the exchange rate, and we have seen that, in the medium term, it is determined by its value, which depends (*a*) on the cost of production plus a reasonable profit for local business enterprises that participate in international trade and (*b*), in the short term, on the supply of and demand for foreign currency, including capital flows. But what is the country's equilibrium exchange rate? What is the exchange rate that guarantees the country's financial stability and favors its growth? We have three candidates: the industrial equilibrium, the current equilibrium, and the foreign debt equilibrium. For those who believe that the country should adopt the policy of promoting growth cum foreign savings, the equilibrium exchange rate is the exchange rate compatible with a current account deficit that does not increase the country's foreign debt-to-GDP ratio. For those who believe that the attempt to grow with current account deficits and foreign indebtedness implies a high rate of substitution of foreign for domestic savings, the equilibrium exchange rate would be the rate that balances the country's current account. Finally, if the country is suffering from the Dutch disease, the equilibrium exchange rate is the rate that makes not only the country's commodity-exporting business enterprises competitive, but all business enterprises using world state-of-the-art technology.

The current account is a fundamental variable because it determines the variations in each country's foreign indebtedness. Whenever there is a current account deficit, there is an increase in the country's foreign debt. The developing countries that adopt a national development strategy and grow fast with stability always manage their exchange rate and avoid chronic current account deficits because they know how dangerous they are, given that foreign indebtedness is denominated in foreign currency. Yet running current account deficits is usually thought to be the "normal" condition for developing countries, insofar as they should benefit from finance from rich countries. This is the origin of the concept of the "foreign debt equilibrium exchange rate" introduced in the beginning of this chapter. The more obvious concept is the "current account equilibrium exchange rate", but, as we will argue extensively in this book, the exchange rate that countries need in order to grow rapidly and to industrialize, that is, to catch up, is the "industrial equilibrium exchange rate" – the exchange rate that is consistent with the neutralization of the Dutch disease, as we will show in Chapter 6.

At this point three things must be clear. First, industrial equilibrium exchange rate is the one that enables a developing country to industrialize. Second, neutralizing the Dutch disease means shifting the exchange rate to a level that makes its competent industrial enterprises competitive. Third, if the country manages to neutralize the Dutch disease by shifting its value or necessary price from the current equilibrium to the industrial equilibrium, making them equal, the country will by definition have a current account surplus, since the exchange rate will be lower than it was before the neutralization, when it was possible to reach a current account equilibrium. This means that other countries will run current account deficits – something that is not an issue for rich countries that become indebted in their own currency. But of those countries only the United States has accepted current account deficits without demur. The other countries and, in general, the liberal orthodoxy strongly resist them.

Both the current equilibrium and the industrial equilibrium are concepts of value. The industrial equilibrium exchange rate is the *competitive* exchange rate of a country that has the Dutch disease; the current equilibrium, the competitive exchange rate when that disease is absent. A competitive exchange rate does not mean that it is a "relatively depreciated" exchange rate; rather it is an equilibrium rate, the market equilibrium being understood in the *strong* meaning of the concept: there is equilibrium when efficient business enterprises make enough profit to continue to invest. The concept of the equilibrium exchange rate is important, because a competitive exchange rate is fundamental to economic growth, insofar as it works as a kind of light switch that turns "on" or "off" technologically and administratively competent enterprises in relation to global demand. An exchange rate is competitive if it encourages export-oriented investment, avoids unfair competition from foreign enterprises in the local market, and correspondingly increases domestic savings. An overvalued exchange rate is an exchange rate that fails to satisfy these three conditions.

Usually we believe that there is a unique relation between the exchange rate and the current account: When the exchange rate appreciates, the current account deficit increases or the current account surplus decreases. But we may, and *must*, think also from the other side of the equation. If the government adopts the policy of growth cum foreign savings, the ensuing current account deficit will cause the exchange rate to appreciate due to capital inflows. If current account deficits result from the decision to grow with foreign savings, they are the exogenous variables that determine the exchange rate appreciation. On the other side, if appreciation of the exchange rate is caused by its adoption as an anchor against inflation, that rate is the independent variable, and the current account deficit the dependent variable.

Summary

Briefly, in this chapter we dealt with exchange-rate regimes. We argued in favor of an exchange rate policy, and we discussed the problem of the determination of the exchange rate. In order to do so, we distinguished the value of the exchange rate from its price – something that we believe will break new ground in economic literature. As happens with goods, foreign currency has a long-term value, and a price that turns or floats around its value. The value of the exchange rate corresponds to the value of the foreign currency, expressed in terms of domestic currency, that allows the country's representative business enterprises that participate in foreign trade to obtain a reasonable (or satisfactory) profit rate and guarantees the equilibrium of the country's current account. Finally, we briefly defined what we understand by the equilibrium exchange rate or competitive exchange rate.

Notes

1 Yet, despite what Surjit S. Bhalla (2012) does in an empirically well-founded book on the role of the exchange rate on economic growth, we don't relate growth with a "misaligned" or a "depreciated" exchange rate, but with an exchange rate floating around the equilibrium – the industrial equilibrium.
2 In other words, it is the "production cost", which includes normal profit.
3 The "relative" PPP is the one determined in real terms (inflation neutralized) throughout time, having as reference the absolute PPP.
4 Observe that here we are not assuming diminishing returns; we are just assuming that we can order business enterprises according to efficiency.
5 Another possibility, which strictly speaking is more realistic, is to consider that business enterprise can replace labour with imported inputs. So it is necessary to consider those inputs as a part of production costs. This strategy can reduce production costs and the value of the exchange rate, but it will also contribute to reducing the share of manufacturing in value added (Marconi and Rocha, 2012). Since this is an undesirable effect, we consider competitiveness based only on unit labour costs.

6 Overvaluation and access to the markets

In the previous chapters we discussed the proposition that the determining factor of economic growth is the investment rate. Investment adjusts to the increase in aggregate demand, provided that the expected rate of return on capital exceeds the opportunity cost of capital by a certain margin. In turn, expectations regarding the return on capital or investment opportunities depend on the expected increase in sales (which depends on the increase in autonomous demand) and on the expected profit margin. Investments may be oriented to both domestic and foreign markets. As for the domestic market, investment opportunities depend on the growth of the demand for consumption, and on the government's spending decisions, particularly investment spending. For investment oriented to foreign markets, the profit opportunities depend on world economic growth and on the income elasticity of the country's exports. Keynes showed that the chronic insufficiency of demand limits investment opportunities, and proposed policies to neutralize this tendency to inadequate demand.

However, just as reality has refuted classical and neoclassical economics, so it has refuted Keynesian macroeconomics, because there are several cases in which demand has initially been guaranteed, but investment opportunities have nevertheless failed to materialize because the exchange rate is overvalued. In this situation, exporters' profit margins are reduced or even negative, and entrepreneurs have no incentive to invest; or imported goods are much more competitive than domestic goods, so demand leaks away (domestic demand will be partially met by foreign competitors) and, again, there is no incentive to invest. Although Keynesian analysis emphasizes the exchange rate's volatility, it assumes, as does the neoclassical analysis, that the country's exchange rate is in equilibrium in the long term. Thus, it assumes that the exchange rate will ensure to technologically competent business enterprises access to both the domestic market and the foreign market – which, however, is not true for developing countries.

Given our claim that markets do not ensure that the exchange rate achieves a medium-term competitive equilibrium, it becomes clear that it is not enough to guarantee effective demand for investment opportunities to emerge;[1] it is also necessary in an open economy that costs and profit margins are internationally competitive. In other words, investments don't depend just on the existence of demand and on the interest rate; they also depend on the exchange rate. In the first chapter of *The General Theory of Employment* (1936), Keynes criticized Say's Law. He demonstrated that supply does not automatically create demand. Leakages may exist that suggest a tendency for demand to be insufficient. Keynes presented a closed economy model. In this book, which assumes an open-economy model, we argue that, in developing countries, besides the insufficiency of demand, there is the problem of the lack of access to this demand, due to the historically observed tendency to the cyclical and chronic overvaluation of the exchange rate in developing countries.

Good economic theory is usually simple; it establishes simple relationships between economic variables. But new theories usually require time to be understood and accepted. It is not obvious that, often, demand exists but business enterprises have no access to it. They lack access not for institutional reasons (because, for instance, the consumption of certain goods was prohibited in the country), but for an economic reason: because the exchange rate tends to be chronically overvalued in developing countries. Once the existence of this tendency is recognized, the problem of access to demand becomes obvious.

The exchange rate either guarantees or blocks access of enterprises to both foreign and domestic markets. If the exchange rate remains chronically overvalued, competent enterprises, which use world state-of-the-art technology, will be disconnected from their markets; access to the markets for which they have been designed and set up will be denied; and they will be uncompetitive not because they are inefficient, but because a mispriced relevant macroeconomic price makes them so.

Generally, when we discuss competitiveness, we discuss business enterprises' technological and administrative capability, the costs they incur in wages and associated workers' entitlements, the quality of the economic infrastructure, and the tax burden. We generally forget what is often the most important factor: exchange rate overvaluation. The same happens in international trade relations. Customs tariffs are extensively debated. Tariffs are normally understood as an acknowledgement by the countries raising them that their business enterprises are inefficient, whereas they may be just an awkward form of compensating them for the chronic overvaluation of the exchange rate.

Tendency to overvaluation

It is time to explain more precisely what we mean by the tendency to the cyclical and chronic overvaluation of the exchange rate that exists in developing countries. When we say that the exchange rate is cyclically overvalued, we mean that there is a tendency to overvaluation, but that, obviously, this tendency is limited; it soon finds a level, a bottom line, from which it is unable to appreciate further; it remains at this level for some time, which corresponds to a current account deficit growth rate higher than the one observed for exports. Consequently, the ratio of foreign debt to exports increases, which causes, first, a credit bubble, insofar as creditors are blissfully happy to finance the country independently of its capacity to honour its debt; and second, an increase in external vulnerability that forces the country to implement "confidence building policy" – that is, to try to regain the confidence of foreign creditors by accepting their recommendations and pressures without demur. Finally, as the debt in foreign currency grows, the creditors, so far euphoric with the loans made, suddenly lose confidence in the country's ability to pay its debts, suspend the debt rollover, and a currency crisis breaks as the domestic currency depreciates violently. This crisis or "sudden stop" happens because it then becomes obvious to all the creditors that they and the government and enterprises of the debtor country have together been involved in what Hyman Minsky called "Ponzi finances", in which additional indebtedness was being used to pay not the principal but the interest on existing debt.

We summarize the tendency to the cyclical and chronic overvaluation of the exchange rate and the three equilibrium levels of the exchange rate in Figure 6.1.

In this figure ε is the exchange rate. The horizontal line is the "current account equilibrium exchange rate" – the level or value of the exchange rate which, given the terms of trade and the country's relative unit labour costs, balances intertemporally its current account. It is the value of the exchange rate around which the market exchange rate should float. The three curves represent, respectively, the typical behaviour of the market exchange rate according to neoclassical economics, Keynesian macroeconomics, and our own developmental macroeconomics; the neoclassical curve floats sweetly around the equilibrium; the Keynesian curve follows a highly volatile pattern around the equilibrium, but, as in the case of the neoclassical curve, the misalignments don't point in any particular direction; but in fact, in developing countries, the market price exchange rate has a tendency to appreciation and the respective curve follows a cyclical trajectory. As Figure 6.1 shows, this curve begins at the time of the currency crisis, when the exchange rate rises violently, devaluing; subsequently, it gradually falls, cuts across the current

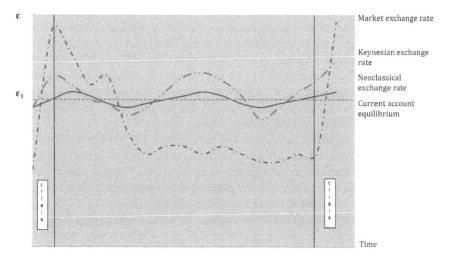

Figure 6.1 The cyclical and chronic tendency to overvaluation

equilibrium lines, and reaches the area of the current account deficit. Eventually, the exchange rate stops appreciating because it has reached its "bottom" – the level below which even exporters of the commodities originating the Dutch disease turn uncompetitive. At this level the current account deficit/GDP will be higher than the GDP growth rate – this means that the foreign debt will increase in relation to GDP, but foreign creditors will continue to be happy. This characterizes the formation of a credit bubble. Only a credit bubble – so common in finance – can explain why the floating exchange rate regime does not correct the misalignment and bring the exchange rate back to the current equilibrium. Creditors keep for a time confidence in the country's and its government's ability to pay back the loans, although such trust ceased to be rational. Actually, after a period of financial health following the currency crises (and the sharp devaluation that they entail), the country now experiences financial fragility – a speculative condition (in Minsky's terms). Creditors continue to trust, but not unconditionally. Now the debtor country will have to pay the "confidence building" game; they will have to follow their recommended policies, particularly the increase in the interest rate and fiscal adjustment. However, as the current account deficit continues high because the exchange rate is overvalued, the country's foreign debt ratio continues to deteriorate, and, finally, following the well-known herd behaviour, the foreign creditors lose confidence, suspend the roll-over of the debt, and a new balance of payment or currency crisis materializes.

Thus the course of the exchange rate is not the gentle fluctuation around the equilibrium that neoclassical economists expect, or the volatile fluctuation predicted by Keynesians; it is one of high volatility with a general tendency – appreciation – which ends in a balance-of-payments crisis. The bubble behaviour prevents the market exchange rate from floating gently around the equilibrium. It is a balance-of-payments crisis, not a well-behaved market, which determines the end of the cycle. But it is not just the market that fails to do its task due to bubble behaviour. As we will see in Chapters 7–9, conventional economic policies – which are usually adopted by developing countries regardless of whether they are orthodox or Keynesian – are an active cause of the cyclical process. A financial bubble made the excessive foreign indebtedness of the country possible; the causes of such indebtedness were policies like the growth cum foreign savings policy, the use of exchange rate as an anchor to control inflation, and exchange rate populism – that is, the policy determined by the preference for immediate consumption that is associated with current account deficits.

Note that the overvaluation depicted in the Figure 6.1 is not just cyclical; it is also a chronic overvaluation, because the exchange rate is overvalued for a much longer time than the short period after the currency crisis in which it is depreciated. The exchange rate is devalued only for a short period immediately after the crisis.

Note also that in this model there is a direct relationship between the exchange rate and the current account deficit or surplus. We cannot, however, infer a cause and effect relationship, because first we need to know which variable was the subject of an economic policy decision – that is, the variable that played the role of independent variable. Let's assume that the exchange rate appreciated and the country's current account deficit increased. If this appreciation resulted from the drop in exports, the decrease in capital inflows, or the increase in capital outflows and, as a result, the exchange rate appreciated, the current account deficit is a consequence of the appreciation. Yet when the government decides to grow with foreign savings, it is deciding that it will have a current account deficit, and this decision then corresponds to the variable that causes the appreciation. Both situations will have effects on the whole economic system, but the latter, as a policy decision, tends to be longer-lasting and therefore has greater impacts on the productive structure of the economy.

An overview of the causes of overvaluation

In Chapter 5 we distinguished the value of the exchange rate from its price. In light of this distinction, we have two types of causes of the tendency to the cyclical and chronic overvaluation of the exchange rate: structural causes, which affect the value of the exchange rate, and policy causes, which affect the exchange-rate market price. The main structural cause is the Dutch disease; wages, productivity, and a reasonable profit rate are the structural factors that determine the value of the exchange rate, but when there is the Dutch disease, the Ricardian rents are the fourth determinant of the value of the exchange rate. But the Dutch disease only appreciates the exchange rate up to the current equilibrium; it does not lead the market exchange rate to the region of the current account deficit in which it falls, as we see from Figure 6.1. Thus we need additional causes to explain why the exchange rate falls below the current equilibrium, and, worse, below the "foreign debt equilibrium" – the limit level of the exchange rate. Consequently, the rate falls below the current account deficit, which is consistent with the constancy of the country's foreign debt to GDP ratio at a level that does not push the country into the financial fragility condition. The policy causes that appreciate the exchange rate and lead the country to incur into current account deficits below the foreign debt equilibrium are related to the supply of or demand for foreign currency. These causes are (*a*) excessive capital inflows as a consequence of the growth cum foreign savings policy, (*b*) the use of the exchange rate anchor to fight inflation, (*c*) the adoption of a high level of interest rates, which is instrumental for the two previous policies and for avoiding a supposed "financial repression", and (*d*) a fiscal policy involving chronic budget deficits inconsistent with the current account surplus, which will materialize insofar that the Dutch disease is neutralized and the exchange rate floats around the industrial equilibrium. The three policies involve a preference for immediate consumption, and, so, are cases of economic populism: the first two, of exchange rate populism, the last one, of fiscal populism.

At this time it is important to observe that the policies causes of the appreciation are policies usually adopted by local politicians with the approval of the international financial institutions. As Olivier Blanchard (2013, p. 2) recognized in an article with a suggestive tittle ("Monetary policy will never be the same"), the orthodoxy have traditionally presented three arguments against exchange rate adjustments, i.e., devaluations, which should be corrected:

> The first is that, to the extent that domestic borrowers have borrowed in foreign currency, the depreciation has adverse effects on balance sheets, and leads to a decrease in domestic demand that may more than offset the increase in exports. The second is that much of the nominal depreciation may simply translate into higher inflation. The third is that large movements in the exchange rate may lead to disruptions, both in the real economy and in financial markets . . . The evidence, however, is that the first two are much less relevant than they were in previous crises. Thanks to macroprudential measures, to the development of local currency bond markets, and to exchange rate flexibility and thus a better perception by borrowers of exchange rate risk, foreign exchange exposure in emerging market countries is much more limited than it was in previous crises.

But we should not minimize the resistance to devaluations. Not only coming from the liberal side, but also from the developmental one. When we emphasize the need of neutralizing the tendency to the cyclical and chronic overvaluation of the exchange rate means, we are recommending in the short term a devaluation of the exchange rate (what does not mean a shock) and, in the long term, the adoption of an exchange-rate policy aimed at keeping the market exchange rate floating around the industrial equilibrium. Besides the resistance of liberal economists, we have also the resistance of developmental economists. They acknowledge the inability of markets to keep the exchange rate competitive, but usually hesitate to recommend devaluation, because, in the short term, it implies a decrease in wages and an increase in inflation. We discuss this issue throughout this book.

Summary

Briefly, the exchange rate is the most strategic of macroeconomic prices. It determines not only imports and exports, but also investment, savings, wages, consumption, and inflation. The presence in developing countries of a cyclical and chronic tendency to the exchange rate overvaluation makes it even more strategic. Its existence raises the problem of access to demand. The presence of demand is not enough to ensure that investment opportunities exist and that investment happens: It is necessary also to have access to demand. The structuralist development macroeconomics of this book tries to focus on this access issue. If there were no tendency to overvaluation, we might still think that either the exchange rate floats around the equilibrium gently, as proposed by neoclassical economics, or in a volatile way, as envisaged by Keynesian economics. In fact, the volatility of the exchange rate is accompanied by a tendency; appreciation is interrupted only by the crisis.

The tendency is expressed in cycles of appreciation, during which a credit bubble is inflated; when the bubble eventually bursts we have a new balance of payment or currency crisis. The causes of overvaluation are both structural, such as the non-neutralized Dutch disease, and policy related, such as excessive capital inflows, the exchange rate anchor policy and exchange rate populism, which we will discuss in the following chapters. All of these factors cause the exchange rate market price to deviate from its value. This chapter serves as an introduction to those that follow, which discuss these causes.

Note

1 The medium term corresponds to the period in which the tendency of exchange rate is more important than its fluctuations in inducing investment decisions.

7 The Dutch disease

The Dutch disease, or the "natural resource curse", results in a permanent over-valuation of the exchange rate, which is key in explaining why some developing countries industrialize and grow rapidly whereas others lag behind. To be sure, there are other explanations for the fact that most oil-exporting countries fail to industrialize and grow, despite the wealth that oil represents; but the Dutch disease is certainly the crucial factor. We may find other explanations for Asian countries developing faster than Latin American countries since they became independent, but a main cause is that Latin America, unlike the fast-growing Asian countries, has an abundance of natural resources. As a result, the Asian countries do not suffer – or suffer only mildly – from the Dutch disease, and can neutralize it relatively easily, while in Latin America the Dutch disease is usually severe, even in non-exporting oil countries such as Brazil.

The cause of the Dutch disease is the Ricardian rents that originate in the exploitation of abundant and cheap natural resources in order to export commodities. Besides paying wages and profits, the exploitation of natural resources gives rise to Ricardian rents for the country insofar as the costs involved in the production of the commodity are lower than those incurred by the least efficient marginal producers admitted to that global market, the ones that set the minimum international market price of the commodity.

The Dutch disease results in the permanent overvaluation of the exchange rates of countries exporting commodities that benefit from abundant and cheap resources and the corresponding Ricardian rents. The overvaluation arises because exports of such commodities are economically viable or can be exported at an exchange rate that is clearly above the level required to make competitive the non-commodity business enterprises producing tradable goods and services that use world state-of-the-art technology. If neutralized through the use of a variable tax on the exports of the commodity, the Dutch disease is a blessing for a country; non-neutralized, it is either a permanent obstacle to industrialization if the country has not yet industrialized, or causes its deindustrialization if the country that is already industrialized has neutralized it in the past but later liberalized its foreign accounts, and consequently no longer neutralizes it.

The Dutch disease afflicts almost all developing countries because, as we will see, it affects not only natural, resource-rich countries, but also countries with cheap labour where wage differential is greater than that which exists in the rich countries. It is a very serious market failure because it does not generate a crisis; in fact, it is consistent with a country's current account equilibrium, such that the exchange rate overvaluation that it causes may persist without causing a balance-of-payment crisis.

The concept of the Dutch disease

The Dutch disease is an old problem. It is essential for explaining development and underdevelopment, but it was identified only in the 1960s, in the Netherlands, where the discovery and export of natural gas appreciated the exchange rate and threatened to destroy the country's manufacturing industry. In the 1980s the first academic studies on the subject appeared, along with the first model of the Dutch disease (Corden and Neary, 1982; Corden, 1984). In their model, the authors assumed an economy with three sectors, two of them related to tradable goods (the "booming" natural resources sector and the "lagging" manufacturing sector), and a third sector made up of non-tradables. Sachs and Warner (2001), summarizing the literature on the Dutch disease, explain it as a wealth shock in the natural resources sector, which creates excess demand in the non-tradables sector, implying a change in relative prices. The appreciated exchange rate reflects the change in relative prices that favours non-tradables. In the model that we present here from Bresser-Pereira (2008), the emphasis is placed directly on the exchange rate and on the existence of two equilibrium exchange rates, two "necessary prices" which correspond to the value of the foreign money respectively for exporters of commodities and for other business enterprises producing tradable goods and services.

We may define the Dutch disease very simply. The Dutch disease involves a chronic exchange rate overvaluation caused by the exploitation of abundant and cheap resources, whose export is compatible with a clearly higher exchange rate than the rate that makes internationally competitive other business enterprises in the tradable sector using the world's most modern technology. The producers of commodities have lower production costs and can be competitive and reach the necessary level of profitability with a higher exchange rate than the rate required by producers of non-commodity tradable goods and services. It is a structural phenomenon that creates obstacles to industrialization or productive sophistication; if it was previously neutralized and the country industrialized, but then it is no longer neutralized, it provokes deindustrialization.

The Dutch disease amounts to a market failure because it distorts a fundamental price – the exchange rate – and because it generates negative externalities for the economy's non-commodity tradable sectors, preventing them from developing even if they adopt the world's best technology and the best administrative practices. It is a market failure that implies the existence of a difference between the exchange rate that balances intertemporally the country's current account and the exchange rate that sustains efficient tradable goods and services sectors besides those benefiting from Ricardian rents. Only when the Dutch disease is neutralized will the market be able to efficiently allocate resources and promote investment and innovation.

Commodities give rise to the Dutch disease because they benefit from Ricardian rents. According to the classic theory of David Ricardo, their market price is defined on the international market by the least efficient marginal producer admitted to the market. The difference between the cost corresponding to this price and the cost to a country of producing the commodity from its natural resources is the Ricardian rent. Usually the Dutch disease is associated with a sole good (oil) or with a limited number of goods produced with these natural resources. Whereas in Ricardo's model the rents benefit only the owners of the most productive lands, in the case of the Dutch disease, if these rents are not neutralized, they will benefit, in the short run, all the country's consumers, who will buy tradable goods more cheaply than the prices that would prevail should the exchange rate be in equilibrium. But these rents will encumber the whole population in the medium term because they compromise industrialization or, more broadly, because they impede the transfer of labour to sectors with greater value added per capita – a transfer that is the primary source of higher productivity and of economic development.

In the model we are presenting here, and in contrast to what happens with the original Ricardian rents, there is no difference in productivity between local producers, but just a difference between the country's productivity and other countries' productivity, which determines the international price of the commodity. If there is a difference in productivity among producers, there will also be Ricardian rents among the producers, insofar as the domestic price of the commodity will be defined by the least efficient local producer, but this does not affect the exchange rate. What is essential to grasp is that the Ricardian rents are earned by the country as a whole, and what is important for growth is what it does with them. If its government fails to manage or to neutralize them, they will be distributed among all the consumers, the exchange rate will remain overvalued, and the manufacturing sector will be rendered unviable in economic terms.

In the first paper by Bresser-Pereira on the Dutch disease (2008), the *value* of the exchange rate was suggested only when he defined the current and the industrial equilibriums as "necessary prices". In his 2013 paper, he defined the value of the foreign money as the value of the exchange rate that covers the costs plus reasonable profits of the business enterprises that participate in the country's foreign trade – a value around which the market exchange rate floats. In the case of the Dutch disease, there are two values or two necessary prices: the current necessary price and the industrial necessary price. In the third part of this book we will also demonstrate more clearly the connection of that value of the exchange rate with the neutralization of the Dutch disease through the imposition of an export tax on the commodities that give rise to it.

This is the second model on the Dutch disease. The first one, by Corden and Neary (1982) and Corden (1984), was a significant contribution, but it is a neoclassical model that does not place the exchange rate at the centre of the problem that the disease creates. Instead, it focuses on the existence of two sectors. In addition, it is a short-term neoclassical model that is concerned with the change caused by the exploitation and export of oil, and it is only a partial macroeconomic model because it has no currency and assumes full employment. In contrast, the model presented here is a structuralist model, which adopts the classic notion of labour value or, more practically, of cost plus a reasonable or satisfactory profit margin, in order to explain why countries where the Dutch disease is not neutralized discourage business enterprises from investing.

Two equilibrium exchange rates

Economics assumes that in reasonably well-functioning markets business enterprises utilizing world state-of-the-art technology are competitive. This is not true where the Dutch disease has struck. Other competitiveness factors being equal, if a business enterprise utilizing the best technology is established in a country affected by this disease, it will be economically viable only if its productivity is so much greater than the productivity of competitors in other countries that it compensates the appreciation caused by the disease. Thus, the Dutch disease is characterized by the existence of two exchange rate equilibriums, one – the current equilibrium – generated by commodities, and the other – the industrial equilibrium – generated by other tradable goods. The current equilibrium exchange rate guarantees a reasonable profit rate for producers of the commodities that cause the disease, and balances intertemporally the country's current account; the industrial equilibrium exchange rate makes competitive those business enterprises producing internationally tradable goods and services using world state-of-the-art technology that don't benefit from Ricardian rents. The two equilibriums are here defined in value terms; there is one value that covers the cost plus reasonable profit of the business enterprises exporting commodities, and another value for the other tradable goods and services. The exchange rate market price will float according to the supply of and demand for foreign money around the current, not the industrial, equilibrium, because the commanding equilibrium is the lower one. Thus, besides those two equilibrium rates there is the market price of the foreign currency, the market exchange rate.[1] The market price may be presented in nominal or in real terms; in this book we are not interested in the short term, and will always work with the real market price. Figure 7.1 (based on Figure 6.1) shows the two equilibriums in value terms and the cyclical and chronically overvalued behaviour of the market exchange rate. The distance between the industrial and the current equilibriums is relatively small in this figure, which means that in this country the severity of the disease or of overvaluation is relatively small – it is typical of a country exporting agricultural goods. In contrast, in a country exporting oil and where the cost of producing oil is low, the Dutch disease will be much more severe, and this would be expressed graphically by a wider space between the two lines.

The market exchange rate may be expressed either in real or in nominal terms. The current equilibrium is the one to which the real market exchange rate converges, but the industrial equilibrium exchange rate is the *true* equilibrium rate; it is the country's *competitive* exchange rate; it is the rate that the country

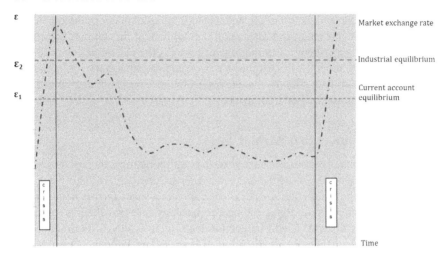

Figure 7.1 Current equilibrium and industrial equilibrium, and the market exchange rate

should pursue in order to develop. Its difference from the current equilibrium rate reveals a serious market failure, because it goes against the basic principle of economic theory according to which, in a market economy, efficient business enterprises are necessarily competitive. In a country free from the Dutch disease, the equilibrium exchange rate corresponds to the equilibrium of relative prices; in other words, it obeys the fundamental law in economic theory – the tendency to the equalization of profit rates. Now, when we have the Dutch disease, it is not the current equilibrium exchange rate but rather the industrial equilibrium exchange rate – the rate resulting from the neutralization of the Dutch disease through exchange rate management – that corresponds to this equilibrium, to this reasonable equalization of profit rates, which is achieved because, as we will see, the correct way to neutralize the natural resources curse is to impose a variable tax on the commodities benefiting from Ricardian rents. Therefore, when a country benefits from Ricardian rents, it will have two equilibrium exchange rates: the current equilibrium exchange rate, ε_c, and the industrial equilibrium exchange rate, ε_i.

In the presence of a non-neutralized Dutch disease, the "potential" competent business enterprises (which could be organized using world state-of-the-art technology) will have a negative expected rate of profit, and the potential entrepreneur will not invest. If the Dutch disease was neutralized in the past and, consequently, industrialization took place, but from a certain moment on this neutralization was abandoned in the name of economic liberalism, those business enterprises in the tradable sector will see their profit rates diminish or become negative (depending on the severity of the disease), and the country will experience premature deindustrialization.[2] In both cases, there will be no equality of opportunity between competing business enterprises, which is the basic condition for the sound operation of world and national markets.

In simple terms, the exchange rate is the price of foreign currency, it is the market exchange rate, ε; it results from the supply of foreign currency generated by exports and capital inflows, and from the demand for foreign currency derived from exports, net profit remittances, and capital outflows. Usually, the exchange rate is in equilibrium when the country's current account is balanced. Capital inflows and outflows endanger its ability to balance the country's current account, but don't change the concept of an equilibrium exchange rate. Measured in domestic currency, the exchange rate is equal to the price in domestic currency of the representative good, $p_{x\#}$, divided by its price in foreign currency, $p_{x\$}$.

$$\varepsilon = p_{x\#} / p_{x\$}$$

But the equilibrium of the exchange depends also on its *value*. The supply of and demand for foreign money just causes the fluctuation of its market price around the current equilibrium. What do we mean by the value of the exchange rate? Just as the value of a good corresponds to the cost plus a reasonable profit margin, sufficient to motivate efficient business enterprises to invest, given the international price of goods and services, the value of the exchange rate corresponds to the rate that enables efficient business enterprises that produce tradable goods to cover their costs and earn a reasonable profit margin. The market exchange rate floats around this value according to the supply of and demand for foreign currency. In the absence of Dutch disease, the necessary price for the exchange rate corresponds to both the current equilibrium exchange rate and the industrial equilibrium exchange rate. For goods in general, therefore, the current necessary price and the industrial necessary price are equal, and correspond to the current equilibrium exchange rate, ε_c.

$$p_{xc\#} = p_{xi\#} = \varepsilon_c$$

Yet, when the Dutch disease is present, there are two values corresponding to the two equilibriums: the *current necessary price*, $p_{xc\#}$, which is the necessary and satisfactory price for business enterprises that produce and export any commodities giving rise to the Dutch disease; and the *industrial necessary price*, $p_{xi\#}$, which is the necessary and satisfactory price for other efficient business enterprises that use world state-of-the-art technology to produce tradable goods. The current equilibrium exchange rate corresponds to the current necessary price, which is, therefore, an exchange rate conceived of in terms of value, in much the same way as the industrial equilibrium exchange rate corresponds to the industrial necessary price

$$P_{xc\#} = \varepsilon_c$$
$$P_{xi\#} = \varepsilon_i.$$

The market exchange rate *floats* around the current necessary price, $p_{xc\#}$, according to the supply of and demand for foreign currency. Capital flows, which have become very high since the 1990s, are part of this supply of and demand for money. As already observed, the market price floats, not around the industrial equilibrium, but around the current equilibrium exchange rate because the current necessary price is the lower value, the one that the market will automatically choose.

$$p_{xc\#} < p_{xi\#}.$$

To sum up, the supply of and demand for money, including capital flows, has no impact on the current equilibrium and the industrial equilibrium, does not change the value of the exchange rate, but affects the market exchange rate. The larger the capital flows, the more volatile the market exchange rate will be; in other words, the more the market exchange rate will diverge from the equilibrium.

Since the market exchange rate will float around the current equilibrium, the other business enterprises in the tradable industries (those not benefiting from Ricardian rents) will become economically unviable even though they use world state-of-the-art technology, because their industrial necessary price is higher (more depreciated) than the current necessary price. The current necessary price and the industrial necessary price are equal when there is no Dutch disease. The two necessary prices or values (the current price and the industrial price) in each country depend (*a*) on the average productivity of the business enterprises that produce, respectively, commodities and other tradable goods and (*b*) on the average wages that they pay compared with the other countries' productivity and wages; in other words, they depend on the unit labour cost (the wage divided by productivity) compared with the unit labour costs of the country's main trading partners.

It is important to observe that the difference between the current price and the necessary price, or between the two equilibriums, should be large enough to characterize the Dutch disease – that is, large enough to inhibit industrialization, or to induce a regression of the productive structure towards primary goods. Otherwise, it would be present whenever there was a comparative advantage and, therefore, whenever there was trade.

The severity of the Dutch disease

The severity or intensity of the Dutch disease, *g*, will increase the greater is the difference between the industrial and the current equilibrium exchange rate. Defining such severity, *g*, as percentage taking as denominator the industrial equilibrium, we have:

$$g = (\varepsilon_i - \varepsilon_c) / \varepsilon_i$$

The severity of the Dutch disease depends essentially on the Ricardian rents involved. The greater the Ricardian rents, the more severe the disease will be. But the Ricardian rents will not be constant: They will vary from moment to moment,

Table 7.1 Severity of the Dutch disease (oil price of US$100.00 per barrel)

Country	1 Industrial equilibrium ($#_i$ per U.S. dollar)	2 Cost of producing oil ($#_i$ per barrel)	3 Current equilibrium ($#_i$ per U.S. dollar) (3-2)	4 Ricardian rents ($#_i$ per barrel) (1-3)	5 Severity of the Dutch disease (3/1)
A	$#_A$2.00	$#_A$140.00	$#_A$1.40	$#_A$60.00	30%
B	$#_B$2.00	$#_B$100.00	$#_B$1.00	$#_B$100.00	50%
C	$#_C$2.00	$#_C$40.00	$#_C$0.40	$#_C$160.00	80%

depending on the international price of the commodity. For a given commodity, they will differ from country to country, depending on the cost of exploiting the natural resource (in the oil industry these costs vary enormously). This is why the Dutch disease affects countries to different degrees or intensities depending on these two variables: the international price (the higher it is, the more severe the Dutch disease is) and production costs (the smaller they are for competent business enterprises, the less severe the Dutch disease is).

To gain a better understand of what we are saying, imagine three countries, A, B, and C, (1) that exploit and export oil at the price of US$100.00 a barrel; (2) their currencies, $#_i$, have different denominations in each country but the same exchange rate to the dollar; and (3) their non-commodity business enterprises are equally efficient, and so the industrial equilibrium exchange rate is equal in the three countries: #2.00 per dollar. Yet they have different costs for producing oil: In country A, the cost plus the reasonable profit margin for the commodity-exporting business enterprises is $#_A$140.00 per barrel; in country B, $#_B$100.00 per barrel; and in country C, $#_C$40.00 per barrel, which will correspond current equilibrium exchange rates of $#_A$1.4, $#_B$1.0 and $#_C$0.40 per dollar, which are satisfactory for the commodity exporters in each of the three countries. Thus, the corresponding Ricardian rents are respectively $#_A$60.00, $#_B$100.00 and $#_C$160.00 per barrel. This means that the severity of the Dutch disease in country A is mild, 30 per cent; in country B medium, 50 per cent; and in country C high, 80 per cent. On the assumption that these countries don't neutralize their Dutch disease, the manufacturing industry in country C and probably also in country B will be simply unviable; in country A, only extremely efficient business enterprises or enterprises whose goods involve high transportation costs will be economically viable.

Extended concept of the Dutch disease

The Dutch disease does not affect exclusively countries that exploit abundant and cheap natural resources. Another source of the Dutch disease, which is becoming significant, is remittances made by immigrants; Mexico and Central American countries are particularly affected by it (Acosta, Lartey, and Mandelman, 2009). Foreign aid also generates Dutch disease in poorer countries. But a cause of the

Dutch disease that dramatically increases its *scope* is the combination of cheap labour and the difference between the average salaries of plant engineers and the average wages of workers that substantially exceeds the equivalent difference in rich countries. This extended concept applies to countries such as China, India, and the other fast-growing Asian countries. They grow fast only because they manage their exchange rates and neutralize the Dutch disease defined according to this extended concept and at the same time achieve current account surpluses (with the exception of India, which has been running deficits). In this case, the Dutch disease is mild, and may be neutralized more easily than in the cases where the Dutch disease is severe.

Why does cheap labour in combination with a wide gulf between salaries and wages cause the Dutch disease? It is not because the value added per capita in the manufacturing sector is higher than that in the primary sector, but because, within the manufacturing sector, there are industries with higher value added per capita and industries with lower value added per capita, which employ unskilled labour and pay low wages. In the case of this extended concept of Dutch disease, the low value added per capita industries play the role of the commodity industry in the classic case of Dutch disease. When the exchange rate is allowed to float freely in a country with cheap labour and a much greater salary–wage differential than exists in rich countries, the equilibrium exchange rate will be determined by the manufacturing sectors that have lower value added per capita and so use less skilled labour and fewer engineers, whereas the high value added per capita industries that use more complex technology and for that reason pay relatively higher wages will not be competitive. Given that salaries make up a greater share of their total salary–wage bill, they would require a more depreciate exchange rate than is satisfactory to the industries that employ only low-wage workers. In other words, given that economic growth implies the transfer of labour to increasingly sophisticated industries that pay higher wages and salaries and involve higher value added per capita, economic growth will be impaired. If the salaries of factory engineers were approximately four times greater than the wages of unskilled workers, as they are in the rich countries, the country benefiting from low salaries and low wages would easily produce all kinds of manufactured goods. But if there is a broader salary–wage differential, for instance salaries 12 times higher than wages in many developing countries, we will be facing a case of the Dutch disease in the extended sense. Sectors that produce low value added goods and hire only unskilled labour require a lower exchange rate to be competitive than sectors producing high value-added goods that involve sophisticated technology in order to be competitive. In this extended concept, the source of the Dutch disease is not Ricardian rents, but rather the salary–wage differential.

The extended concept of the Dutch disease is not the only reason, but is certainly the fundamental reason why the fast-growing Asian countries manage their exchange rates so firmly, preventing their appreciation, and, consequently, often achieving current account surpluses. China, for instance, would never export the increasingly sophisticated products that it does if it did not manage its exchange rate. Thereby, it keeps the exchange rate at the *necessary* level – that is, at the level of the industrial equilibrium exchange rate.

Note that, in the case of the narrow concept of Dutch disease, the commodity-exporting industry may be technologically sophisticated. This is the case with the oil industry, whose value added per capita is usually high since it involves high scientific and technological intensity. But a country cannot just produce oil as a tradable good unless it is very small, first, because the oil sector is capital intensive, thus lacking the capacity to absorb the country's workforce, particularly the engineers and skilled workers that characterize a rich country, and second, because all the other potential tradable industries that are eventually more sophisticated technologically will remain economically unviable. Employment opportunities will be limited mainly to low value added per capita non-tradable industries.

The Dutch disease and deindustrialization

We can identify three paradigmatic scenarios that trigger the Dutch disease: the discovery of natural resources that incorporate Ricardian rents in a poor country, which will undermine this country's industrialization where a neutralization policy is not adopted; the same discovery in an industrialized country that does not take care to neutralize it; and finally, trade and financial liberalization that implies renouncing the existing neutralization policy that successfully opened the way for industrialization. In the second and in the third scenarios the outcome will be premature deindustrialization. The first scenario embraces the cases of Saudi Arabia, Venezuela, and many other poor countries. The second scenario for a while covers the case of the Netherlands (where the policymakers adopted no measures to neutralize the Dutch disease); the case of Mexico, whose rate of growth started to fall in the mid-1970s when oil began to be exported in large quantities; and probably the case of the United Kingdom where the oil discovered in the North Sea was not exhausted. The third scenario was acted out in the case of Brazil after the trade and financial liberalization in the early 1990s. It is true that, sooner or later, technological progress causes deindustrialization, because richer societies shift demand towards modern and highly sophisticated services, and transfer simple manufacturing industries to developing countries. In this case of "non-premature" deindustrialization labour is transferred to service industries where the value added per capita is greater than that in the manufacturing industries that are being transferred to less-developed countries. But this is not the case with the aforementioned deindustrializations. As Gabriel Palma observed (2013, p. 14), in the countries affected by the Dutch disease under the second and third scenarios (United Kingdom and Brazil, respectively), "the fall of manufacturing employment was clearly greater than could be anticipated".[3]

In Brazil, as well as in the other more developed countries in the region, industrialization was possible only because of the formation of a developmental state whose policies were understood by their policymakers as "industrial policies" and by their liberal critics as "protectionism"; but in fact, although the import tariff could be understood in part as legitimate industrial policy reflecting the "infant manufacturing industry" argument, for the most part it was the outcome of an intuitive exchange rate policy aiming at the neutralization of the Dutch disease on the import side. Certainly, in Latin America, trade liberalization in the late 1980s and early 1990s implied that the country was ceasing to neutralize the Dutch disease and beginning premature deindustrialization.

Stopping the neutralization of the Dutch disease hampers the manufacturing industry insofar as it appreciates the exchange rate. But manufacturing industries import inputs. A key characteristic of globalization is the global integration of chains of production. Thus, when there is devaluation, this benefits exports but makes imports more expensive. For that reason it is commonly said that the smaller the local content of a manufacturing good is, the less sensitive the gross production of each business enterprise will be to the devaluation (or appreciation) of the exchange rate. This is a false argument. The devaluation will always benefit this enterprise; however, it will benefit less in terms of total production than another business enterprise that uses fewer imported inputs, but both will benefit in proportion to the respective local value added.

We saw that intuition inspired the neutralization of the Dutch disease in some Latin American countries. Such intuition manifested itself in multiple exchange rates systems and in the combination of high import duties and subsidized exports of manufacturing goods. In both cases, an implicit tax was imposed on the export of commodities – a tax that, as we will see in Chapter 13, is the correct way to neutralize the Dutch disease. Originally the neutralization was effected only on the import side, both with multiple exchange rates (by imposing a relatively high exchange rate on the export of commodities and a relatively low exchange rate on imports of manufactured goods) and with tariffs (by making them higher than would be required by a legitimate industrial policy). Later on, when some countries realized that they could export manufactured goods, the high tariff on imports was complemented by an equally high subsidy for exports of manufactured goods. In this way, between 1967 and 1985 Brazil increased the share of manufactured goods in its total exports from 6 per cent to 65 per cent.[4]

In fact, the adoption as well as the removal of tariffs and export subsidies changes the effective exchange rate. Suppose that, under international pressure, and accused of "protectionism", a country abandons tariff neutralization of the Dutch disease in the name of trade liberalization. As a consequence, the effective exchange rate appreciates. The appreciation is not immediately perceived, since part of the appreciation results from the elimination of taxes and subsidies. However, the country's manufacturing sector soon begins to suffer from the effects of the appreciation, and premature deindustrialization begins. If the disease is not very severe, as in country A, the symptoms of deindustrialization will not be clear, although they will be reflected in the falling share of the manufacturing sector in GDP, in total employment, and in net exports (in terms of value added).

If the country stops neutralizing the Dutch disease, it will be able to preserve its manufacturing sector and tradable service sector with a zero import duty only if the

Dutch disease is mild enough to be compensated by the achievement of a higher level of productivity than the country's international competitors. Usually, however, the newly overvalued exchange rate will gradually damage business enterprises in tradable industries, one by one. Faced with the fact that their foreign sales are no longer profitable and that imports of competing goods are growing, the enterprises will first redouble their efforts to increase productivity; later they will reduce or suspend exports; third, they will increase the share of imported components in their production, in order to reduce costs; finally, as this process continues, they will become mere importers and assemblers of the goods, which they re-export or sell in the domestic market. In other words, the country's manufacturing industry gradually becomes a "maquiladora" industry.[5] Domestic sales of the manufacturing industry (and even its exports) may continue to grow, but their value added will decrease, because their components with higher technological content will increasingly be imported. At the final stage of this process, entrepreneurs decide to cease production and to import the final goods; they cease to be industrial entrepreneurs.

When the economy reaches this point, and premature deindustrialization becomes obvious, liberal economists often deny that deindustrialization is taking place. Yet the symptoms of the Dutch disease and of deindustrialization continue to appear through the decreased share of the manufacturing sector in the domestic product, through a growing trade deficit in manufactured goods, through the increase in imported components in production, and through the relative or even the absolute reduction in the exports of manufactured goods measured by value added, not by their final value. For some time, the share of exports of manufactured goods may decrease not in volume but just in value added, as business enterprises are transformed into "maquilas", but sooner or later the share of exports of manufactured goods in the total volume of exports will also fall.

Sometimes, manufacturing industries with a high share of cheap labour remain competitive when the country ceases to neutralize the Dutch disease. But it would be a mistake to attribute this fact to the international division of labour. It is well-known that rich countries transfer standardized or codified activities to developing countries, and keep within their borders activities with higher value added per capita that demand more skilled labour. This process of division of labour gave rise, for instance, to the maquila business enterprises that long ago were set up on the Mexico–U.S. border. The premature deindustrialization that happens in a country that has long been industrialized is a different issue. The transformation of its manufacturing industry into a large maquila is a consequence of its ceasing to neutralize the Dutch disease. In the period of accelerated industrialization, the country managed to improve the technical quality of its workforce. But when trade and financial liberalization eliminates the country's control over its exchange rate, the jobs of this more skilled workforce will be put at risk. Premature deindustrialization and the country's transformation into a large maquila characterized by low growth rates will go hand in hand with the underemployment or straight unemployment of skilled personnel.

Briefly, the most important symptoms of the Dutch disease are the low growth of the manufacturing industry, a smaller share of manufactured goods in total exports, premature deindustrialization, artificially high real wages, and unemployment in the manufacturing sector. Since the Dutch disease is a market failure on the demand side – more precisely, on the access side – that limits investment opportunities in the manufacturing industry, it will cause the unemployment of skilled workers when the country has achieved the technical and administrative conditions to invest in the production of goods with more sophisticated technology, which implies higher wages, but the overvalued exchange rate prevents these investments from being made. In the vast majority of the developing countries, the workforce is underemployed, despite the claim that low levels of education and expertise characterize these countries. This low level obviously exists, yet at the margin unemployment of highly skilled workers exists.

Insofar as the Dutch disease is not neutralized, real wages will be artificially high in the sense that they would be lower if the exchange rate was at the industrial equilibrium (and imported goods were more expensive). However, what we actually observe are very low wages, indeed subsistence-level wages for unskilled workers because, insofar as the domestic workforce is abundant and unorganized, wages are defined in classical terms by the cost of the reproduction of labour. In this case, who does capture the Ricardian rents of the Dutch disease? None other than the political and business elites, including the uncorrupted elites. Such capture will not only be the outcome of rent-seeking, because the simple fact of an unlimited supply of labour keeps wages just a little above the subsistence level. Thus, rents will be necessarily captured by the elites. The corrupt elites will probably benefit more, but the elites as a whole benefit from the rents. Besides directly capturing the rents through salaries and profits, they will take advantage of the exchange-rate overvaluation to consume luxury goods imported from or directly bought in the rich countries to which they often travel.

Why not specialize in commodities?

The Dutch disease can be dismissed by appeal to the concept of the natural resource curse associated with rent-seeking. But there is another way of doing so. It is to say that the Dutch disease does not damage a country because industrialization is not a condition for economic development. This is a traditional idea of neoclassical economics – an idea always refuted by historical experience but always repeated by the followers of hypothetical–deductive theory who do not respect reality. This claim was made by Lederman and Maloney (2007), who wrote a whole book to show that the Dutch disease does not exist and that there is nothing wrong with a country specializing in the production of commodities. According to neoclassical thought, it is not wrong for a country to specialize exclusively in the exploitation of its natural resources. It is simply benefiting from its "comparative advantages" and rationally allocating its resources where they are more profitable. Industrialization is not necessary for economic growth.

We will not discuss here this argument, whose criticism has a long history in economics, particularly in developmental economics. We simply observe that a developed country such as the Netherlands does not seem to have reasoned in neoclassical terms, because it identified the problem as a disease that was destroying its manufacturing industry, and decided to neutralize it. As well, the Norwegians were not persuaded by the absurd neoclassical reasoning and, when they discovered oil, they decided to neutralize the disease competently by imposing a high tax on oil exploitation and by setting up a sovereign wealth fund in which to invest the revenues from the tax.

What history really tells us is that economic development begins with the industrial revolution and is characterized by industrialization. The Dutch disease is an obstacle to economic development because it prevents industrialization; more precisely, because it prevents the diversification and productive sophistication of the economy: the transfer of labour to industries with higher value added per capita. Therefore, when we talk about "industrialization" and associate it with economic development, we are using this concept in a broad sense. Industrialization occurs whenever labour is transferred to sectors with higher value added per capita. The productivity increase, which is practically synonymous with economic development, is brought about through the higher efficiency in the production of the same good or service, or through the transfer of labour to technologically more sophisticated sectors, which require a more educated and trained workforce and, for that reason, pay higher wages. Of the two methods of increasing productivity, the second is evidently the more important. As countries develop, they relegate the sectors with lower value added per capita to the less developed countries.

When a poor country specializes in natural resources because the Dutch disease makes it economically unviable to implement economic activities other than those that give rise to it, we really are in the presence of a disease because, in this case, the country is limiting its ability to create jobs and giving up the production of any good with a higher value added per capita than exists in the commodities that it produces and exports. When a middle-income country which, in order to industrialize, neutralizes the Dutch disease, but later, in the name of a misguided economic liberalism, ceases to do so, it engages in a process of premature deindustrialization.

The Dutch disease model assumes that the commodity that gives rise to it has a lower value added per capita than most of the country's manufacturing sectors. However, this assumption is not always right, but we cannot conclude from this that the Dutch disease is not really a disease and that it does not damage the country. Although the value added per capita of agricultural and mining production is traditionally lower than that of industrial production and of exportable services, it does not have to be. There is no reason why agricultural and mining production must always be less productive or less efficient than manufacturing production. Besides, we have observed since the 1970s a huge increase in agricultural productivity worldwide; at the same time, mining is becoming increasingly technologically sophisticated. This is also the case with oil, which is the natural resource that most often gives rise to the Dutch disease. However, even if the exploitation of natural resources involves a higher value added per capita than certain manufacturing sectors, the country will be damaged, provided that the manufacturing sectors offer jobs that the commodities sector – which gives rise to the Dutch disease – is not able to offer. On the other hand, the country will be forgoing the diversification of its economy into other activities with higher scientific and technological content that it is already able to engage in, and – even more seriously – it will be forgoing all the other activities with higher value added per capita in which it could engage.[6]

In a country where the Dutch disease originates mainly in agricultural commodities, we must take into account the industrial production generated by them, particularly agricultural machinery. But the Dutch disease will make these industries unprofitable too. It may affect them less severely than it affects other manufacturing industries, but unless the transportation costs are too high, even such complementary industries will become unviable due to the overvaluation of the exchange rate.

The Dutch disease and the natural resource curse

The Dutch disease involves a contradiction. On one hand, natural resources represent a huge benefit to a country – their exploitation is usually the way a developing country achieves its primitive accumulation and may start to grow. But on the other hand, natural resources represent a curse because they prevent the country from industrializing and diversifying its economy if policymakers don't recognize the problem and act to neutralize it. Usually triggered by the discovery of, for instance, oil, the Dutch disease brings a sudden and large windfall of wealth for a backward country. But, as this country lacks the values and institutions corresponding to this new level of prosperity, it soon sinks into corruption surrounding (*a*) the concessions to foreign business enterprises to exploit the new wealth and (*b*) the tax imposed on its export. This is why some economists and political scientists draw a distinction between the Dutch disease and the natural resource curse. Whereas the Dutch disease would be a market failure, the natural resource curse would result from weak institutions that facilitate corruption or rent-seeking – phenomena that are known to be more widespread in backward societies exporting commodities, particularly oil.[7] Consequently, these economists and political scientists attach more importance to the institutional and moral problem than to the economic problem, namely the structural overvaluation of the exchange rate; they focus on the need to reform institutions (something that has no cost for their own rich countries), instead of focusing on the need to make developing countries' exchange rates competitive – something that is not in the interest of other countries.

Inequality, the absence of cohesion or of a true nation, poorly defined institutions, and high levels of corruption are the rule in the poor countries that have not yet undergone their national and industrial revolutions, that have not yet formed their nation-state and industrialized; but, for them to develop, more important than modifying their laws and educating their people is to set the exchange rate at the industrial equilibrium and, thus, make possible their industrialization.

The theme of the natural resource curse has also been discussed in the political science literature. Its most distinguished expression is in Terry Lynn Karl's book

The Paradox of Plenty (1997). We would have no objection to the use of this expression to identify the high level of corruption often found in oil-exporting countries, if it did not involve disregarding the economic curse involved: the permanent overvaluation of the national currency. The book by Karl (1997, pp. XV, 6) is an excellent analysis of rent-seeking in political terms, but it is questionable in that it ignores the major economic problem involved. Corruption is a moral and political problem in all countries, and particularly in the poor ones; yet it is not corruption but the overvaluation of the exchange rate that is the fundamental obstacle that poor countries face in industrializing and developing. For that reason, we understand the Dutch disease and the natural resource curse as synonyms. Karl asks: "After benefiting from the largest transference of wealth ever to occur without war, why have most oil-exporting developing countries suffered from economic deterioration and political decay?" What is her answer to the "puzzle"? She ignores the exchange rate and attributes the problem simply to the country's weak institutions. Even if she manifests a clear awareness of the contradictory nature of the relationship between economic development and institutional change, she turns the Dutch disease ultimately into a consequence of weak institutions: "Because the causal arrow between economic development and institutional change constantly runs in both directions, the accumulated outcomes give form to divergent long run national trajectories. Viewed in this vein, economic effects like the Dutch disease become outcomes of particular institutional arrangements and not simply causes of economic decline". This reasoning makes no sense, since the Dutch disease has strictly economic causes: It is caused not by weak institutions but by Ricardian rents. We could attribute her mistake to her being a political scientist; yet orthodox economists make the same mistake. Rodrik, Subramanian, and Trebbi (2004), for instance, assert the priority of institutions over natural resources in explaining economic backwardness. Sometime earlier, Sala-i-Martin and Subramanian (2003) concluded from their long study of Nigeria that the causes of its backwardness lay in institutions corrupted by the natural resource curse and did not make a single reference to the overvaluation of the country's exchange rate.

In order to avoid this kind of error, we reject the alleged distinction between the Dutch disease and the natural resource curse. They are the same phenomenon, seen from two angles: the economic one and the moral and political one. When a country is poor, its society is unstructured, its institutions are weak, its public moral standards are low; and its corrupt elites, usually associated with the interests of rich countries, will capture some of the Ricardian rents through rent-seeking. We will have the Dutch disease and the natural resource curse. The poorer the country is, and the more exposed it is to global capitalism, the more disorganized is its society, the weaker are its institutions, the more difficult it is to govern. On the other hand, among poor countries, the richer a country is in mineral resources, the more likely it is to be at the mercy of corruption and civil wars. The studies of Collier and Hoeffler (2004) and of Collier (2007) are conclusive on the subject.

The fundamental cause of political instability, civil war, corruption, and the lack of democracy in poor countries is that, in this kind of country, the economic surplus is appropriated not in the market, through profits, but in politics, through control of the state. Therefore, in order to keep control over a country's economic surplus, the local elites will need to be in the government, will need to control the state. It is not surprising, therefore, that corrupt and authoritarian elites besiege the state and are permanently trying to capture it in order to serve their interests; or that the political regimes are authoritarian. This is one of the reasons why poor countries are faced with the "poverty trap".

When a country is finally able to neutralize the Dutch disease and industrialize, this is a sign that it has also neutralized the natural resource curse. The Dutch disease is an essentially economic phenomenon that has, obviously, political and ethical consequences. Distinguishing between the Dutch disease and the natural resource curse simply draws attention away from the fundamental economic problem. Even if we believed that poor countries' major problems are ethical in nature, even if we ignored the endogenous nature of the institutions, and even if we believed that institutional reforms would solve a country's ethical problems; if we adopted this nonsense, which is very common among the educated elites of the rich countries, and if we managed, thanks to it, to "moralize" a country, that country would not develop because it would not be solving its true economic problem: the chronic overvaluation of the exchange rate caused by the Dutch disease.

The Dutch disease is a serious disease amidst abundance. It usually appears when a country is still very poor, its society shows little cohesion and its institutions are weak. At first, it looks like manna from heaven: Its negative aspects are not yet evident, because the country is still unable to diversify its economy. As time passes, however, the country gradually finds itself in a trap. Instead of the natural resources promoting growth, they become the great obstacle to it: an obstacle that, as we shall see, is very difficult to overcome, in view of the economic and political problems involved. Since the discovery of the natural resources and the beginning of their exploitation, the new wealth on the one hand appreciates the domestic currency and on the other hand causes rent-seeking and becomes a major source of corruption. The problem is different when a rich country, such as the Netherlands or Norway, discovers natural resources. Since these countries have more political resources to cope with the economic problem involved and to neutralize it, their national currency does not become overvalued or their wages artificially high. Nor is the country engulfed by corruption. So the problem of rent-seeking or widespread corruption associated with the Dutch disease arises mainly in poor countries, since institutional development is endogenous to economic growth. Rich countries that contract the Dutch disease, as in the examples quoted above, usually count with institutions and with economic and a political culture that allow them to neutralize it.

Notes

1   In this book we deal only with the real market exchange rate, not with the nominal market exchange rate. Moreover, if in some cases we fail to say "real", nevertheless we are referring to the real market interest rate, in order to avoid monetary illusion.

2 In this second case are middle-income countries such as Brazil. Brazil industrialized between 1930 and 1980 through the use of several mechanisms that neutralized the Dutch disease, usually involving multiple exchange rates or high import taxes and high subsidies to exports of manufactured goods. However, as of 1990 it liberalized its trade and financial account, and premature deindustrialization became established in the country.

3 As Gabriel Palma (2013, pp. 51–52) remarks in that same paper, in Latin America since the 1990s the Dutch disease or syndrome "was basically the outcome of a radical program (extremely strict and without any pragmatism) of trade and financial liberalization, undertaken in the setting of a general process of institutional change".

4 In this period, in Brazil the average tariff on imports of manufactured goods was 45 per cent, and the average subsidy to exports of manufactured goods was also 45 per cent. How much of the import duty is protectionist and how much is the necessary neutralization of the Dutch disease is difficult to evaluate.

5 The "maquiladoras" are originally manufacturing business enterprises that were created on the Mexican–American border in order to profit from cheap labour. The productive processes transferred to Mexico were very simple, neither demanding skilled labour or contributing to technological development.

6 It must be noted that we are not taking into account a number of other negative effects resulting from the specialization in the commodity that gives rise to the Dutch disease, such as the concentration of political and economic power or the economy's increased vulnerability – as well as issues arising from wealth distribution among the several sectors of society.

7 Sachs and Warner (1999); Torvik (2001); Larsen (2004).

8   Domestic, not foreign savings

In the previous chapters we saw that the market does not guarantee that the exchange rate floats around the competitive equilibrium – the industrial equilibrium – because in developing countries there is a tendency to the cyclical and chronic overvaluation of the exchange rate. There are structural and policy causes for such tendency, namely the Dutch disease (a secondary cause is the fact that the profit and the interest rates tend to be higher in developing countries), whereas the policy causes are the growth cum foreign savings policy including the practice of high interest rates to attract capitals, the use of the exchange rate to control inflation, and a fiscal policy involving budget deficits inconsistent with the current account surplus, which will materialize insofar as the Dutch disease is neutralized and the exchange rate begins to float around the industrial, not the current equilibrium. In the previous chapter we discussed the Dutch disease; in this chapter we discuss the policy causes of the overvaluation, which are associated, directly or indirectly, to excessive or unnecessary capital inflows.

We begin with the growth cum foreign savings policy. This policy is the basic explanation of why net capital inflows are negative and often excessive in developing countries. It is justified morally by the argument that rich countries are supposed to transfer their capitals to capital-poor countries; it is justified economically by the fact that developing countries face a foreign constraint that can be overcome by resorting to "foreign savings" – that is, by developing countries running current account deficits financed either by direct investment or by loans. In our discussion of this foreign constraint in Chapter 4, we saw that it is real, but that it has lost most of its relevance for middle-income countries that have already industrialized, and also that the best way to overcome the remaining foreign constraint is not to try to grow with foreign savings but to keep the exchange rate competitive, floating around the industrial equilibrium. Yet developing countries usually adopt conventional policies that cause the exchange rate to appreciate, hamper investment, stimulate consumption, and, in consequence, imply a high rate of substitution of foreign savings for domestic savings rather than additional investment. In fact, as we argue in this chapter, foreign savings are not complementary to domestic savings but mostly *replace* domestic savings, which entails a high rate of substitution of foreign for domestic savings. More broadly, we argue that capital is made at home. Countries that resort to foreign finance follow a perverse path, whose first phase is the substitution of foreign for domestic savings; the second phase is the increase in the country's external financial vulnerability; and the third phase is the bursting of the credit bubble and the balance-of-payments crisis. In this chapter we discuss, first, the concept of foreign savings; second, its effect on the exchange rate (raising it); and third, the substitution of domestic for foreign savings and the variables that determine the rate of this substitution.

Foreign savings

In national accounting terms, and on the simplifying assumption of an economy without government, GDP is the sum of investment, consumption, and exports minus imports; national income is gross income minus profits and wages sent abroad; and investment is equal to domestic savings plus foreign savings or the current account deficit.

$$S_i + S_x = I.$$ [8.1]

Foreign savings are equal to the current account deficit, which, in turn, corresponds to the trade balance plus services and income balances. Yet, as these are all *ex post* concepts, mere accounting identities and not economic relationships, there is no direct relationship between foreign savings and additional investment, even if the expression "foreign savings" suggests otherwise. Although, for a few brief years when the economy is already growing fast, foreign savings may contribute to growth; all the currently developed countries achieved development thanks to their own domestic savings – that is, without incurring consecutive current account deficits. In the well-known words of Ragnar Nurkse, one of the founders of developmental economics, "capital is made at home". This claim accurately reflects empirical observation, but Nurkse didn't offer a theoretical explanation for it. Naturally, it is easier to believe that foreign savings add to domestic savings and increases a country's rate of investment. Common sense tells us that foreign savings add to domestic savings, and this is consistent with the view that investment and the sum of domestic and foreign savings are basic accounting identities. But we need to be careful with common sense. In principle, science progresses when it goes against common sense. If things were as simple as a mere accounting identity suggests, developing countries would have discovered the magic formula for growth. Given the abundance of capital in the world, it would be enough to obtain foreign savings from the rich countries for growth to accelerate. This is what orthodox economics teaches, because it is apparently true and because it is in the best interest of developed countries to finance the current account deficits of developing countries with loans and direct investment. They are remunerated for loans by high interest rates, and for direct investment by *occupying* developing countries' domestic markets and earning profits from them, while these countries are unable to reciprocate by occupying the domestic markets of developed countries.

Foreign indebtedness is a long-standing and serious problem that the Internal Monetary Fund (IMF) since it was created viewed with concern. Yet, beginning in the early 1990s, when the neoliberal policy regime turned fully dominant, the growth cum foreign savings policy, which implies either financial or patrimonial indebtedness,[1] turned into an essential part of the policy agenda that the rich countries *recommended* to the developing countries with the support of the IMF.[2] At the same time, as developing countries opened their financial accounts, there was a huge increase in capital flows into these countries in order to finance their current account deficits – the desired "foreign savings". The assumption, which was so self-evidently true as not to brook discussion, was that "capital-rich countries should transfer their capital to poor countries", whereas the current account deficits that such transfer of capital involved were forgotten or ignored. The only caveat appeared in the concept of "original sin", the term adopted to refer to the fact that developing countries are unable to borrow in their own currencies, and are therefore subject to balance-of-payment crises or currency crises.[3] But the economists that made this caveat didn't change their assumption about the "natural" character of transfers of capital from rich to poor countries, even though, at that moment, China, among other countries, was demonstrating the opposite insofar as it was financing the current account deficits of rich countries that have no problem incurring them – countries, that is, whose national currencies are reserve currencies, particularly the United States.

"Foreign savings" is a deceptive expression, which neoclassical economics uses to convey the idea that they are essentially the same as domestic savings. In fact, foreign savings are the foreign resources needed to finance the current account deficit; they are the savings of other countries, raised in order to finance the current account deficit; they add to a country's external debt, but they are not necessarily converted into investment: more often they add to consumption. Even if direct investment finances the current account deficit, there is no guarantee that it will add to the country's total capital accumulation. Since direct investments are financial investments, they don't need to have real investments as their counterparts. Or these real investments may have occurred, but they may have merely replaced the investments that nationals would have made if the capital inflows caused the exchange rate to appreciate.

Foreign savings and exchange rate appreciation

Why do foreign savings fail to add to domestic investment? What ensures that part or even the entire current account deficit is transformed into consumption? In order to answer this question, we must distinguish foreign from domestic financing. When a business enterprise obtains investment finance in the national currency, this finance will directly add to total investment. In contrast, when a business enterprise obtains investment finance in foreign currency, it does so through an intermediate variable: the exchange rate. Foreign finance will appreciate the exchange rate and, for that reason, may eventually turn into additional consumption, not additional investment.

Financial theory as taught in business schools clearly distinguishes foreign finance from domestic finance, because the former presents an additional risk – the exchange rate risk. It recommends, therefore, that financial institutions carry out matched operations in foreign currency. The "mismatching" of currencies is a danger, but this is *not* the problem that we are interested in. From the standpoint of developmental macroeconomics, what matters is the fact that foreign indebtedness implies *capital inflows* and, therefore, an increase in the supply of foreign currency that causes exchange rate appreciation, besides producing additional indebtedness in a currency that the country cannot issue.

Therefore, when a country decides to grow with foreign savings, it decides at the same time to make its currency appreciate and brings on itself all the problems associated with an overvalued exchange rate. The exchange rate becomes, thus, the endogenous variable resulting from that decision. When a country decides to go down this path, it decides that its exchange rate will be chronically overvalued, because the exchange rate that matches a current account deficit is higher than it is when the current account is balanced.

Neoclassical economics is not concerned with the capital inflows involved in the financing of chronic current account deficits, because it assumes that the equilibrium exchange rate is not the current equilibrium, much less the industrial equilibrium, but the "foreign debt equilibrium" – the rate at which the current account deficit (i.e. the increase in total foreign debt) is equal to the growth of GDP, and so the current account deficit does not imply an increase in the ratio of foreign debt to GDP. According to this view, the only source of concern is short-term hazard "misalignments". The idea of a tendency to such misalignments, as well as the idea that the resulting overvaluation is chronic, is wholly absent. From this perspective, all that economic policymakers can do is to choose between fixing and floating the exchange rate, without regard to the direction of misalignment, its chronic character, and the fact that there are many intermediate points between the pure fixed and floating regimes. Equally false is the idea that, in the long run, the real exchange rate cannot be managed.[4]

In practice, within certain limits, all countries manage their exchange rates effectively, influencing both their value and their market price.[5] Notwithstanding the assumption of the liberal orthodoxy that the exchange rate cannot be managed or subjected to policy, exchange rate management is in place when neoclassical economists decide that a country *should* grow with foreign savings. When a country accepts this policy recommendation, it is agreeing to make its currency appreciate. On the opposite side, when a country grows with negative foreign savings (i.e., with a current account surplus), as is usual among the fast-growing Asian countries, it is managing its exchange rate so as to keep it competitive, and, in this way, it is promoting an increase in domestic savings. In both cases, the exogenous variable is an economic policy – the decision whether or not to try to grow with foreign savings. And the *endogenous* variable is the exchange rate. It is true that countries that accept the growth cum foreign savings policy usually do not realize that it implies an appreciated exchange rate; but this lack of perception does not alter the fact that they are managing their exchange rates downwards (they are causing it to appreciate) by accepting finance in foreign currency.

Will the exchange rate appreciate whenever the country runs a current account deficit financed by capital inflows? Yes, this is what the market tells us. Can the exchange rate appreciation associated with current account deficits be compatible with growth? Yes, provided, first, that the country does not suffer from the Dutch disease; second, that this deficit is relatively small; and third, that the rate of substitution of foreign for domestic savings is at that moment low because the country is already growing fast, investment opportunities are abundant, and the marginal propensity to consume is low. This is what happened in the 1970s in South Korea. We will return to this issue at the end of the next section.

Rate of substitution of foreign for domestic savings

The degree of appreciation of the national currency caused by the policy of growth cum foreign savings depends fundamentally on the elasticity of the exchange rate in relation to foreign savings, e_{lS_x}, in which e is the exchange rate, l the elasticity, and S_x the foreign savings. How high will this elasticity be? It differs from country to country. In general, it rises with a country's propensity to consume. In its turn, the increase in wages as a result of the appreciation depends on the *wage elasticity* of the exchange rate, w_{le}, in which w is the wage rate. The greater the price and income effects of the appreciation are, the higher the elasticity. Like exchange-rate elasticity, wage elasticity is relatively stable, changing only over the long term.

The fundamental consequence of the policy of growth cum foreign savings is that foreign savings do *not* add to domestic savings but mostly replace them, insofar as a good part of the corresponding foreign finance is transformed into consumption, not investment; in other words, there is a high rate of substitution of foreign for domestic savings. The causes of this high rate are the price and income effects and lack of access to markets due to the appreciation of the domestic currency.

We can see the substitution of foreign for domestic savings in income or supply terms and in demand supply terms. On the income side, the substitution takes place because the exchange rate appreciation causes an artificial increase in wages and in consumption; on the demand side, it happens because business enterprises lose access to markets. The more appreciated the domestic currency is, the higher the real wages will be, because, with the appreciation, the prices of internationally tradable goods and services fall relative to the prices of non-tradable goods and services (price effect), the most important of which are wages. Consequently, the purchasing power of workers increases (income effect); depending on the share of tradable goods in their consumption basket, the profit share will fall and wage share will rise. Since the propensity to save out of profits is higher than the propensity to save out of wages, this distribution of income from profits to wages will decrease the aggregate propensity to save, resulting in a reduction in domestic savings; it will also increase the average propensity to consume and, consequently, aggregate consumption. On the demand side, investment opportunities for local business enterprises will fall because they will lose access to foreign and domestic markets.

In both cases – on the income side and on the demand side – the consequence of the appreciation is an increase in real wages and, therefore, in consumption. On the income side, this directly causes a decrease in domestic savings; on the demand side, savings drop because the profit expectations of entrepreneurs decline and, hence, do investment and savings, which depend on the difference between the interest rate and the expected profit rate. Consumption varies along with the variations in wages and in profits, and investment varies conversely to the difference between the expected profit rate and the interest rate or cost of capital. This expected profit rate drops insofar as, on the income side, wages increase, and, on the demand side, investment opportunities oriented towards exports decline. So, as foreign savings are "imported" and foreign indebtedness increases, the exchange rate appreciates, wages and consumption increase, and domestic savings fall, thus configuring the process of substitution of domestic for foreign savings. In other words, the two processes of exchange rate appreciation, one on the income side and the other on the demand side, validate one another, cause exchange rate overvaluation, and entail a reduction in investment.

But such substitution is not instantaneous. In the very short term the increase in real wages caused by the exchange-rate appreciation increases domestic consumption. But this surge in demand is strictly temporary; competent business enterprises will hardly be fooled by it, and will not invest. Soon the products of business enterprises that are possibly less efficient than the domestic ones begin to enter the domestic market in the form of imports.

In the medium term, the artificial increase in wages caused by the temporary appreciation is not sustainable. As costs increase and profits fall, business enterprises will try to pass through the wages increases to prices, and the consequent cost inflation will force wages to fall in real terms and the profit rate to return to *equilibrium*. This equilibrium refers to the profit–wage relationship that guarantees a satisfactory or "satisficing" profit rate, as Herbert Simon called it – that is, a profit rate sufficient to stimulate business entrepreneurs to invest. When wages are artificially high – that is, when they grow faster than the productivity increase due to the exchange rate appreciation, the profit rate is no longer satisficing.

So far we have seen that the attempt to grow with foreign savings – in the hope that the investment rate will increase when a country incurs current account deficits – does not necessarily succeed, but always results in exchange rate appreciation. Even when the foreign resource takes the form of direct investment, there is no guarantee that it will add to total investment. There will always be a substitution of foreign for domestic savings; and this substitution will tend to be high. It will not necessarily be 100 per cent. Some proportion of foreign savings should eventually result in an increase in investment, but this increase will be much smaller than the presumed zero substitution (which corresponds to additivity) implicit in the growth cum foreign savings policy.

We may define the rate of substitution of foreign for domestic savings as the variation in domestic savings divided by the variation in foreign savings:[6]

$$z_t = -dS_i \, / \, dS_x.$$ [8.2]

The rate of substitution, z, in the period t, is, therefore, negative, since we are comparing a decrease to an increase. In order to measure the rate of substitution of foreign for domestic savings, we need to define the relevant period and the amount of variation in foreign savings and in domestic savings. If in the chosen period foreign savings increase by R$1,000 billion (covered by capital inflows of that amount) and domestic savings decrease by R$800 billion, the rate of substitution will be 80 per cent, because only R$200 billion of this foreign savings will have been added to total investment, the remaining R$800 billion having financed consumption. Thus, in the example, which is far from unrealistic, a large proportion of the foreign savings eventually financed not investment but rather consumption.

What is the meaning, in practice, of the rate of substitution of foreign for domestic savings? If we ignore the signal, and if the rate is equal to 100 per cent, it means that the increase in foreign savings corresponds to a decrease in domestic savings by the same amount. In this instance there is full substitution. If the rate is equal to 0 per cent, there is no savings substitution. In the first case, the additional foreign savings does not cause an increase in the rate of investment; in the second, it is entirely transformed into an increase in investment and, therefore, in the rate of investment. In intermediate cases, the foreign savings will be channeled partly into consumption and partly into investment. If it is equal to 50 per cent, and if the return on the investments financed by the capital inflows is 15 per cent, the foreign investors will receive this return, but the country will be paying a return of 30 per cent, since only half of the foreign savings has financed investment.

On what does the rate of substitution of foreign for domestic savings depend? What is the variation in domestic savings due to the appreciation of the currency of a country that ensures that it will grow with foreign savings? Basically, it depends on the *difference* between the propensity to save out of profits and the propensity to save out of wages. Since we assume that there is a basic correspondence between the exchange rate and the current account deficit, on the supply or savings side the rate of substitution of foreign for domestic savings depends on the elasticity of domestic savings in relation to the exchange rate, S_{ile}, which, in turn, depends, first, on the elasticity of real wages in relation to the exchange rate, and, second, on the difference between capitalists' propensity to save and workers' propensity to save. The greater the elasticity of real wages in relation to variations in the exchange rate, and the greater the difference between the propensity to save out of profits and the propensity to save out of wages, the greater will be the elasticity of savings and investments in relation to the exchange rate, and the higher will be the rate of substitution of foreign for domestic savings.

The most relevant of these three components is the elasticity of the expected profit rate in relation to the exchange rate, which, unlike the other components, varies enormously. If the country is growing very rapidly, if it is experiencing a "miracle", and there are great profit opportunities, the capitalist class will use a greater portion of its expected and earned income to invest, increasing its marginal propensity to invest. Besides, given the wage increases and (especially) the salary increases that are under way, the workers and the professional middle class will also increase their marginal propensity to save and invest. As a result, the rate of substitution of foreign for domestic savings will fall.

On the demand side, the rate of substitution of foreign for domestic savings depends on the elasticity of the expected profit rate (which is associated with exports) in relation to the exchange rate. Given a higher elasticity, if the exchange rate appreciates, exports will fall more than otherwise, and so the greater will be the fall in the investment rate.

Therefore, demand and supply (intermediated by income) operate in the same direction: On the demand side, the exchange rate appreciation precipitates successively a decrease in exports, in investments intended for export, and in savings; on the income or supply side, the direct decrease in domestic savings sanctions the decrease in investment.

The rate of substitution of foreign for domestic savings will be particularly high the smaller the difference is between the expected profit rate and the interest rate – that is, the fewer the investment opportunities. In this case, not only will the workers show a high propensity to consume, but also the middle class will tend to consume practically all the increase in its salaries, and the capitalists, facing a non-satisficing profit rate, will stop investing instead of reducing their consumption. Therefore, if the differential between interest and profit is small, we will have "normal" investment opportunities, which will not stimulate the middle class to transfer part of its salary to investment or persuade the capitalists to consume less. Consequently, the inflow of foreign savings will be strongly compensated by the decrease in domestic savings resulting from the increase in consumption. In addition, profits themselves and their reinvestment will be modest. The result of those two outcomes is that there will be no new investment, despite the inflow of foreign savings. At the other extreme, if the differential between the profit rate and the interest rate is large and the variation in consumption is small, a substantial share of the increase in wages and salaries will be directed not towards consumption but towards investment.

Giving the mediocre expected profit rate and the high marginal propensity to consume that exists in developing economies, the rate of substitution of foreign for domestic savings tends to be high in these countries. It will be nearly 100 per cent when the current account is in deficit without any connection with investment and economic growth is particularly slow, as happened in Latin America in the 1990s. However, we know that, historically or empirically, under certain circumstances some countries have developed with foreign savings. This happened, with a rate of substitution of less than 50 per cent, when, for different reasons, the countries experienced high rates of growth, or a "miracle". Then, a favourable combination of externalities and increase in demand gave rise to huge investment opportunities that generated high expected profit rates. In so saying, we are assuming that during episodes of high growth the rate of substitution of foreign for domestic savings falls, and, for that reason, foreign savings contribute to growth. We could be tempted to reverse the causality and say that the inflow of capital produced the high rates of growth that reduced the rate of substitution; but such a move implies a rejection of something that we hope is now obvious to the reader: that the appreciation of the exchange rate reduces investment opportunities.

It is important to note that, in much the same way as there is a substitution of foreign for domestic savings when the current account deficit increases, the opposite may happen – that is, a substitution of domestic for foreign savings when the current account deficit or foreign savings are diminishing. In that case, on the supply side wages and salaries will fall; on the demand side, exports and investments will rise, causing the reverse substitution.

Summary

We have seen in this chapter that foreign savings – that is, current account deficits financed by loans or by direct investments, are not just added to domestic savings, thus increasing investment (as the economics establishment suggests). Rather, they mostly replace domestic savings, resulting in increased consumption rather than increased investment. This happens because the decision to adopt the growth cum foreign savings policy causes the exchange rate to appreciate, since for each level of current account deficit or surplus there is a corresponding exchange rate. The greater the current account deficit resulting from the growth cum foreign savings policy, the higher will be the exchange rate.

An appreciation of the exchange rate causes an increase in real wages and in consumption, and a decrease in domestic savings; it also causes a decrease in investment opportunities, a decrease in investments decided domestically, and therefore, a decrease in domestic savings.

The rate of substitution of foreign for domestic savings depends on the elasticity of the exchange rate in relation to the current account deficit. The greater this elasticity, the higher will be the exchange-rate appreciation caused by a current account deficit. This elasticity varies from country to country and from moment to moment according the variables discussed in this chapter.

The growth cum foreign savings policy is not always negative, because the rate of substitution is not always high. When the country grows fast and investment opportunities become particularly attractive to business enterprises, and even to the middle class, the propensity to invest will increase, and the rate of substitution of foreign for domestic savings will decline. In such episodes, foreign savings have a substantial positive effect on investment.

Notes

1 For us, "financial" indebtedness results from foreign loans, and "patrimonial" indebtedness results from direct investments.
2 This change of the IMF's stance in relation to current account deficits led Bresser-Pereira (2002) to claim that the "Second Washington Consensus" was formed in the early 1990s. The first consensus, which John Williamson (1990) summarized in the late

1980s, did not include the opening of countries' financial account or the growth cum foreign savings policy.

3 Of this vast literature, we mention here only Calvo, Leiderman, and Reinhart (1995), Rodrik (1998), and Eichengreen and Leblang (2003).

4 See Montiel (2003, ch. 16)

5 The idea that the real exchange rate cannot be managed in the long term is true only if the time interval implicit in this "long term" is very large – over 20 years – but in this case the restriction becomes irrelevant. The important thing is to manage the exchange rate over a reasonable period, which would, relatively speaking, be under the control of the economic policymaker.

6 The rate of substitution may also be expressed as follows:

$$z_i = \frac{\partial S_i}{\partial S_x} = \frac{\partial S_i}{\partial e}\frac{\partial e}{\partial S_x} = \frac{(\partial S_i/\partial e)}{(\partial S_x/\partial e)}.$$

In words, the rate of substitution may be expressed as the ratio between the elasticity of domestic savings in relation to the real exchange rate and the elasticity of foreign savings in relation to the real exchange rate.

9 Inflation, interest, and exchange rate appreciation

Inflation is a macroeconomic problem that requires constant surveillance, but there are healthy and unhealthy ways of controlling it. If it is demand-pull inflation (which is its normal condition), the *healthy* ways of controlling it in the developing countries are (*a*) fiscal policy and (*b*) the management of interest rate policy by the central bank, in order to keep it at a reasonable *level* (slightly above the international level, since the assets of developing countries are, in general, at greater risk than those of developed countries). The *perverse* or unhealthy way of controlling inflation is mainly the utilization of an exchange rate anchor by the central bank, usually combined with high level of the interest rate around which the central bank tracks its monetary policy, instead of managing the interest rate to keep it slightly above the international level.

In this chapter, before discussing these issues, we say a few words about the theory of inflation.

Some comments on the theory of inflation

Theories of inflation usually try to explain the *acceleration* of inflation, but it is also necessary to take into account the factors that *sustain* a given level of inflation. These factors are essentially the formal and informal indexation of the economy that results in inertial inflation, and the factors that *sanction* inflation, among which the most relevant variable is the increase in the supply of money. The basic reason for the acceleration of inflation is excess demand, although other factors may be considered, such as monopolistic increases in prices, wage increases above productivity increases due to the power of trade unions, the existence of bottlenecks on the supply side (especially in the presence of a closed economy and a poorly developed domestic market), and the occurrence of supply shocks that affect productivity or change relevant prices such as those related to food, energy, or the exchange rate.

Excess demand usually explains the acceleration of inflation in normal situations in which the inflation rate is relatively low and there is no intense distributive conflict. In this case, we don't have to pay special attention to the factors that maintain and sanction inflation. But when the inflation rate and its rate of acceleration increase, distributive conflict becomes relevant to the explanation because the substantial change in relative prices generates significant losses for economic agents.

Since in Latin-American countries the inflation rate is higher than that in developed countries, the structuralist tradition has established that the acceleration in inflation derives from supply bottlenecks and, particularly, from the distributive conflict associated with the monopoly power of either enterprises or unions. Economic agents always aim to increase their share in the national income, and the less costly and faster way of doing so, in the short term, is by marking up the prices of the goods and services they offer on the market (including real wages on the part of workers). This would be impossible in a capitalist economy in which economic agents had no power, but in actual capitalist economies economic agents do have power, and when they exercise it inflation accelerates. Since the productive structure is reasonably complex and interconnected, production costs also vary as a result of these price markups, and therefore profit margins fluctuate among the different industrial sectors or categories of workers that have power over the market.

These fluctuations in entrepreneurs' profit margins and in workers' real wages define their shares of income. When entrepreneurs' margins are equalized, and real wages are at an acceptable level for the workers, where wages keep pace with productivity, the distributive conflict between (and within) the social classes is mitigated because the economic agents are relatively satisfied with their income shares. Certainly they would like to have larger shares, but a number of obstacles prevent this, such as the degree of organization of the social classes and the possible shortfall in aggregate demand that would result from a decrease in investment (when the profit rate falls below the minimum level expected by the entrepreneurs) or in consumption (when real wages are sharply reduced). Given these constraints, a mitigation of the distributive conflict would serve to balance or align relative prices, since both wages and the profit margin are preponderant factors determining the share of income assigned to business enterprises and workers, and prices are composed precisely of an average unit cost – one of whose main components is remuneration for work – and of a profit margin on that cost.

High inflation is usually explained (*a*) by the factor that *accelerates* inflation – the struggle of economic agents to increase or recover their income shares; (*b*) by the factor that *sustains* inflation – the struggle of all agents to preserve their income shares (thus maintaining the equilibrium of relative prices) through indexation mechanisms to correct prices and wages; and (*c*) by the factor that *sanctions* inflation – the endogenous increase in the supply of money through which the economy maintains its real liquidity, preventing the ongoing high inflation from reducing the real amount of money that it is needed for economic transactions. This is a factor that sanctions inflation because otherwise the reduction in the real quantity of money would prevent the previous total number of transactions from being accommodated, and would strongly suppress aggregate demand and income. If the rate of ongoing inertial inflation is very high, the monetary adjustment that would be required would be so big that the economy would protect itself from it by developing mechanisms such as the endogenous creation of money by the banks and the government.

Exchange rates, inflation, and real wage

It is well known that variations in nominal wages above productivity increases are a basic cause of the acceleration or deceleration of inflation. Labour unit costs increase, reducing the profit margin, and firms react by raising their prices. This can happen when the demand for labour exceeds supply (caused either by aggregate demand pressures or by a reduced workforce) or when unions have monopoly power. But when productivity is constant and prices increase at the same rate as wages, the real wage becomes constant. In the same way, if the nominal exchange rate is also rising at the same rate as domestic inflation, and foreign inflation is constant, the real exchange rate will also be constant. So, in order to keep the exchange rate stable in an economy where prices and wages are formally or informally indexed, increases in nominal wages and the exchange rate should be similar, on the assumption that productivity and foreign inflation are also constant. On the other hand, given that the wages are the key price for non-tradable goods, and if prices and wages are not fully indexed to each other, the appreciation of the real exchange rate (due to smaller increases in the nominal exchange rate than in domestic prices) implies a fall in the prices of tradable goods and an increase in real wages, while the inflation rate declines. This is why exchange rate appreciation is so attractive to policymakers: It performs the "miracle" of increasing wages and lowering inflation. But at a price: The fall in the price of tradable goods implies a fall in the expected profit rate and in investment in the sectors that produce those goods.

In order to better understand the relationship between the exchange rate, inflation, and the real wage, consider a small open economy that produces a homogeneous good, which serves as both a consumption good and an investment good, using labour and intermediate inputs imported from abroad. The business enterprises that operate in this economy have the power to form prices, which are therefore determined by a *mark-up* on the direct unit costs of production, as can be observed in equation (9.1):

$$p = (1 + z)[wa_1 + ep^* a_0] \tag{9.1}$$

where p is the price of the domestic good, z is the *mark-up* rate, w is the nominal wage rate, e is the nominal exchange rate, p^* is the price of the imported input in the currency of the country of origin, a_0 is the imported inputs share, and a_1 is the labour share in production. We assume that labour productivity is constant in order to explain the relation that interests us, since changes in wages will be equal to changes in labour unit cost in this situation.

We presume that the final good produced by the business enterprises of the economy in question is an imperfect substitute for the final goods produced abroad, so that the trade opening does not impose the *law of one price* for internationally tradable goods; that is, purchasing power parity does not apply. However, the monopoly power of domestic business enterprises is affected by the price of imported goods. More specifically, the ability of domestic business enterprises to determine a price above the direct unit costs of production depends on the real exchange rate, which is defined as the ratio between the price of imported goods in the domestic currency and the price of domestic goods in the domestic currency. In this setting, a devaluation of the real exchange rate allows domestic business enterprises to increase the markup on production costs in line with the decrease in the competitiveness of the final goods imported from abroad.[1]

Consequently, we may express the markup as a function of the real exchange rate, as follows:

$$z = z_0 + z_1 \theta \tag{9.2}$$

where $\theta = \dfrac{ep^*}{p}$ is the real exchange rate.

Dividing the expression (9.1) by p, we have:

$$1 = (1 + z)\,[Va_1 + \theta a_0]. \tag{9.3}$$

Equation (9.3) presents the distributive locus of the economy in question – that is, the combinations between real wage (V), exchange rate (θ), and rate of markup (z) for which the added value produced in the economy is entirely appropriated as wages and profits. We must note that, given the markup and the technical coefficients of production (a_0 e a_1), there is an inverse relationship between the real wage and the real exchange rate – that is, a devaluation in the real exchange rate is necessarily followed by a decrease in the real wage because it allows for a higher mark-up, which means that prices increase faster than wages. Since the mark-up rate depends positively on the real exchange rate, it follows that the required decrease in the real wage will be even greater than if the mark-up is fixed.

Actually, by replacing (9.2) in (9.3) and by distinguishing the resulting expression regarding V and θ, we have:

$$\frac{\partial V}{\partial \theta} = -\left\{ \frac{a_0\left(1+z_0\right)+z_1\left(a_1 V + 2a_0\theta\right)}{a_1\left(1+z_0\right)+z_1 a_1\theta} \right\} < 0. \tag{9.4}$$

Equation (9.4) points to the existence of an inverse relationship between the real exchange rate and the real wage rate, given the technical coefficients of production.

The relationship between real exchange rate and real wage is illustrated in Figure 9.1.

In this setting, assume that the workers, organized in trade unions, have a real wage target equal to $\bar{V}$.[2] This real wage target defines a value for the real exchange rate that is compatible with a stable inflation rate, which we will call $\theta^{eq\,inf}$. If the government tries to force a depreciation of the real exchange rate, so as to promote an alignment between the current equilibrium exchange rate and the industrial equilibrium exchange rate, the resulting drop in the real wage will lead the trade

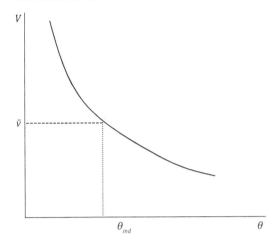

Where: *V* is the real wage rate, θ is the real exchange rate,
θ_{ind} is the industrial equilibrium exchange rate, and
$\bar{v}$ is the target real wage.

Figure 9.1 The real wage-real exchange rate locus

unions to demand increases in the nominal wage. These increases will be transferred to the prices of goods, since business enterprises are unwilling to accept a
decrease in their profit margins. Therefore, there will be an increase in the inflation
rate.[3] Due to the acceleration of inflation, the trade unions will demand further
wage increases, particularly if employment contracts are indexed to past inflation,
thus producing a wage–price spiral that will ultimately lead to hyperinflation.

The validity of this reasoning can be attested by a simple mathematical model.
Consider an economy in which the rate of increase in nominal wages is determined according to this equation:

$$\hat{w}_t = \alpha_0(\bar{V} - V_t) + \hat{p}_{t-1} \tag{9.5}$$

where $\hat{w}_t$ is the rate of variation in the nominal wage in the period t, and $\hat{p}_{t-1}$ is the
inflation rate of the previous period.

The inflation rate will be a weighted average between the rate of variation in
nominal wages and the rate of depreciation of the nominal exchange rate, since
the unit cost of production of business enterprises, according to equation (9.1),
depends both on the nominal wage and on the nominal exchange rate.[4] Therefore,
we have:

$$\hat{p}_t = \alpha_1\hat{w}_t + (1 - \alpha_1)\hat{e}_t \tag{9.6}$$

where $\hat{e}_t$ is the rate of variation in the nominal exchange.

The variation in the real exchange rate can be expressed by the following equation:

$$\hat{\theta}_t = \hat{e}_t + \hat{p}_t^* - \hat{p}_t \tag{9.7}$$

where $\hat{p}_t^*$ is the foreign inflation rate.

Finally, we will presume that the government adopts a policy of managing the real exchange rate so as to produce a gradual adjustment of the exchange rate to the industrial equilibrium level by means of consecutive and controlled devaluations of the nominal exchange rate. This way, we have:

$$\hat{\theta}_t = \alpha_2 \left(\theta_{ei} - \theta \right). \tag{9.8}$$

After a few algebraic operations, we arrive at the following expression:

$$\hat{p}_t = \hat{p}_{t-1} + \alpha_0 \left(\bar{V} - V \right) + \left[\left(\frac{\alpha_2}{\alpha_1} \right) (1 - \alpha_1) \right] \left(\theta_{ei} - \theta \right). \tag{9.9}^5$$

Equation (9.9) shows that the current inflation rate depends on the inflation rate of the previous period (inflationary inertia), on wage misalignment, and on the degree of overvaluation of the real exchange rate (since the target for the real exchange rate is the industrial level).

If the trade unions oppose the reduction in real wages, that is, if the phenomenon of *real wage resistance* prevails, then $V = \bar{V}$ and the expression (9.9) becomes:

$$\hat{p}_t = \hat{p}_{t-1} + \left[\left(\frac{\alpha_2}{\alpha_1} \right) (1 - \alpha_1) \right] \left(\theta_{ei} - \theta \right). \tag{9.10}$$

In equation (9.10) we can observe that, in a context of real wage resistance, the overvaluation of the real exchange rate ($\theta_{ei} > \theta$) will result in a continuous acceleration in the inflation rate ($\hat{p}_t > \hat{p}_{t-1}$) if the government decides to try to eliminate the overvaluation of the real exchange rate through consecutive devaluations of the nominal exchange rate. The reason is that the decrease in real wages induced by the depreciation of the exchange rate will lead the trade unions to demand increases in nominal wages above the inflation of the previous period. In order to protect their profit margins, business enterprises will transfer the wage increases to prices, accelerating inflation. The real exchange rate will not be devalued since the inflation will also rise. The only way to make the real exchange rate float around the industrial equilibrium (the informal exchange rate target) is to control nominal wage increases to keep them below the variations in the nominal exchange rate. To achieve this it is necessary either to conclude an agreement with unions or to reduce the demand for employment for a short period.[6]

So, for inflation to remain constant over time and the real exchange rate to be devalued, the workers must be willing to accept the reduction in the real wage that is necessary for the adjustment in the real exchange rate. Actually, if we make $\hat{p}_t = \hat{p}_{t-1}$ in equation (9.9), we arrive at the following expression:

$$V = \bar{V} + \frac{\alpha_2}{\alpha_0 \alpha_1}(1 - \alpha_1)(\theta_{ei} - \theta). \tag{9.11}$$

In equation (9.11) we observe, first, that the other side of the coin of the phenomenon of exchange rate overvaluation ($\theta_{ei} > \theta$) is an overvaluation of the real wage – that is, $V > \bar{V}$. In other words, a real exchange rate appreciated up to the industrial equilibrium level generates an artificially high real wage rate – that is, a real wage that is high relative to the target wage that would be consistent with the industrial equilibrium. Second, we verify that the end of the exchange rate overvaluation implies the consequent elimination of the overvaluation of the real wage – that is, a reduction in the real wage to the level $\bar{V}$.

Rational expectations and inflation

There is a large economic literature on the general theory of inflation, and there is no need to re-examine it here. However, it is necessary to point out that in the 1980s, a period of hegemony of monetarist macroeconomics, the idea prevailed that inflation was an exclusively monetary phenomenon and that, to control it, it was enough to control the supply of money. This orthodoxy, which initially manifested itself in American universities, later reached the central banks. However, since policies based on the manipulation of monetary aggregates to control inflation repeatedly failed, the central banks abandoned them, and began to pragmatically adopt an inflation-targeting policy. The economic mainstream, realizing that it had been relegated or discarded by the central bankers, reacted with what was called the New Macroeconomic Consensus, which considered the inflation-targeting policy adopted by the central banks to be basically correct and gave to it a rational expectations theoretical wrapping.

Under inflation targeting, governments and their central banks set a level of inflation that they would seek to achieve through a combination of fiscal policy and interest rate policy. This practice was formalized through a simple rule – the "Taylor rule" – a reaction function that correlates the inflation target with ongoing inflation and, given the capacity utilization or the output gap, estimates the interest rate that will bring the inflation down to the target level.

$$r = r_e + 0{,}5\,(\pi_t - \pi^*) + 0{,}5\,y \tag{9.12}$$

where r is the short-term interest rate, r_e is the equilibrium interest rate that keeps the inflation rate on the target, π_t is the current inflation rate, π^* is the central bank's inflation target and y is the output gap.

Although this rule, originally formulated by John Taylor (1993), is a simple historical–deductive formalization of how central banks act in relation to the inflation target, and not a deduction stemming from *homo economicus* as would be consistent under a fully neoclassical approach, the inflation targeting policy was soon co-opted by the different currents of neoclassical rational-expectations macroeconomics through the subordination of monetary policy to the principle of "constrained discretion". Based on this principle, monetary policy would be able ideally to deal with inflation shocks, allowing central banks to react to unexpected recessions by adequately changing short-term interest rates without losing credibility. Central banks would act, therefore, by adjusting the interest rate in order to minimize output fluctuations in line with its long-term trajectory in compliance with predefined rules. The freedom of central banks to spring "inflationary surprises" was thus reduced.

The neoclassical matrix of the debate about inflation-targeting regimes is traditionally based in the literature on "rules versus discretion" within a monetary economy. A vast literature emerged following the 1970s dispute between discretion and rules, which pitched neoclassical monetarists against Keynesians. The prevailing mainstream notion was that successful monetary policy must be disciplined and transparent and must also communicate credibility, so as to demonstrate a strict commitment to austerity – conduct that central banks should observe in light of the problem known as "time inconsistency" and of the inflation bias of several elements of economic policy. At the theoretical level, this kind of behaviour by central banks is validated by models of "reputation and credibility", in which it is argued that the central bank minimizes the loss function resulting from the trade-off between inflation and unemployment (both can generate losses to society) and plays with economic agents a proper game by adopting policies and responding to the reactions of economic agents.

Trust is a moral quality fundamental to social life. But credibility cannot be gained just by combining the good reputations of the government and the central bank with stabilization plans that are considered consistent or rational from an economic point of view, as assumed by the theory of rational expectations. In fact, government or central bank credibility is not enough; it is also necessary for each agent to be convinced that other economic agents will equally behave according to what has been defined as "rational". Now, there is no easy way to do so, because all agents are involved in a distributive conflict that inflation accentuates; they are all trying to maintain (not necessarily to increase) their income shares, and nothing is more rational than this.

In this book, we are not interested in debating and criticizing this attempt to find the perfect neoclassical equilibrium through classic moral virtues such as transparency and credibility. Post Keynesian economists such as Paul Davidson, Jan Kregel, and Philip Arestis have already undertaken the criticism of this theory, in the case of the relatively low inflation existing in the developed countries. Instead, in this chapter we limit ourselves to discussing how policies aiming to control inflation (which today are mostly identified with inflation targeting) play a direct or indirect role in generating the tendency to the cyclical and chronic overvaluation of the exchange rate. In this book, what is relevant is to understand how, in practice, central banks in developing countries (which adopt the policy of inflation targeting and the theory that underlies it) end up causing the domestic currency to appreciate, whether because they use the perverse resource of the exchange rate anchor to meet the target, or because they establish a high level of interest rate to attract foreign capital, which also results in exchange rate appreciation.

Exchange rate anchor policy

The use of the exchange rate to control inflation is an old practice, and it has always been required in order to stabilize episodes of hyperinflation. In the countries that faced inflation rates higher than 50 per cent per month (which defines hyperinflation), the classic way of dealing with it was for the government to fix or "freeze" the exchange rate. The policy will be successful, or in other words will enjoy a degree of social credibility that persuades economic agents to cease raising prices independently of demand, if the government (*a*) has raised international loans to guarantee the policy and (*b*) has adopted a firm fiscal policy of expenditure reduction. Hyperinflations in Germany and in other Eastern European countries in the 1920s ended this way.

In Brazil it has been argued that price stabilization succeeded in 1994 ("Plano Real") also because of an exchange rate anchor. But this is not the case, mainly because Brazil did not have hyperinflation but rather a high inertial inflation resulting from delayed increases in prices that were formally and informally indexed. In the presence of such inflation, it is necessary to neutralize the imbalance in existing relative prices, which was carried out by using, over three months, an index currency pegged to the dollar. Inflation was not yet high enough for the gap in price increases to become so small as to render unnecessary the mechanism of neutralizing inflationary inertia, and all that was needed was to determine the exchange rate. Inflation had reached a level at which price increases were still desynchronized, each increase correcting the imbalance in relative prices caused by the previous increase and generating a new imbalance to be corrected by the next agent.

The use of the exchange rate anchor to control hyperinflations is, therefore, legitimate. The exchange rate that results from the stabilization remains overvalued due to the inflationary residue that will always exist after the exchange rate shock, but that is a problem that the economy will have to solve after the stabilization is achieved. Yet the use of the exchange rate anchor simply to meet the inflation target, as is usual in developing countries, is unacceptable. In everyday economic management, keeping the exchange rate floating around the competitive or industrial equilibrium is as important as controlling inflation. There is no reason to sacrifice the informal exchange rate target that every country must set to help meet the inflation target. Models of inflation-targeting policy obviously include the exchange rate, but those models treat exchange-rate appreciation or depreciation as an exogenous variable, which is not subject to policy. If, for example, the national currency is depreciating, the central bank will be required to respond by further raising the interest rate. The problem that concerns us here, however, is the use of the exchange rate as an instrument for controlling inflation in addition to the instrument of the interest rate.

For inflation control, it is undoubtedly desirable that the central bank gains credibility. But there is a circular problem that the use of the exchange rate anchor perversely "solves". After all, the credibility of the bank and of its policy eventually depends on the inflation target being met. Since the efficacy of the interest rate in controlling inflation is limited and takes time, the temptation to profit from an exchange rate appreciation to meet the target becomes difficult to resist. Therefore, we often have an inflation target, an explicit interest rate policy to reach it, and an implicit exchange rate policy. This latter is never avowed, because neoclassical economics assumes that the only legitimate instrument to be used by central banks is the interest rate, and that the price of foreign currency would be adequately defined by the market.

An exchange rate guideline (a kind of anchor) combined with the assumption that economic agents will act according to rational expectations was adopted in Argentina in 1978, and in Chile in 1981, in the context of authoritarian military regimes, and resulted in extremely violent balance of payment crises. The local policymakers were persuaded by the new (at the time) neoclassical ideas that inflation could be controlled by managing the rational expectations of economic agents and that the instrument for this management, in the context of a crawling peg regime (the exchange rate adjusted for the inflation rate) prevailing at that time, would be an exchange rate that would decline month by month according to a predetermined scale. In embarking on this radical policy, they "transparently" informed the population of their goal and how they would reach it "rationally", and began to correct the exchange rate month by month according to the plan. At the same time, they adopted strict fiscal and monetary policies in order to ensure more credibility for their policy. However, economic agents, very reasonably, did not believe that other agents would act in the "rational" way predicted by the economic policy, and did not reduce their prices proportionately to the exchange rate guideline. Inflation fell, but substantially less than expected, and the exchange rate in each one of the countries appreciated strongly. The consequence was an increase in current account deficits and in foreign indebtedness and, in the end, each country experienced a brutal balance-of-payment crisis during which, once again, the currency depreciated and inflation increased.[7]

Traumatic experiences with exchange-rate anchors such as these two have not been repeated for a long time, but the use of the exchange rate as an instrument as important as the interest rate in reaching the inflation target continues to be a regular practice in emerging countries. Theoretically and officially, the interest rate is still the sole instrument available to the central bank; but, in practice, the exchange rate is another instrument that central banks use to control inflation.

But how would the government authorities appreciate (or depreciate) the domestic currency, given that today most countries have adopted a floating exchange-rate regime? There are several ways to achieve an appreciation under such a regime, but the simplest way is for the government to do *nothing* – to allow the exchange rate to be overvalued, as is its natural tendency. Ineffective ways to achieve an appreciation include neutralizing the Dutch disease, stopping the adoption of the policy of growth cum foreign savings, stopping use of the exchange rate as an anchor to control inflation, and rejecting exchange rate popu-lism. Besides, to achieve appreciation the central bank is supposed to sell interna-tional currency reserves.

We must observe that, *after* balance-of-payment crises that are characterized by violent devaluations of the exchange rate, there is scope for a relatively short period of "healthy" exchange rate appreciation – up to the point where it reaches the industrial equilibrium. From then on, further appreciation is perverse from the standpoint of efficient resource allocation and economic growth, but is welcomed by economic policymakers who prioritize inflation control over employment and growth.

High interest rate levels and appreciation

A second policy associated with the control of inflation that eventually results in the appreciation of the exchange rate is the policy of a high interest rate *level* – a level substantially higher that the average interest rate prevailing in rich coun-tries. We considered including in this book a special chapter on the interest rate, but we concluded that we would have little to add to what has already been researched and written on the subject. Suffice it to note that a low interest rate is a significant factor in promoting investment, and that the adoption of a high level of interest rate basically reflects the influence of rentier capitalists and financiers. High interest rates, which attract foreign capital and cause the cyclic appreciation of the exchange rate, are justified by liberal orthodoxy with several arguments. The most common argument is that a high interest-rate level is nec-essary to control inflation. This kind of argument, which is intrinsically absurd, can continue to be made only because both the economists who defend and the economists who attack a high interest-rate monetary policy do not mention the *level* of the real interest rate, but only its *oscillations*. Undoubtedly, monetary policy should be able to operate by raising the interest rate when the economy is heated and inflation is rising, and by reducing it when the economy cools down. But it is one thing for the central bank to conduct its interest rate policy by mak-ing it vary in real terms, for instance between 2 per cent negative and 4 per cent positive (a 1 per cent average in real terms), and another thing to make it float around 5 per cent in real terms, as often happens when liberal-orthodox policies of "financial deepening" and attracting foreign capital are adopted.

A policy that keeps the interest rate at a high level indeed attracts capital and consequently is a significant cause of the exchange rate appreciation to which the developing countries are prone. But, as we saw in Chapter 8, it does not promote an increase in the investment rate, first because, when the exchange rate appreci-ates, lucrative investment opportunities diminish and we have a high rate of sub-stitution of foreign for domestic savings, and second because the rise in the cost of capital discourages investment. And we must also remember that a high level of interest rate for a country with a large internal public debt implies an increase in public expenditures that weakens the government, and therefore does not increase effective demand and investment opportunities; on the contrary, it reduces them.

According to neoclassical economics, prices in countries that adopt developmental policies are "wrong" – not only the prices of goods and services as a result of industrial policy, but also the interest rate, which would be too low, a characteristic of "financial repression". Thus, in order to improve economic performance, developing countries should carry out "financial de-repression", that is, increase the level of the interest rate. The theoretical framing of this policy is old, dating from the 1970s, when two neoclassical economists, Ronald McKinnon (1973) and Edward Shaw (1973), realized that in several Asian and Latin American countries, which at that time were industrializing and experiencing high rates of growth, interest rates were low if not negative. These low rates derived from the developmental policies that the countries were successfully pursuing at that time, which involved public banks offering investment subsidies. The aforementioned economists argued that such subsidies prevented private banks from financing investment; this was a serious problem because the "financial repression" would constrain funding for private investments and render the financial system "shallow". The proposed solution was immediately given a pompous name: "capital deepening". But all it meant was legitimizing an increase in the interest rate in order to make it positive and satisfying for savers, that is, for rentier capitalists, who would then increase their savings and place them at the disposal of the private banks; these private financial institutions could then finance investments and make higher profits at the expense of capital accumulation. "Capital deepening" was based on the neoclassical assumption, endlessly disproved by reality, that a rise in the interest rate increases savings. The assumption has been disproved again and again. In modern capitalist societies, marginal savings (which high interest rates would stimulate) are not relevant when compared with the accumulated stock of money-capital available to finance investment or consumption. Instead of recognizing that the developmental system of financing private investment with public finance worked well, so much so that investment rates were high and the countries were growing fast, these economists reasoned from their hypothetical and ideal model of market economy and did not hesitate to argue in favour of higher interest rates. In the 1970s, those economists were unable to persuade countries to change their developmental policy and to embark on de-repression or capital deepening. And that is why those countries continued to grow. But in the 1990s, when the liberal orthodoxy became dominant, most developing countries (particularly the Latin American ones that in the previous decade had been weakened by the foreign debt crisis) surrendered to the new orthodoxy and accepted the arguments of capital deepening. Credit subsidies were eliminated or greatly reduced, but private banks increased long-term finance only marginally.

A fourth argument in favour of a high level of interest rate is that such a level is necessary to finance public debt. Unlike the previous arguments, this is a legitimate justification if the government is highly indebted. In this case, the level of interest rate will tend to be higher than it would be otherwise. High interest rates are among the many problems caused by fiscal irresponsibility. However, high interest rates are often justified in this way even when the country's level of public indebtedness is not high. On the other hand, it is necessary to consider the causes of an increase in public debt, which results from nominal budget deficits (primary balance plus interest payments). Its causes are usually irresponsible fiscal policies characterized by high primary deficits, but they can also be explained by high interest rates on the public debt. As a result of either of the two cases, of fiscal populism or of the imposition of onerous interest rates by the central bank, the government may become a kind of Ponzi debtor, and may have to offer securities with a constantly increasing level of remuneration. This dynamic, besides destroying a government's capacity to raise finance, places additional upward pressure on the exchange rate, and results in a currency crisis.

Carry trade causing appreciation

The exchange rate appreciation associated with a high interest rate and with excessive capital inflows is also expressed in the "carry trade" phenomenon, in which a high interest rate is combined with the tendency to the overvaluation of the exchange rate and the prospect of currency appreciation. A financial crisis is characterized by a sharp and large depreciation of the exchange rate. Subsequently, when (mostly on account of this devaluation) the country's economy is reorganized and stabilized, foreign financial agents can safely predict that the country's currency will appreciate in the following months and years. In making this projection they do not need to explicitly take into account the tendency to the cyclical and chronic overvaluation of the exchange rate. Since the exchange rate immediately after the crisis is highly overvalued, the prospect of its appreciation is clear. When foreign speculators recognize it, they see a huge opportunity for financial gain resulting from the carry trade, in which they realize a double gain (based on the interest rate and on the currency appreciation).

In the financial literature, the carry trade has a broader meaning than the one used here. It means an operation in which the cost of carrying a given asset is smaller than the gain that could be made in the future thanks to its appreciation. In our case, we have in mind the carry trade conducted by foreign investors, who use the dollar or another hard currency to buy financial assets of the middle-income country. Insofar as this financial operation involves a self-fulfilling prophecy, a new financial bubble develops that causes exchange-rate appreciation. Since the interest rate is high and foreign financial investors anticipate that there is scope for the exchange rate appreciation, they gain twice: both from the interest rate and from the appreciation of the local currency caused by the capital inflows involved in the operation.

Eventually the real exchange rate achieves the bottom below which even the exports of commodities become economically not viable. The credit bubble remains strong, which explains why, in a floating regime, the exchange rate does not depreciate the demand for foreign money and increases in relation to the supply, but the gains from the carry trade stop being warranted. During the period in which there was scope for appreciation, the country had become very popular among foreign investors. Once the exchange rate has reached the bottom, the gains from the appreciation end, and a slow process of deterioration of the prestige of the country among foreign creditors begins.

Budget deficits and overappreciation

Finally we must consider high budget deficits as a policy cause of overvaluation of the exchange rate. A fiscal policy involving high budget deficits is inconsistent with the current account surpluses that arrive when the country dully neutralizes its Dutch disease. In this case, the exchange rate is in the equilibrium, and the twin deficits hypothesis will hold. Actually, since the equilibrium is the industrial equilibrium, not the current equilibrium, if the accounts of the private sector are balanced, the accounts of the public sector will have to present a surplus.

It may be surprising that, being Keynesian economists, we come to the conclusion that budget deficits are not normally welcome. But good Keynesian economists don't welcome chronic and high budget deficits. The normal condition is the one in which the public debt is moderate and constant in relation to GDP. An expansive fiscal policy is only required when the economy is in recession, i.e., when the private sector is expending insufficiently for the many reasons that macroeconomics discussed at length. The normal condition for the country, which has the Dutch disease and neutralizes it, is a current account surplus (which is a direct consequence of the industrial equilibrium) and a balanced budget (or a surplus), which is a consequence of the fact that the private accounts are balanced, i.e., that the private indebtedness is not increasing and getting out of control.

Summary

The exchange rate tends to appreciate in developing countries and to lead them into a current account deficit, increasing foreign indebtedness and, ultimately, a currency crisis, for several reasons. First, most developing countries do not neutralize the Dutch disease (from which almost all of them suffer).[8] Second, the interest rate tends to be higher than in developed countries, not only because there is a relative capital shortage in developing countries, but mainly because the shortage is often strongly increased in times when inflation is rising, and is timidly reduced when the inflation surge ends, which results in a high interest rate. Third, the exchange rate anchor policy is adopted to control inflation. Fourth, foreign financial investors take advantage of the tendency to currency appreciation, combined with high interest rates, to apply the carry trade strategy. Fifth, almost all the heads of government succumb to exchange-rate populism, though in different degrees.

In this chapter, after a brief reference to the theory of inflation, to the relation between real wages, inflation, and exchange rate, to inflation targeting policy, and to the neoclassical New Consensus, we analyzed the relation between the interest rate and the excessive priority given to the control of inflation. We discussed the arguments that are often presented to justify high levels of the interest rate. The first argument – that interest rates should be high in order to attract capital – has a direct effect on currency appreciation. The second is that a high interest rate is necessary to fight inflation – an argument that does not make a distinction between the level of inflation (which is crucial) and its oscillations. The third is that a low interest rate implies "financial repression". The only reasonable argument is the fourth one: indeed, in the presence of fiscal irresponsibility and a very high level of public indebtedness, the interest rate will tend to be high.

The adoption of all these policies or non-policies which cause the chronic overvaluation of the exchange rate reveals – on the part of a large number of policymakers, regardless of whether they are liberal or developmental – a high preference for immediate consumption. A more depreciated level for the exchange rate – one that arrives at the industrial equilibrium level – will reduce wages and consumption in the short term.

Notes

1 The depreciation of the real exchange rate will also push up the cost of imported inter-mediate goods, but since this cost is just a small fraction of production costs, the price (in national currency) of the domestically produced final good increases less than the price of the imported final good.

2 It is not necessary to assume that the trade unions' real wage target is constant over time. In fact, we may admit that the real wage target increases from period to period in line with productivity increases. Consequently, the real wage target in the period t may be written as $\overline{V}_t = (1+g)\,\overline{V}_{t-1}$, in which g is the rate of labour productivity growth. If the real wage increases at the same rate as productivity, the real unit labour cost remains constant.

3 The price increase will not happen only if labour productivity variation is similar to the wage variation, and, so, the unit labour cost is held constant.

4 In practice, firms consider that the unit labour cost – nominal wages divided by labour productivity – fixes not only wages but prices too. So this is the relevant variable for calculating the inflation rate. In our price equations we consider productivity to be constant in order to aid understanding of the relation between real wages, inflation, and the exchange rate.

5 For sake of simplicity we are also assuming that $\hat{p}_t^* = 0$.

6 The other alternative would be a productivity increase similar to the nominal exchange-rate variation: In this case, wages could increase at the same rate as the nominal exchange rate and, in order to keep the profit margin constant, prices would rise to reflect past inflation. But productivity takes too long to improve, and firms will raise their prices before it does.

7 The canonical analysis of the financial crises caused by those stabilization plans based on rational expectations and on the pre-fixing of the exchange rate was made by Carlos Diaz Alejandro (1981).

8 Even when a developing country does not export commodities that reflect abundant natural resources, as is true of many Asian countries, it has cheap labour and a wide variation between wages and salaries, and, therefore, it could be included among the victims of the extended concept of the Dutch disease.

10 Balance-of-payment crises

The exchange rate is the most strategic and also the most dangerous macroeconomic price. As an outstanding Brazilian economist, the late Mario Henrique Simonsen, used to say: "inflation cripples, the exchange rate kills". As we saw in earlier chapters, the governments of developing countries do not neutralize the tendency to the cyclical and chronic overvaluation of the exchange rate, but rather worsen it with their economic policies. The most serious effect of this is the currency crises that mark the end of cycles of indebtedness. Capitalism is a basically unstable economic system. In this respect, the Great Depression of the 1930s was a great source of social learning. In the 1930s, John Maynard Keynes and Michael Kalecki developed new theories that better explained how to work with economic systems and made economic policy much more effective in stabilizing economic cycles, while wise commentators alerted economists and politicians to the dangers of uncontrolled markets. Likewise, John Kenneth Galbraith published in 1954 his book on the Great Depression, *The Great Crash, 1929*; and in 1978 Charles Kindleberger published the first edition of his remarkable historical survey of the crises, *Manias, Panics, and Crashes*. Based on what they learned from the Great Depression, governments built institutions, particularly central banks, and developed competent regulatory systems at national and international levels (the Bretton Woods system) to control credit and prevent financial crises or reduce their intensity and scope.

On the other hand, since the beginning of the 1970s Hyman Minsky had developed the fundamental Keynesian theory that connects finances, uncertainty, and crises. Before Minsky, the literature on economic cycles focused on the real or production side – on the inconsistencies between demand and supply. Even Keynes did it. Therefore, when Minsky (1975, p. 128) identified financial fragility as the agent of the crises, and associated it with the Keynesian concept of uncertainty, he took a decisive step to the understanding of economic cycles. For him, "the essential difference between Keynesian and both classical and neoclassical economics is the importance attached to uncertainty". The growing instability of the financial system is the consequence of a process of growing autonomy of credit and financial instruments in relation to the real side of the economy, both production and trade. In his paper "Financial instability revisited", Minsky (1972) showed that financial crises are endogenous to the capitalist system and that major economic crises were always associated with equally endogenous *financial* crises; the financial crisis is a particular moment of the cycle, and may be the immediate cause of cyclic reversion or recovery.

Minsky (1986) argues that indebtedness and financial fragility tend to worsen in the boom phase, but this does not mean that the fundamental problem – financial fragility – derives solely from indebtedness, because payment deadlines may be relaxed during the boom, giving rise to increasingly fragile financial credit conditions even if the level of indebtedness has hardly changed. With the increase in financial fragility, the debtor goes from the "hedge" condition to the "speculative" condition and finally to the "Ponzi" condition. In the hedge condition, the debtor preserves full liquidity and solvency; in other words, financial charges (interest and amortization) can be paid from the profits resulting from the financed investment. In the speculative condition, the debtor's liquidity is in doubt, because he now lacks the ability to repay all his debts on maturity, and he begins to count on his creditors rolling over the debt. Finally, the Ponzi condition is one of insolvency: The debtor lacks funds even to pay the interest on his debts. The same reasoning applies to financial institutions, but it is more difficult to determine in which of the three conditions a bank is, because its solvency depends not simply on the loans/capital ratio but mostly on the quality of its loans – that is, the extent to which the enterprises and individuals to which it has lent are in a hedge or Ponzi condition, information they hide as carefully as possible. Ponzi finance is a key concept in Hyman Minsky's thought, because to him deregulated financial markets tend endogenously to move towards this condition.

Minsky said that financial crises were essentially crises of excess indebtedness, but historical experience shows that financial crises may derive from a mismatch of currencies, even when total indebtedness is not excessive. Minsky analyzed financial crises in the United States and other rich countries with hard currencies. He therefore thought in terms of *banking* crises. Yet for developing countries the major financial crises arise not from banks but from the balance of payment crises or exchange rates (currency crises), because, unlike in rich countries, they involve foreign currency. The crises follow the logic analyzed by Minsky, and are usually associated with the formation of credit and speculative asset bubbles. Banking crises may occur both in rich and in developing countries; yet balance-of-payment crises are, in principle, confined to the developing countries, because these countries become indebted in foreign currency – a currency which, in contrast to the national currency, the countries concerned can neither issue nor devalue – the two defenses that a sovereign debtor can resort to when it is indebted in its own currency. If they have not dollarized their economies, sovereign debtors in foreign currency can resort only to the devaluation of their own money.[1]

Orthodox economists maintain that currency crises occur only in countries which have adopted the fixed exchange rate regime. They would not occur under a floating exchange rate regime because, if the country lacks dollars and loses foreign credit, the domestic currency gradually depreciates, which restores equilibrium to the inflows and outflows of dollars. But the experience of countries that have let their exchange rates float freely contradicts this thesis. The countries' credit or the confidence of creditors does not end gradually, but in a relatively sudden way. Governments and business enterprises become indebted through the formation of *credit bubbles* which, like all bubbles, grow because creditors' expectations of earning high interest returns, and are confirmed insofar as they finance payments of the interest and create a Ponzi condition. But, as also happens with all bubbles, when they burst there is a sudden suspension of credit.

Balance-of-payment crises are usually the consequence of current account deficits and of the accumulation of foreign debt, which, after reaching a certain critical level, lead foreign creditors to suddenly suspend the foreign financing of a given country. "Sudden stops" are like this. Current account deficits are followed by high and growing foreign debt, but the sudden stop may also happen when foreign debt is not so high but the current account deficit is growing rapidly and, from the creditors' perspective, dangerously.[2] When the current account deficit affects a country's ability to meet the conditions of solvency and liquidity, the crisis breaks. The liquidity constraint is related to the country's short-term ability to honour its current obligations, while it is presumed that in the medium term it will be able to pay them; but the solvency constraint requires that the present value of future payments must be sufficient to redeem the present stock of debt. When a country is insolvent, this indicates that it has become seriously indebted and that it will not be able to overcome the problem without first undergoing a financial crisis. From these two definitions, we can see that solvency is a structural problem associated with a Ponzi condition, whereas liquidity refers to economic circumstances and is associated with the speculative condition. The failure to heed either of the two constraints leads to financial crisis, but the crisis will be deeper in the solvency case and will require debt "restructuring" – that is, an extension of deadlines and a discount.

When there is a balance-of-payment crisis, the developing country finds itself suddenly unable to meet its debt obligations because the financial institutions of the rich countries, having sponsored a credit bubble for the country, lose confidence in its ability to pay and suspend the debt rollover. In the 1990s and the early 2000s, in the context of the Washington Consensus, financial crises in developing countries became much more frequent and severe. All these countries, before the crisis, significantly presented high and recurring account deficits insofar as they hoped to grow with foreign savings. Thus, the crises were caused by exchange rate irresponsibility, sometimes (*not* always) combined with fiscal irresponsibility. Yet this is not the story that neoclassical economics teaches.

Neoclassical explanations

The neoclassical models of balance-of-payment crises can be divided into three different "generations", beginning with the Krugman model (1979), which explained the crisis by reference to the inconsistency between the variables that determine the exchange rate and the value determined by the country's monetary authorities. Among these variables, the high public deficit stood out: Fiscal policy would be incompatible with the parity of the exchange rate.[3] The second-generation models, such as those of Obstfeld (1986, 1994), tried to demonstrate that exchange rate crises cannot be identified or foreseen only by macroeconomic indicators. Self-fulfilling prophecies, for instance, might be part of the explanation. In a setting of accelerating inflation caused by expansive fiscal policies, creditors might predict the abandonment of the exchange parity to keep the country growing, and thereby they help fulfill the prophecy. Finally, the third-generation models (Krugman, 1998) resorted to the argument of the "financial surplus" or, simply, of excess financing (ultimately, the cause of all financial crises). In this case, the crisis would be mainly a banking crisis. The process begins with huge capital inflows that increase the ability of the domestic banks to lend. The banks, in turn, adopt high-risk lending practices. The problem with these models is that they don't take into consideration the crucial cause of currency crises in developing countries: the growth cum foreign savings policy or the high current account deficits, which appreciate the national currency and causes the increase of the foreign indebtedness ratio to GDP.

The key assumption of these models is that the local banks are subject to moral hazard: They have little incentive to adopt more prudent lending policies because they assume that even high-risk loans will be guaranteed against default by the local authorities, which will not hesitate to bail out the banks if they are in danger. In other words, they – especially the major banks – assume that they are "too big to fail" – the big problem that regulators have been trying to solve after the 2008 global financial crisis, so far without success. This is why those models are part of a scenario of financial bubbles, moral hazard coupled with loose or irresponsible fiscal policies that would prevail in developing countries. Speculative bubbles and financial crises would be mainly caused by governments' fiscal irresponsibility and by the low quality of the loans made by the banks, and would explain the banking crises.

These models overestimate both the role of budget deficits in causing currency crises in developing countries and the significance of the assumption that their politicians are essentially populist, while they underestimate the role of the current account deficits and ignore their main cause: the growth cum foreign savings policy. The crises are believed to originate in banking, not in the balance of payments, although currency crises are different in developing countries because foreign debt is denominated in foreign money. Evidently both crises can appear together. An appreciated exchange rate in a context of highly mobile capital is associated with large capital inflows, through which business enterprises become indebted in foreign currency, with the local banks acting as intermediaries. When the balance-of-payment crisis breaks, the banking crisis tends to break simultaneously, insofar as business enterprises are unable to repay their debts to banks that have lost the ability to roll them over due to the suspension of international credit. And a fiscal crisis also tends to follow (not to precede) the balance-of-payment crisis, because the government bails out the banks, so incurring high fiscal costs.

In all these models the current account deficit is understood to be a consequence of the budget deficit, on the assumption (which is not borne out by the facts) that (*a*) the exchange rate is in the equilibrium and, in consequence, (*b*) the finances of the private sector are balanced – the two conditions to which the twin deficits hypothesis hold. According to this assumption, the policymakers should worry only about the public sector's imbalances. In other words, according to the models, optimal intertemporal decisions on savings and investments made in a decentralized way will give rise to an equally optimal balance in the current account, compatible with an intertemporally balanced exchange rate, and, so, the private sector is always in equilibrium. If the current account shows a deficit, this deficit will also be optimal, because it is the result of rational maximizing decisions on the part of economic agents. The culprit in this narrative is the government, which is often guilty of populism or fiscal irresponsibility.

According to the neoclassical way of thinking, there is no reason to imagine that the government would have better information about how much money private agents should save and invest than the agents do themselves. This reasoning would not apply only with regard to the state and the public deficit: Whereas the private sector could become indebted without endangering the national economy, the same would not be true of the public sector, because we cannot assume the rationality of public agents. Corden (1994, p. 78) summarizes this view as follows:

> It follows that an increase in a current account deficit that results from a shift in private sector behaviour should not be a matter of concern at all. On the other hand, the public budget balance is a matter of public policy concern and the focus should be on this.

It is true that politicians are sometimes guilty of populism, but in middle-income countries they are increasingly less prodigal. They learned the electoral consequences of fiscal misbehaviour. On the other hand, there is no reason to assume that the private sector is always in equilibrium. As we see also in rich countries, the overvaluation of the exchange rate is often associated with excess indebtedness of households and/or of business enterprises. When there is a current account deficit and the public sector is balanced, the exchange rate will be appreciated, and the reason why will be excessive expending of the private sector. Whereas the press and the political opposition are able to permanently control the profligate politicians, only the market could, theoretically, control the profligate individuals and firms, but we know well how limited is the power of the market when the banks and other financial institutions are ready to finance their expenses. On the other hand, the liberal orthodoxy recommends that developing countries control budget deficits, while it welcomes current account deficits. If the developing country follows the recommendation, it will leave the private sector unbalanced, and the exchange rate, overvalued.

According to this neoclassical approach, our theory would make no sense, since we argue that the adoption of the growth cum foreign savings policy or of deliberate current account deficits is the primary cause of financial crises in the developing countries. Only "bad quality" current account deficits would be reproachable, but they would be the consequence of fiscal imbalance and of the fact that national governments ignore the moral hazard involved in sustaining banks and business enterprises at any cost. Macroeconomic policies were derived from these models. In 1981, when the current account deficit in Chile hit 14 per cent of GDP, a high IMF official argued that there was no reason for concern, since the public accounts were under control and domestic savings was growing (Robischek, 1981). Months later, Chile suffered a serious balance-of-payment crisis and heavily devalued its currency. A few years later, the "Lawson doctrine", named after Nigel Lawson, the British Finance Minister from 1983–89, became part of the neoclassical macroeconomic orthodoxy. According to this doctrine, private deficits were no cause for concern, because the market would automatically balance them; financial crises would always have their origins in the fiscal imbalances of the public sector.

Although the Lawson doctrine is not a theory, it assembles the various theoretical arguments that combine the twin deficits hypothesis with the intertemporal approach to the current account, ignoring that private sector accounts may be unbalanced and the public accounts, balanced. Therefore, it is not surprising that in the early 1990s the IMF, which previously had exercised caution in relation to current account deficits, recommended that developing countries should open their financial accounts and adopt the policy of growth cum foreign savings. Whereas orthodox policies correctly rejected fiscal populism (government spending more than it collects and incurring irresponsible budget deficits), they now had no objection to exchange rate populism (the nation-state spending more than it earns and incurring current account deficits).[4]

Mexico is a good example of the application of this doctrine. In the period from 1992–94, the average current account deficit amounted to almost 7 per cent of GDP. However, according to data from Mexico's Central Bank, during that period the country's public finances were balanced, even though the country suffered from a balance-of-payments crisis during that period. The same happened in the 1997 financial crisis in four Asian countries (Thailand, Indonesia, Malaysia, and South Korea). Before the crisis they all had their public deficits under control, but the private sector incurred high current account deficits in the course of financing investment in real estate. And the same occurred in Italy, Spain, and Ireland before the 2010 euro crisis; their budget deficits were under control, below the 3 per cent of GDP ceiling, but in the previous ten years their current accounts ran huge deficits to which the European Commission and the European Central Bank paid no attention.

In summary, the neoclassical explanation of financial crises in developing countries identifies public deficits as their main cause and ignores the dangers of current account deficits. It uses the concept of the twin deficits in order to maintain that, once the public deficit is under control, the current account deficit must be automatically controlled, because the market ensures the intertemporal equilibrium of the current account: The current account will be permanently and reasonably balanced provided that the floating exchange rate regime prevails. However, when we examine the neoliberal years, we observe that many countries faced major balance-of-payment crises in spite of presenting reasonably balanced fiscal budgets; the only explanation was excessive private expending and an overvalued national currency.

Foreign savings and financial crises

We understand that financial crises in developing countries stem mainly from the growth cum foreign savings policy and the use of the exchange rate as anchors to achieve inflation targets, or, in other words, they are the consequence of exchange rate populism. A balance of payment crisis in those countries breaks out when the foreign creditors lose confidence and decide to suspend the rollover of public and private debts, which are denominated in foreign money. This decision is conditioned by the expected return $E(R)$ from credit operations. When the return becomes negative, the flow of finance is ruptured. The creditor evaluates the probability of receiving back its loans. Let us call P this probability of success, R the expected return, K the amount lent, and i the interest rate. ER^e is the expected exchange rate (currency in the destiny's resources country / currency in the origin's resources country) at the end of a loan, and ER is the exchange rate at the time of the grant of a loan, which we may write in a simplified way[5]:

$$E(R) = P[K(1 + i) - (ER^e - ER)] - K(1 + i^*) \tag{10.1}$$

in which i^* is the international interest rate and represents the creditor's opportunity cost. In making its decision the creditor considers the interest rate, the variation in the exchange rate and the probability of success (or default by borrowers). Given a positive interest differential $[(1 + i) - (ER^e - ER)] - (1 + i^*) > 0$, the probability P will determine the signal of the creditor's expected return. The probability P depends on the country's liquidity and solvency conditions. Those conditions – or the perception of them – can rapidly deteriorate so as to generate a negative expected return. The crisis arises when neither the liquidity constraint nor the solvency constraint is any longer satisfied. The expected exchange rate will also influence the foreign creditor's decision: When the probability of default arises, capital outflow increases and the investor's interests or profits, which are achieved in the local currency, fall in the investor's currency. So he will try to avoid this loss, ceasing the inflow and anticipating the outflow; this behaviour contributes to a sudden depreciation of the currency and to the outbreak of a balance-of-payments (or currency) crisis.

When a country adopts the growth cum foreign savings policy, it incurs high and continuous current account deficits that will have negative effects on both the liquidity and the solvency constraints. As we have seen, the process of mounting foreign indebtedness leads to a high rate of substitution of foreign for domestic savings, followed by foreign financial fragility; and, finally, if the government does not intervene with a combination of monetary, exchange rate, and fiscal policies, the high level of indebtedness in foreign money and/or high current account deficits will lead the country into a currency crisis.

Our explanation for a balance-of-payment crisis is, therefore, relatively simple: it results from the growth cum foreign savings policy – that is, from the policy of growing by resorting to foreign finance, in the form of loans. In each country, the excessive public expending and budget deficit may contribute to the current account deficit, but not necessarily, because twin deficits do not always occur. Whenever the exchange rate is overvalued, there will be a current account deficit without a budget deficit. This will happen because the overvalued exchange rate will stimulate the private sector to import and to finance its imports with foreign finance. Consequently, the current account may become negative, whereas the fiscal accounts may remain positive or, at least, under control. In the event that the public accounts are balanced, the cause of the current account deficit will be excess expenditure of the private sector – an event that neoclassical economists seldom took into consideration. The currency crisis will be accompanied by a banking crisis, where the banking system mediates between foreign resources and the domestic private sector. Consequently, local banks will be pressured by foreign creditors to repay the loans they raised abroad to finance domestic business enterprises and household consumption, which will lead the banks to stop rolling over their loans to the domestic private sector – loans that the private sector is unable to repay. This will give rise to bankruptcies in the domestic private sector, with corresponding loss of assets in the banking sector. Since the major banks are "too big to fail", as became very clear in the 2008 global financial crisis, the government will be forced to bail out the banking system. And, finally, since the government is the lender of last resort, although its finances were originally balanced, it too will move into (fiscal) deficit.

The intertemporal solvency constraint in a country is similar to the one faced by business enterprises when they take on loans. Creditors will evaluate the country's intertemporal solvency in much the same way as they do loans to business enterprises. They will evaluate the country's ability to repay the loans. They will determine the potential present value of the cash flow generated by the financed investments (defined as operational assets). A company is insolvent when this present value is not enough to meet its liabilities, including loans.

When we transfer this reasoning to the evaluation of a country's external solvency, the most appropriate measure of its ability to repay is the present value of the transfers of funds capacity, calculated in view of the surplus that originates in trade and non-factor services balance. It can be expressed as follows:

$$(1+i)D_{s-1} = \sum_{s=t}^{\infty} \left[\frac{1}{1+i} \right]^{s-t} TLR_s \qquad (10.2)$$

Therefore, this country's surplus corresponds to the operating cash flow generated by a business enterprise. The insolvency situation is the limit situation in which the present value of the transfers (TLR) is insufficient to liquidate the stock of the debt (D) existing at that moment.

But the concept of intertemporal solvency in the strict sense is not very useful for creditors, because there are endless trajectories that guarantee a country's intertemporal solvency. We should bear in mind, therefore, the possible trajectories that creditors usually demand from debtors in order to maintain the debt rollover. As the late Mario Henrique Simonsen used to say, creditors conventionally use the ratio between foreign debt and exports (D/X) to control solvency. A country will be in a comfortable situation if this ratio is below 2, in an uncertain situation if it is between 2 and 4, and in a critical situation if the ratio is higher than 4. These are rules of thumb, but they are widely accepted. Consequently, the point is to know how the growth cum foreign savings policy affects this ratio. It negatively affects the ratio D/X because a current account deficit is compatible with a more appreciated exchange rate than the rate that balances the current account, so that, if the current account deficit increases and the debt grows faster than exports, this ratio will increase.

The second financial constraint – the liquidity constraint – can be defined as the discrepancy between the country's short-term foreign debt and its international reserves (the difference corresponds to net external liabilities). If this ratio is lower than 1, the country has a low level of liquidity, being therefore exposed to financial crises due to self-fulfilling prophecies. Another way of defining it, given the accumulation of current account deficits, is by reference to the inconsistency between the potential dollars that are judged to be in the liabilities of local financial institutions (local FIs) and the international reserves. According to this approach, the local banks and the central bank can lead the country from a hedge condition to a speculative condition as a consequence of the growth cum foreign savings policy.[6]

The above assumptions lie behind the claim that the liquidity constraint may bring about (*a*) a floating exchange rate that, however, does not respond rapidly to the variations in the market;[7] and (*b*) balance-of-payment crises. In addition, we have to take into account the well-known arbitrage equation in which the expected profit rate or return on investment (r) is equal to the international interest rate (r_f), which is the cost of the financing plus the expected devaluation of the local currency (e) plus the risk premium (p):

$$r = r_f + e + p. \tag{10.3}$$

Given these assumptions, we can evaluate the impact of the growth cum foreign savings policy on the liquidity. According to Neftci (2002), the process of indebtedness, together with the exchange rate appreciation, coincides with the early phase of the liquidity cycle. Beginning with the local FIs,[8] the financial opening increases the rate of introduction of financial innovations and the supply of differentiated "products" for rentier capitalists. The elimination of the barriers to capital flows allows local FIs to raise funds in hard foreign currency that are sold to the central bank, the counterpart being invested in securities and/or generating assets against the private sector.

From the standpoint of systemic risk, the increase in debt does not substantially affect the amounts initially raised or the consolidated asset structure of the local FIs and of the central bank. However, since the returns encourage the entry of new institutions into the market, the balance sheets of the local FIs typically display speculative features. In order to understand why this happens, we must take into account the evolution of the balance sheet of the central bank, insofar as capital inflows over and above those needed to finance the growing current account deficits make it possible to accumulate international reserves and to give a false impression of lower foreign vulnerability. The accumulation of reserves can be followed by an increase in the money supply, depending on the degree of sterilization implemented by the monetary authority. When the money supply increases, the neoclassical argument is that the fall in the interest rate will make the country less attractive to foreign creditors, and capital inflows will slow down. This is a typical assumption of the "efficient markets hypothesis". What really happens is that the increase in systemic risk – the risk premium as defined above – tends to grow, stimulating the continuation of the funding process, in fact the creation of a credit bubble. But foreign creditors monitor the increase in the debt ratio and, at a certain moment in time, lose confidence and raise the red flag. From then on, the loans finance only debt repayments – that is, the net capital inflows stop, and the euphoric phase of the cycle comes to an end. Since there is a current account deficit to be financed, a discrepancy is created between the foreign obligations incurred by the FIs and the reserves. In other words, the FIs' balance sheets now typically display speculative characteristics.

It would be reasonable to assume that the central bank may somehow intervene on the market. But the financial fragility of the banks, whose assets will now comprise mainly of nonperforming loans resulting from speculative credits, will impose constraints on the actions of the central bank. This is the classic "too big to fail" trap. On the other hand, the national economy will be undergoing a boom. Therefore, although foreign creditors understand the incentives and constraints facing the central bank, they are also infected by the existing euphoria. What's more, they will be making money from high interest rates and from the constant appreciation of the indebted country's currency, so that their bets will be self-fulfilling prophecies. Their loans – or in other words, the capital inflows – will appreciate the local currency, validating the financial bet. Consequently, the local currency will most probably continue to appreciate or, at least, will remain over-valued for a long time – which means that the foreign debt will continue to grow until the creditors' confidence is exhausted, they raise the red flag (as observed above), and the economy goes into a crisis.

Although creditors are subject to "herd behaviour", changing their views in moments of crisis together, the crisis usually requires a few months to materialize. The first sign of the crisis is the fact that the net inflow of foreign resources is no longer sufficient to finance the current account deficit, and the foreign reserves start to steadily, although discreetly, shrink. For the central bank, a fall in the foreign exchange reserves means a downgrading of the country's credit, since it was previously believed that foreign loans to the country were guaranteed by a growing stock of international reserves. Now, in view of the reversion to the mood of the financial market, the flow of potentially necessary money to finance the growing liabilities existing in the balances of the local banks exceeds the amount of reserves of foreign exchange in the central bank. The decision of a single creditor to sell off in part or in full its position is enough to trigger the herd behaviour, which will later trigger the crisis – a crisis whose causes are directly related to the growth cum foreign savings policy, liquidity, and external solvency constraints.

Summary

To summarize, contrary to the tenets of neoclassical economic analysis, financial crises in the developing countries are not primarily caused by budget deficits, but rather by current account deficits. The corresponding capital inflows that, according to the conventional wisdom, benefit the developing countries actually follow a three-stage process: first, they cause the substitution of foreign for domestic savings, a small increase in the rate of investment and a substantial increase in the country's foreign indebtedness; second, they cause international financial fragility, entailing a policy of confidence building; and third, they ultimately provoke a balance-of-payments crisis. Public deficits can provoke crises, but only when the twin deficits hypothesis is confirmed. Yet usually that hypothesis is not confirmed because the exchange rate is rarely in equilibrium in the developing countries: It is usually overvalued and, whenever that happens, current account deficits may emerge without corresponding public deficits. In this situation, the imbalance usually occurs in the private sector.

In view of the tendency of the exchange rate to chronic overvaluation, the exchange rate may remain overvalued for relatively long periods, which will imply the increase in foreign debt to unsustainable levels The overvaluation is exacerbated not only by the growth cum foreign savings policy, but also by the policy of capital deepening and exchange rate populism. As foreign indebtedness increases and comes up against the liquidity and solvency constraints, the probability of a financial crisis increases. Thus, sooner or later, creditors will lose confidence and begin to suspend the rollover of debts, while financial speculators, knowing that the country cannot issue the currency in which the loans were denominated, will mount a speculative assault on the country, leading to a sudden stop or a currency crisis, defined by a sharp devaluation of the local currency and either a moratorium on the debt or an IMF rescue. In this process, foreign creditors attracted by high returns underestimate the liquidity and solvency constraints to which these countries are subject.

Notes

1 Balance-of-payment crises also occurred to the developed Eurozone countries in 2010 and 2011 because in those countries, the implicit or internal exchange rate had appreciated during the previous 10 years against the German euro in that their unit labour costs increased in relation to those of Germany. By creating the euro, they mistakenly established for themselves a *foreign currency* and became vulnerable to the kind of financial crisis that is characteristic of developing countries. As the European Central Bank is able to issue money, it offered guarantees to the countries' sovereign debt, and the financial crisis was overcome, but the economic crisis remained because the imbalance in internal exchange rates or in unit labour costs could not be corrected by exchange rate depreciation. Given this constraint, the indebted countries instead chose austerity programs, aiming to reduce real wages by means of recession and unemployment.
2 This is what, for instance, happened during the 1997 Asian crisis. The four affected countries did not have huge foreign debts, but their current account deficits were increasing dangerously.
3 Among the numerous studies that have tested this model are Flood and Garber (1984), Ötker and Pazarbasioglu (1995) and, in Brazil, Miranda (2006).

4 Liberal-orthodox policymakers partially revised this position after the 2008 global financial crisis.
5 The recovery tax – that is, the portion of the loan that is recovered after the "default", is ignored here.
6 The concepts of "hedge", "speculative", and "Ponzi" used here are from Hyman Minsky (1986). A financial institution is regarded as a "hedge" if its liabilities are small in relation to sales or exports, and as speculative if the institution becomes dependent on creditors' goodwill. The Ponzi condition is a condition of insolvency.
7 By including this condition, we are rejecting the conventional "fixed versus floating" alternatives because in fact this choice does not exist empirically. Countries always manage their exchange rates, although to different degrees. In addition, experience shows that a floating regime does not prevent balance-of-payment crises.
8 We use the expressions "local FIs" and "local banks" interchangeably.

11 The closing of the model

We now are ready to present a formal model of economic growth that synthesizes the state of the theoretical discussion so far. As seen in Chapter 3, the long-term growth of middle-income countries depends on the investment rate and on the growth of exports. This growth, however, is subject to three kinds of constraints. The first is the foreign constraint, analyzed by the growth models à la Thirlwall. If we take into account the effect of the exchange rate on the economy's productive structure, the income elasticities of exports and imports of Thirlwall's model are endogenous, so that, if the exchange rate is duly aligned (that is, at the level corresponding to the industrial equilibrium), any growth rate will be sustainable from the standpoint of the equilibrium of the balance of payments (that is, the foreign constraint will never be an obstacle to long-term growth). But there will be an exchange rate constraint because, if the country leaves its economy at the mercy of the international market, of the policies of growth cum foreign savings, of the exchange rate as an instrument to control inflation, and of exchange rate populism, and if it fails to neutralize the Dutch disease, the exchange rate will be overvalued most of the time rather than at the industrial equilibrium level.

The second constraint is given by the guaranteed growth rate, derived from Harrod's growth model, which presents the real output growth rate that is compatible with the normal level of productive capacity utilization. Since the distribution of income and the profit rate depend on the real exchange rate, it follows that, if the real exchange rate is depreciated (because we presume that it is usually overvalued) and later kept balanced, it will encourage business enterprises to invest more, causing the productive capacity growth rate to accelerate, given the output–capital ratio. This way, the productive capacity constraint can also be "relaxed" through adequate variations in the real exchange rate.

The third constraint, fundamental to this model, is the tendency to the chronic overvaluation of the exchange rate and particularly the Dutch disease, which determines the difference between the industrial equilibrium and the current equilibrium. In this chapter, we present the model first without this constraint and, later, with the constraint.

The Keynesian–structuralist model of growth

The Keynesian–structuralist model of growth comprises, therefore, the following system of equations:

$$g = u^n [v(\vartheta (\theta, R(\theta) - r)) + \delta]. \tag{11.1}$$

$$\theta = \theta_{ind}. \tag{11.2}$$

The system composed of equations (11.1) and (11.2) has two equations and two unknowns, namely the real output growth rate (g) and the actual value of the real exchange rate (θ). It is, therefore, a determinate system from the mathematical point of view.

The exogenous variables of the model are the industrial equilibrium exchange rate (θ_{ind}), the normal degree of capacity utilization (u^n), the output–capital ratio (v), the real cost of capital (r), and the rate of depreciation of the stock of capital (δ).

So equation (11.1) presents the combinations of the rate of growth of the stock of capital and the real exchange rate, for which the degree of productive capacity utilization is equal to the normal one, so that business enterprises will be satisfied with the current level of capacity utilization. It follows that the growth rate determined by equation (11.1) amounts to the guaranteed growth rate.

Equation (11.2) presents the level of the real exchange rate at which the economy's productive structure, measured by manufacturing industry's share of GDP, is kept constant over time. It is, as seen in Chapter 7, the industrial equilibrium exchange rate.

The long-term equilibrium of the economy in question is defined as the twin values of the real output growth rate and of the real exchange rate, for which productive capacity is growing at the same pace as aggregate demand, so that the degree of productive capacity utilization remains constant and equal to the normal level, and the economy's productive structure is constant over time. The determination of the long-term equilibrium (g_{ind}) is illustrated by Figure 11.1.

We also observe in Figure 11.1 the importance of the real exchange rate for long-term growth. In fact, the real exchange rate plays the role of reconciling the growth rate that makes possible the normal degree of productive capacity utilization with the long-term stability of the productive structure. This way, the Keynesian–structuralist model presented here situates *the real exchange rate at the centre of development economics*.

Dutch disease and deindustrialization

In the Keynesian–structuralist or new-developmental approach that we adopt in this book, the constraint on long-term growth does not derive mainly from the foreign constraint, but, on the supply side, from the capacity constraint, and, on the demand and access side, from the tendency of wages to grow below the productivity rate (which is overcome when the country achieves the Lewis point), and from the tendency to the overvaluation of the exchange rate, which originates in the Dutch disease and in policies that induce excessive capital inflows.

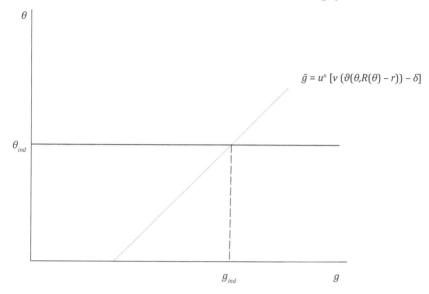

$$\bar{g} = u^n \left[v \left(\vartheta(\theta, R(\theta) - r) \right) - \delta \right]$$

Figure 11.1 Long-run equilibrium without Dutch disease

If the exchange rate is persistently overvalued in a primary-export economy, the country will not industrialize; if it happens in a middle-income country that has already undergone its industrial revolution, it will deindustrialize. In this case, it previously industrialized only because the Dutch disease was neutralized during the industrial revolution. This is the case, for instance, with Brazil, which industrialized between 1930 and 1980 by imposing on commodity exports a disguised tax[1] that neutralized the Dutch disease.

In order to understand this claim, consider a medium-development economy that industrialized by neutralizing the Dutch disease through a tax on commodity exports and other mechanisms of exchange rate management in the context of a developmental political coalition, but that, for reasons that are not relevant to the discussion, abandons this policy and, in the context of a neoliberal political coalition, allows the exchange rate to float freely. In this setting, the Ricardian rents arising from the commodities that the country exports enable its current account to remain balanced (at the current equilibrium) but overvalued with regard to the industrial equilibrium. A perverse structural change then takes place in the economy. More precisely, the economy undergoes a process of deindustrialization and of re-primarization of the export portfolio, which leads to a reduction in the income elasticity of exports and to an increase in the income elasticity of imports. The foreign constraint then reappears, so that growth will be limited by the requirement of the equilibrium in the balance of payments, as illustrated in Figure 11.2.

In Figure 11.2, the current equilibrium exchange rate is below the industrial equilibrium exchange rate. The country suffers, therefore, from the Dutch disease.

The exchange rate must therefore appreciate, dropping to the level θ_{cc}. This appreciation of the real exchange rate will lead to a decrease in private investment, as a result of its effect on the profit margins of business enterprises and,

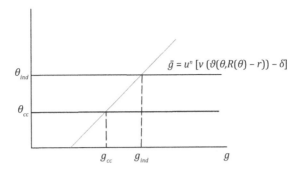

Figure 11.2 Long-run equilibrium with Dutch disease and deindustrialization

consequently, on the long-term profit rate. In addition, the real exchange rate appreciation will also shift the productive structure of the economy towards less value-added goods, requiring less sophisticated manpower, which will reduce the income elasticity of exports and increase the income elasticity of imports. In other words, the Dutch disease will unleash a gradual process of deindustrialization or, more precisely, it will cause the gradual productive *de-sophistication* of the economy. Due to the decrease in the pace of expansion of productive capacity and to the process of deindustrialization, the long-term equilibrium growth rate of real output will decrease, from g_{ind} to g_{cc}, as shown in Figure 11.3.

Excessive capital inflows

Excessive and unnecessary inflows of foreign capital may worsen the exchange rate overvaluation resulting from the Dutch disease. Capital flows are said to be excessive when they do not satisfy the national economy's need for stability and growth. As we saw before, if the real exchange rate is at the appropriate level – that is, at the industrial equilibrium level – then any output growth rate is sustainable from the standpoint of the balance of payments because it will imply a current account surplus, and there will be no need for net capital flows.

Speculative capital flows are, in general, the result of interest rate differentials and of the adoption of a growth model based on a current account deficit or foreign savings. As regards interest rate differentials, we should stress that the real interest rate tends to be higher in middle-income countries, for a number of reasons. First, capital markets are less organized in middle-income countries than in developed countries, which makes the liquidity premium on long-term securities greater in the former than in the latter. Second, middle-income countries generally become indebted in foreign currency – in currency that they cannot issue in the event of crisis. This "original sin" (the expression that Barry Eichengreen used to refer to indebtedness in foreign money) of developing countries is the reason why these countries are often threatened by a balance-of-payment crisis (a problem unknown to rich countries able to incur debts in their own money), and so they increase the domestic interest rate in order to attract foreign capital.

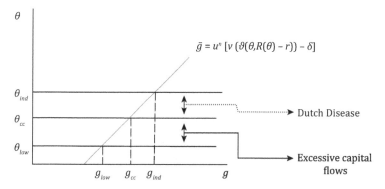

Figure 11.3 Long-run disequilibrium with Dutch disease and excessive capital flows

Finally, since the adoption of the growth cum foreign savings policy implies that the government takes the decision to incur current account deficits through the deliberate overvaluation of the real exchange rate, the financing of this deficit involves keeping the domestic interest rate at a higher level than that prevailing in developed countries.

As a result of excessive capital flows, the real exchange rate appreciates up to the level θ_{low}, lower than the level of the current account equilibrium. This means that the middle-income country that suffers from the Dutch disease and from excessive capital inflows will simultaneously present a current account deficit and deindustrialization. This situation is illustrated in Figure 11.3.

Exchange rate overvaluation and *falling behind*

If the reduction in the long-term equilibrium growth rate due to the presence of the Dutch disease (and also of excessive capital inflows) is big enough, it may cause the medium-development economy that we are analyzing to begin a process of *falling behind* – that is, to present an economic growth rate systematically lower than that of the developed countries.

Consider Figure 11.4. Let z^* be the developed countries' growth rate. Assume that the population of the developed countries grows at the rate γ^*. Therefore, the growth rate of the per capita income of developed countries is equal to $z^* - \gamma^*$. Given the output–capital ratio, the real interest rate, the degree of productive capacity utilization (equal to normal), the rate of depreciation of the stock of capital, and the population growth rate of the middle-income economy (equal to γ), the real exchange rate should be equal to θ^* for the growth rate of the per capita income of middle-income countries to be equal to the growth rate of the per capita income of developed countries.

In this case, the difference in the per capita incomes of the middle-income country that we are analyzing and of the developed countries would persist indefinitely. For *catching-up* to happen, the real exchange rate must be above this critical value, so as to lead to an acceleration in the process of capital accumulation.

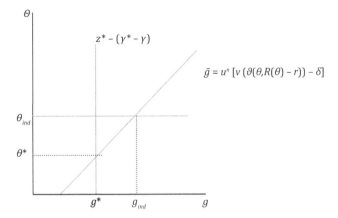

Figure 11.4 Long-run equilibrium and catching-up: no-supply constraint

On the other hand, if the real exchange rate is lower than this value (θ^*), then the country will begin a process of falling behind – that is, it will begin a growth path in which the difference between its per capita income and that of the developed countries will progressively widen.

In Figure 11.4 we consider that the exchange rate at which the gap between per capita incomes remains constant over time is lower than the real industrial equilibrium exchange rate; that is, the middle-income economy faces no supply-side obstacle to carrying out the *catching-up* process. In fact, if the exchange rate is at the industrial equilibrium level, the growth rate of per capita income determined by the pace of capital accumulation induced by this level of exchange rate will be higher than the growth rate of the per capita income of the developed countries, thus allowing *catching-up* to happen.

The failure to neutralize the Dutch disease may result in a current equilibrium exchange rate lower than the level of the real exchange rate at which the gap between per capita incomes remains constant over time. This situation is illustrated in Figure 11.5.

In Figure 11.5 the middle-income economy did not succeed in neutralizing the Dutch disease, so that the current account equilibrium rate is lower than the industrial equilibrium rate. In addition, the magnitude of the Dutch disease can be so large that the current equilibrium exchange rate would be lower than the value of the real exchange rate at which the gap between per capita incomes remains constant over time. In this case, even in the absence of speculative capital inflows, the economy in question not only will not be able to achieve *catching-up*, but will also start to slide into a *falling-behind* trajectory – that is, a low-growth trajectory where the gap between its per capita income and that of the developed countries will progressively widen.

What about the supply constraints?

So far we have assumed that in a middle-income economy economic development is essentially constrained by aggregate demand. In this context, the real exchange

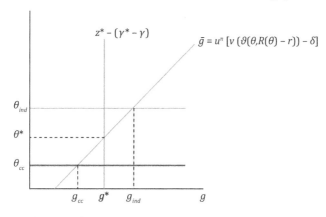

Figure 11.5 Falling behind due to Dutch disease

rate plays a fundamental role in the process of economic development. If the real exchange rate is at the industrial equilibrium level, then capital accumulation will take place fast enough to enable a process of *catching-up* with the developed countries. The failure to neutralize the Dutch disease may, however, prevent this process, as the chronic and profound overvaluation of the real exchange rate induced by it will discourage capital accumulation, thus reducing the growth rate of per capita income, which may eventually fall permanently below the growth rate of the per capita income of the developed countries. In this case, the middle-income economy will begin a process of *falling behind*.

However, it is possible that the process of economic development is constrained by the economy's supply conditions. This will happen, as shown in Figure 11.6, if the level of the exchange rate for which output growth rate is equal to the required level to keep constant the gap of per capital income over time (θ^*) is higher than the industrial equilibrium exchange rate. In this case, as illustrated by Figure 11.6, the mere neutralization of the Dutch disease and controls on capital inflows will be insufficient to enable the process of *catching-up*.

A situation such as the one illustrated in Figure 11.6 may occur in a middle-income economy in which (*a*) the normal degree of productive capacity utilization is relatively low, (*b*) the output–capital ratio is relatively low (that is, the capital–output ratio is relatively high).

In the first case, we are dealing with an economy characterized by a high degree of market concentration and high barriers to entry in the industrial sector; this often causes industrial investment to stagnate. Here, the most suitable economic policy to stimulate growth will be trade liberalization in order to reduce the market power of domestic enterprises and thus reduce the chosen overcapacity. In the second case, the most probable cause of low capital productivity is the inefficiency of the capital goods sector. Indeed, if the capital goods sector is inefficient, then the price of capital equipment will tend to be high and will increase the supply price of the capital equipment. In this case, the solution will be to stimulate the import of capital goods produced abroad or to implement policies to encourage

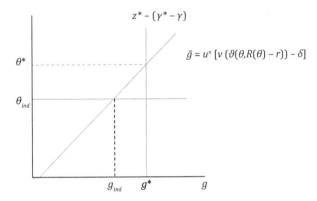

Figure 11.6 Falling behind due to supply constraints

the technological modernization of the domestic business enterprises that produce this kind of equipment. The exchange rate policy that we propose in this book doesn't aim to protect inefficient business enterprises but to make competitive the ones that are efficient. Another interpretation of the situation described in Figure 11.6 is that the required level of exchange rate is higher than the industrial equilibrium level in order to compensate for the negative impacts of the high interest rate over the investment rate and to enable the process of *catching up*.[2]

An alternative graphic closing

The close of the model may also be represented in an exclusively graphic form. To this end we refer back to Figures 6.1 and 7.1, and to Figure 11.7 we add a third equilibrium line below the current equilibrium, the "foreign debt equilibrium exchange rate". As we saw in Chapter 5, the foreign debt equilibrium is the level of the exchange rate that stabilizes the ratio of foreign debt to GDP. In contrast to the other two lines, this line does not represent a value of the exchange rate, but just a level – a level that becomes important when the foreign debt ratio starts to worry creditors. We could also imagine a fourth equilibrium line, one that depicts the level of current account deficit that, in a given country, is usually financed by foreign direct investment. But this kind of "equilibrium" is just a rule of thumb often used in middle-income countries.

   Figure 11.7 involves some of the main models that form our developmental macroeconomics, in which the exchange rate plays a key role because it is the macroeconomic price that assures access to demand to competent business enterprises. It depicts the market exchange rate that reflects the tendency to the cyclical and chronic overvaluation of the exchange rate, and the three relevant exchange rate equilibriums. The current equilibrium is what, in principle, should be *the* equilibrium; it is the price that balances the foreign accounts and to which the market tends. The foreign debt equilibrium is the sustainable equilibrium below which the country will face financial instability and eventually a

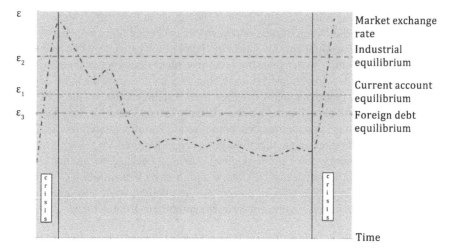

Figure 11.7 Current equilibrium, industrial equilibrium, foreign debt equilibrium, and market exchange rate

currency crisis; it is the equilibrium that neoclassical economics usually defends in light of the intuitive "truth" that capital-rich countries are supposed to transfer their capital to capital-poor countries; it is the equilibrium that ignores the high rate of substitution of foreign for domestic savings. The "real" equilibrium in the model is the industrial equilibrium, the one that is consistent with the more general equilibrium in economics: the equilibrium of relative prices. At this level the Dutch disease is neutralized, and business enterprises that utilize world state-of-the-art technology are competitive. In fact, this is the "right" price for the exchange rate.

This figure shows not only the cyclical but also the *chronic* character of the overvaluation of the national currencies of developing countries. If we take into account the comparison with the industrial equilibrium, only in a very short period, after the balance-of-payments crisis, is the exchange rate relatively devalued; for the rest of the period it is overappreciated. How long will the cycle take to complete its course? How much time will elapse between one crisis and the next? This depends on how far below the foreign debt equilibrium the exchange rate lies. The more overvalued the market exchange rate is in relation to this equilibrium, the sooner the currency crisis will break. For sure, the occurrence of the crisis will depend on other variables, such as wars, price shocks, and sudden policy changes in rich countries; but in our model the key and relatively predictable variable is the degree of overvaluation of the exchange rate.

Obviously, Figure 11.7 does not show the whole story. It does not say that growth depends essentially on the investment rate, which determines the savings rate; or that the investment rate depends on profit opportunities, which, for competent business enterprises, depend on the exchange rate being competitive, floating around the industrial equilibrium. The figures in this chapter show that a country that has the Dutch disease and keeps its exchange rate competitive will present a current account surplus (since the level of exchange rate that balances the current account is lower than the level that makes enterprises competitive, which corresponds to the industrial level), but they do not show the main consequence, which is that the country does not need foreign capital; on the contrary, and counterintuitively, despite being relatively capital-poor, it will transfer resources to capitalrich countries (via consumption and income remittances, for example). Despite their name, the "foreign savings" required for the net transfer of capital to a country don't add to domestic savings, because, as another model shows, developing countries usually show a high rate of substitution of foreign for domestic savings. The price of current account deficits is an overvalued currency which disconnects competent business enterprises from demand.

Summary

In this chapter we closed our macro-developmental model in two ways: in a more abstract way, through a mathematical model combined with a graphic model, and in a simpler way, just with a figure which we have been developing throughout the book. In this model, the exchange rate is at the core of development macroeconomics, because investment and savings depend on that rate. The strategic role of the exchange rate should be obvious, but economics, independently of school of thought, has paid little attention to it insofar as it assumed that exchange rate misalignments were short term and lacking direction. Insofar as we have demonstrated that this is not true, that the Dutch disease and conventional policies make the exchange rate cyclically and chronically overvalued, the picture changes from top to bottom, and only policies that neutralize such a tendency are consistent with fast growth and catching-up. If this neutralization is not dully undertaken, the country may experience some growth, because capitalism is essentially dynamic, but it will fall behind other countries.

Notes

1 The disguised tax, which coffee growers used to call "exchange rate confiscation", was collected either through multiple exchange rates or through a system of high customs duties combined with equally high subsidies to exporters of manufactured goods.
2 It is necessary to control the capital inflows to allow for the exchange rate to be higher than the industrial equilibrium level and, at the same time, the interest rate to be fixed in a high level.

Part II
Policymaking

12 Wage, export, or balanced-led?

In the first part of this book we reviewed the definition of economic growth, related it to wages and to investment, and showed that it is demand-led insofar as investment depends on the existence of lucrative investment opportunities. That section also covered the core model of our developmental macroeconomics, we argued that in developing countries the existence of effective demand is not enough to stimulate investment; it is also necessary that efficient business enterprises have access to that demand, which is not automatically assured because in these countries there is a tendency to the cyclical and chronic overvaluation of the exchange rate (if the exchange rate was merely volatile and subject to misalignment, as is usually assumed, the problem of access to markets would not arise). Then we discussed extensively the causes of the overvaluation, and summarized the findings in the chapter on the close of the model. In this second part of the book we discuss policymaking.

In this chapter, we enquire whether the overall strategy should be wage-led, export-led, or balanced from the new-developmental perspective. The definition of those strategies will be based in the behaviour of the import coefficient (imports/GDP) and the export coefficient (exports/GDP). The strategy will be domestic-led when the import coefficient is decreasing and export-led when the export coefficient is increasing. When both coefficients are stable, the economy is on a balanced growth path.

It is important to differentiate between a growth strategy and the source of economic growth. According to the theoretical framework adopted in this book, growth is demand-led, which means that economic growth is driven by the rate of growth of autonomous demand. In middle-income countries that do not have a convertible currency, exports are the only autonomous and sustainable source of demand growth. Consumption can drive aggregate demand in the middle term by means of an increase in the wage share. However, as we have already discussed, continuous increases in the wage share are not sustainable in the long run, since they would force a decrease in the profit rate and, consequently, a reduction in the rate of capital accumulation. Public spending, especially public investment, is another source of autonomous demand, but it is not sustainable in the long run due to fiscal constraints (it can generate a high public debt and an increase in the interest rate, and is a disincentive to private investment). Private investment is induced by the rate of economic growth by means of the so-called accelerator effect if the (expected) profit rate (which depends on the exchange rate) is higher than the cost of capital. So in our model, growth is driven by export growth in the short phase during which the economy makes its transition to the industrial equilibrium exchange rate and to a constant level of openness coefficient, and is always sustained by capital accumulation. This does not mean, however, that middle-income countries have to adopt a strategy of export-led growth in the long run (but for a certain period it can be necessary, as we will discuss later). As a matter of fact, in a balanced growth (long-run) equilibrium (where Dutch disease is neutralized) exports, GDP, imports, consumption, and investment are all growing at similar rates, which means that the export and import coefficients are reasonably constant through time. But when we are discussing growth strategies, the issue at hand is not the source of economic growth, but how to achieve a higher rate of GDP growth. For this purpose we can visualize two alternative growth strategies: an export-led growth strategy (which requires an increase in the rate of exports growth) or a domestic or import substitution strategy (which means a decrease in the income elasticity of imports). In the first case, during the transition from a lower to a higher rate of growth, the exports coefficient will increase, since export growth will be temporarily higher than GDP growth. In the second case, the import coefficient will decrease since the growth rate of imports will be temporarily lower than GDP growth. Once the economy has achieved a higher rate of growth, the export and import coefficients will be constant, and the growth strategy is "balanced". Adoption of an export-led growth strategy requires a competitive exchange rate and the neutralization of the Dutch disease. On the other hand, the adoption of domestic or import-substitution growth strategies requires the adoption of trade tariffs and trade protection, which is forbidden by existing rules of the World Trade Organization (WTO) and which increases productive inefficiencies in the long term.

Under normal conditions, the best strategy for a middle-income country is neither wage-led nor export-led, but balanced; in this strategy, wages and exports have a fundamental role on the demand side, as profits do in encouraging entrepreneurs to invest. It is only during the brief initial period of industrialization that backward countries successfully adopt an import-substitution model in which the degree of openness decreases or, in other words, the share of the domestic market in aggregate demand increases. Under normal conditions, exports are an essential part of economic development, and economic policy should strive to make them grow at the same rate as the increase in the national income, since a stable degree of openness, in which the GDP growth rate is equal to the exports growth rate, characterizes the "normal" development typical of this country.

Why would the balanced strategy be the "normal" strategy for a country? The domestic-led and export-led strategies are ultimately part of the historical process by which the market and economic policy try to find the best degree of openness for the country, which uses its resources most effectively and results in higher economic growth. When the country reaches this level of openness, which also contributes to a satisfactory GDP growth rate, exports should grow at this same rate.

Domestic-led strategy

The domestic-led strategy makes sense when applied to economies that export primary goods and are still in the phase of import-substitution industrialization. Since there are no exporters of manufactured goods, the overvaluation of the domestic currency will exert only negative effects on the profit margin of the primary exporting sector that, in principle, is already well remunerated and whose exports respond poorly to the exchange rate (they respond much more to the cyclic fluctuations of world economy). Therefore, as long as there are no prospects of industrialization, there would be no reason to advocate devaluation. The strategy of devaluing the exchange rate in order to shift it to the industrial equilibrium, therefore, is proper for a national economy in the process of industrialization. However, if there are tariff restrictions on imports, as is proper for the import-substitution model, the overvalued exchange rate will not become an obstacle to investment in manufacturing industry because the entrepreneurs in this sector will not face competition from imports.

The domestic-led strategy begins with a policy of increasing wages, particularly the minimum wage, which the government controls. In this situation, the strategy can also be considered wage-led. The idea is to create investment opportunities and to increase the rate of investment through expanding the domestic market. This strategy presupposes that investment is less sensitive to the profit margin and more elastic to variations in the amounts sold and, therefore, to the degree of capacity utilization; therefore, entrepreneurs' revenue would increase as a function of the amounts sold rather than of the profit margin. Thus, the profit rate could be higher even if the profit margin was low. But this assumption makes little sense in the long term. In the short term, a fall in the profit margin may be compensated by an increase in sales, so the profit rate may not fall. However, this does not happen in the long run because there is no increase or decrease in capacity. In other words, in the long run we cannot think about a continuous reduction in profits' share of national income, since in order to keep the profit rate constant, the reduction would have to be compensated by a continuous increase in the degree of capacity utilization, which is impossible since its limit is 1.[1] Instead, wages would increase faster than productivity, which would raise unit labour costs, appreciate the real exchange rate (since prices rise), and reduce investment opportunities. Besides, this strategy implies a higher increase in imports than in exports, which could be implemented only in an economy that imposes quantitative and tariff restrictions on foreign purchases in order to constrain imports and prevent a sharp deficit in the current account. Nowadays, however, such controls are not feasible. Consequently, when one tries to apply this strategy of increasing the minimum wage the domestic market actually expands, but after two to three years (the time it takes for importers of manufactured goods to become organized) this increase ceases to benefit domestic manufacturing industry and begins to benefit importers, since the real exchange rate appreciates: There is a "leak" of aggregate demand towards foreign producers.[2]

The domestic-led strategy is possible only if domestic producers are protected or rendered less subject to foreign competition. In addition, this kind of strategy in the end stimulates imports considerably, so that, despite import restrictions, current account deficits will emerge that have to be financed by foreign indebtedness – which is undesirable, as we discuss in this book – or reversed by an exchange rate devaluation, which implies abandoning the strategy since there will no longer be an increase in the coefficient of imports, and exports will grow again at the same rate as (or faster than) GDP. So long as the currency is not devalued, domestic producers will try to offset the increase in unit labour costs by increasing their imports of inputs. In this case, the damaging effect on the current account balance will be exacerbated and the need for adjustment in the foreign accounts will increase, right up to the process of deindustrialization.

The domestic-led strategy makes sense in a middle-income country only if there is good reason to believe that the profit rates expected by entrepreneurs are clearly above the satisfactory level and, of course, if there is unemployment, so that economic policy can include minimum wage adjustments higher than increases in productivity and the market is able to absorb not only those adjustments but also those resulting from the consequent revival of the labour market without damaging investment, since unemployment constrains large wage increases and there is room for reductions in the profit rate. However, this is a very special situation because, if the expected profit rate is high, investment will be high and, thereafter, unemployment will fall. Therefore, this is not a mid-term strategy, as growth strategies should be, but a short-term strategy that assumes the existence of unemployment, widespread idle capacity and high profit rates, in addition to engendering balance-of-payments constraints in the medium term. It can be justified as a temporary measure, therefore, as long as these conditions prevail and, consequently, the impact on the current account balance does not result in excessive foreign indebtedness. It is not realistic to expect that wages in the medium term will continue to grow more than productivity and that the expected profit rate and investment will not fall only because the volume of sales will increase. In order to grow fast, a reasonable equilibrium is necessary between the profit rate, the wage rate, aggregate demand, and aggregate supply (productivity capacity) of the economy. At this point, the scenario for a middle-income country, such as the developing countries that we are assuming, is no different from the scenario that would unfold in the rich countries.

Balanced strategy

In the 1940s and the 1950s, Latin-American structuralist economists advocated a model of development that is *inward oriented* because the import-substitution model was succeeding at that time, and because an export-led strategy would be oriented to the export of commodities or primary goods – precisely what these economists had criticized in the alternative prescriptions of orthodox economists. However, in 1963, Maria da Conceição Tavares published her classic paper showing that the import-substitution model was exhausted in Latin America. In following years, it became increasingly clear that, in fact, this model was a temporary and short-lived development strategy. It was a valid model for a country that was beginning its industrial revolution but it could not provide sustained development, for several reasons. First, even in relatively large countries such as Brazil or Mexico, the domestic market was too small for enterprises to benefit from economies of scale; second, it was a model that did not assist in evaluating and promoting the efficiency of industrial enterprises through foreign competition; third, it always kept the country short of dollars, given the foreign constraint (the asymmetric two elasticities).

Therefore, the countries should turn to the export of manufactured goods. In the late 1960s, Brazil and Mexico started to do so very successfully, as, since the beginning of that decade, the small dynamic Asian countries then called "tigers" had been doing: South Korea, Taiwan, Singapore, and Hong Kong. This fact demonstrated the possibility of backward countries exporting manufactured goods, something that was inconceivable for the structuralist economists of the 1940s and the 1950s.

These two new facts (the exhaustion of the import-substitution model and the viability of exporting manufactured goods) signaled that it was the time for structuralist theory to engage in a strategy oriented not only to the domestic market but also to the export of manufactured goods – under a balanced strategy, because this was the only way to continue to transfer labour to sectors of higher value-added per capita and to grow fast. Insofar as the enterprises of a developing country were capable of using world state-of-the-art technology to produce, technologically, relatively simple goods, but already with higher value-added per capita than that prevailing in the production of commodities, this country would be increasing its productivity and begin to develop. Later, in the 2000s the successful experience of India would show that not only manufactured goods but also services with higher value-added per capita could be exported, particularly services associated with information technology and communication sectors.

Given the practical demonstration of the viability of developing countries exporting manufactured goods, another argument appeared, namely that developing countries should adopt a wage-led rather than an export-led strategy because this would prevent economic development leading to an increase in inequality. This argument makes no sense in terms of the theory of income distribution. In reality, distribution may remain constant once the exchange rate has been devalued to the right level – the industrial equilibrium level. When the exchange rate is at that level, employment and income can grow from then on, with the profit rate remaining constant and the wage rate growing at the rate of productivity increase. The initial drop in real wages will be compensated by subsequent wage increases and by increases in investment, employment, productivity, and income after the depreciation of the exchange rate. The conditions are then created for competent enterprises to achieve the desired profitability and for real wages to increase without placing downward pressure on profitability.

Export-led strategy

But, one might ask, why not an export-led strategy rather than a balanced strategy? For the same reason that the wage-led strategy is usually mistaken: because it is an inherently temporary strategy, designed to achieve an increase in the rate of economic growth. The export-led strategy is not based on an expansion in private consumption and consequently in the domestic market because, unlike with the wage-led model, it is not the initial increase in wages that will stimulate demand (wages will grow as a consequence of the increase in investment and productivity), but rather exports. Whereas the wage-led strategy implies an increase in the wage–profit ratio and a decrease in the coefficient of imports, the export-led strategy implies an increase in the profit–wage ratio – an increase that is necessarily temporary.

The export-led strategy does not imply the need for a trade-off, by an increase in the volume of enterprises' sales to keep the amount and the rate of profit stable, because there is no reduction in the profit margin; on the contrary, there is an increase. But once again, this fact makes it obvious that the strategy is necessarily transitional, because a permanent reduction in real wages – the consequence of an increase in profit margins – is not sustainable, since it will reduce aggregate demand, and is not socially desirable in the long run.

The export-led strategy is appropriate if, in a given national economy, investment and growth rates are low and below the country's potential, and its government decides to devalue the exchange rate in order to increase exports and investment opportunities. In the theoretical framework of the developmental macroeconomics, this assumption is realistic, given that the exchange rate tends to be cyclically and chronically overvalued in developing countries. Once the depreciation is achieved through a series of interventions, let us assume that the exchange rate is at the industrial equilibrium level and that the government is able to keep it there. Export-oriented investment opportunities will increase because enterprises will no longer compete at a disadvantage at the international level, or, in other words, because real wages, which were artificially high relative to the country's productivity level, have declined (which implies the correction in unit labour costs) and competent enterprises have become competitive. Very well, we adopted a successful export-led strategy but, by definition, it was temporary. Once the process of correcting the exchange rate and the wages level has ended, the economy will grow again in a balanced way, with wages once again growing along with increases in productivity. But now, with a higher rate of investment, the increase in productivity will be considerably higher, and wages will grow faster than before.

Export-led strategy as a transition

The export-led strategy is justifiable, therefore, when it is a transition strategy, designed to change the level of a country's rates of investment and growth that are generally deemed as unsatisfactory. The level of "unsatisfactory" rates will vary from country to country but, for instance, investment rates of 18 per cent and growth rates of 3 per cent, very common in developing countries such as Brazil, are usually considered as unsatisfactory because they fail to make it possible to catch up with developed countries. The adoption of the export-led strategy begins with a depreciation of the domestic currency towards the industrial equilibrium, which makes tradables more expensive than non-tradables. This change in relative prices implies a reduction in purchasing power and consequently a reduction in actual real wages (at first), an increase in the profit–wage ratio and an increase in the expected profit rate. Policymakers bet, however, that this reduction will be temporary. They also bet that, subsequently, due to the increased profitability of export-oriented investments, the rate of investment will increase in a sustained way, the country's output and employment will increase at a faster rate, and wages will soon return to, and exceed, their level before the exchange rate devaluation. As we can see in Figure 12.1, which shows the effect over time of an exchange rate devaluation, wages and other remunerations decline but, later, due to the increase in the rate of investment, the growth rate of GDP, and wages, they are higher than before, and soon the workers return to, and surpass, the previous level of wages.

The reduction in wages as a result of the depreciation happens, therefore, only once, whereas the later growth rate of the economy and of wages is higher than that before the depreciation, and remains so in a permanent or sustained way. The government that takes this decision incurs the political cost of temporarily reducing wages, but knows that the economy will later achieve a higher and more sustainable growth rate. In Figure 12.1 we actually have two figures. Alternative # 1 is the more optimistic alternative, in which the recovery in the wage tendency occurs in three years; under the more pessimistic alternative # 2, this recovery in the tendency takes six years. The bravest policymaker will bet on the first alternative. Obviously, a preliminary agreement between workers and entrepreneurs greatly helps to make the policy viable.

A second cost of the depreciation is its impact on inflation. This is also a cost that is incurred only once. And provided the economy is not formally or informally indexed, inflation will soon return to its previous level. For this increase to be temporary, it is also important that, besides de-indexation, the expansion in the level of activity is initially reduced in order to avoid the transfer of the costs of currency depreciation to the prices of tradables and, later, of non-tradables (when inflation begins to rise). This control of aggregate demand must be effected through fiscal policy, since monetary policy cannot be strongly restrictive in this setting since otherwise pressure for the appreciation of the domestic currency will be intense (which would be incompatible with the purpose of the strategy), as we will see when we analyze the determinants of the exchange rate level.

Currency devaluation stimulates exports and, consequently, domestic production itself. The increase in domestic production revives the labour market, and wages, both nominal and real, grow again. Since the country continues to export, the import growth resulting from the increase in income can be fully funded by the earnings in foreign currency, without the need to incur foreign indebtedness.

To summarize, the change in the level of a country's growth rate from, for instance, 3 per cent to 5 per cent per annum is possible with an export-led strategy. But, later, this strategy should be balanced once again. It will continue to be based on the export of goods and services with growing value-added per capita, and on the balanced growth of wages and profits, exports and GDP, and it should bring greater financial stability.

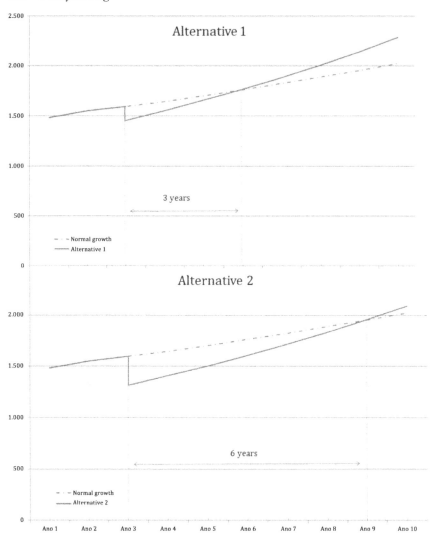

Figure 12.1 Wages and exchange rate devaluation: alternatives

Reducing inequalities without reducing the profit rate

Progressive economists are always trying to find a way of reconciling growth with the reduction in inequalities. However, the obstacles to achieving this objective are considerable. If we take into account only the supply side and, more specifically, technical progress, this is possible only when technological development is capital-saving – that is, when economic development takes place by making capital cheaper. In other words, it possible only as long as technical progress is characterized less by mechanization or the substitution of capital for labour, and more by the substitution of new, more efficient or cheaper machines for old ones and, therefore, by an increase in capital productivity or by cheaper capital, which offsets the wage increases in excess of productivity gains that would be necessary to allow income redistribution in favour of wages.

In the short term, one of the reasons why Keynesian thought attracted social-democratic economists was that, through the transition from unemployment to full employment, or from idle capacity to full capacity, it became possible to increase wages above productivity without damaging profits and, therefore, without endangering capital accumulation. The Bhaduri and Marglin model (Bhaduri and Marglin, 1990) embodies this hope by identifying a number of restrictive conditions in which the model could apply. Schumpeterian thought is equally attractive because, through the idea of innovation, it ensures that entrepreneurs will invest even if the normal profit rate is low.

However, we have just seen that, in the long run, the recommended viable strategy is the balanced one, in which there is neither an increase nor a decrease in inequality, but the profit–wage ratio is preserved. This is because the *reasonable* level of the profit rate is neither the "normal profit" level of microeconomics textbooks, which is very low, nor the level of monopolistic profit for which every enterprise strives, but is the viable profit for normal entrepreneurs who are efficient in their activity; it is the profit rate that, in conditions of reasonable competition in the market, is *satisfactory* for these enterprises and stimulates them to invest, and is higher than the opportunity cost (the interest rate).

For the structuralist economic theory on which the old developmentalism was based, this was a moral issue because most of its economists were progressive or social-democratic and wished to reduce inequalities; but it was not a key political issue because the political regimes in place at the time when the countries achieved their national and industrial revolution were usually authoritarian, and the workers had limited power. Yet for the economists associated with developmental macroeconomics and the new developmentalism, the picture changes because now practically all of the middle-income countries are democratic, and the workers' or voters' demands must be heard, particularly because in those countries the distribution of income used to be very unequal. What to do in this case? Isn't there a way of promoting redistribution without adversely affecting entrepreneurs' profit expectations?

Yes, there is, but it implies giving up the simple equation of the national income with wages plus profits ($Y = W + P$) and accepting that the national income also comprises the revenues from rentier capitalists (R), the high wages and bonuses of financiers and top executives of the big multinational corporations (B), and the state, insofar as it incurs social expenses that in the end represent indirect wages (G_w).

$$Y = W + G_w + P + R + B.$$

Given this slightly more complex identity, there are three ways of reducing inequality: a reduction in the gains of rentier capitalists, a reduction in wage inequalities through the taxation of high wages and bonuses, and an expansion of the welfare state. The three approaches make it possible to reduce inequality without reducing the profit rates of entrepreneurs and, therefore, without reducing investment and growth rates.

The rentier capitalist is the idle capitalist, who is remunerated by interest, rents, and dividends, apart from gains from speculation in assets. Marx clearly distinguished the active from the idle capitalists in volume 3 of *Das Kapital*, but the Marxists, focused on the class struggle, attached no significance to this distinction. The rentier capitalist is a mere burden on modern societies, as Keynes pointed out when he referred to the "euthanasia of the rentier". Every policy that can reduce interest rates and rents in the medium term, and tax them and distributed dividends more heavily, reduces inequalities without reducing the profit rate.

As we well know, the interest rate does not depend solely on the market. On the other hand, the "satisfactory" rate aimed by developmental macroeconomics should be seen in relation to the cost of capital. The important thing for the business entrepreneur is the difference between the two rates. Therefore, the remuneration par excellence of the rent-seeking or idle capitalists – the interest rate – should be as low as possible. Resistance to this kind of policy will come from the rent-seekers themselves and from the professionals of the financial sector, the financiers, who are paid to manage rent-seekers' wealth. The remuneration that concerns them – interest, rents, and dividends – does not contribute to economic development: it is just the price that entrepreneurs or active capitalists need to pay to use their capital. For these two groups, to which can be added foreign lenders for developing countries, the fundamental purpose of economic policy is to keep nominal interest rates relatively high and inflation as low as possible, because the result – the real interest rate – will increase their remuneration. Most of the economic policies supported by liberal or orthodox economists meet these demands.

A second way of reducing inequality is to reduce the differences in remuneration between the top professionals, specifically financiers and the top executives of the big enterprises, and the workers' wages. The policy par excellence to achieve this result is progressive taxation of their revenues, which was imposed with excellent results in the golden years of capitalism, but rejected, in the neoliberal years that followed, when rentier capitalists and financiers, as well as the neoclassical economics that legitimizes neoliberal policies, were in the ascendant. Better education and training will also help to reduce this inequality, but it takes too long to have an effect. Progressive taxation is necessary to accelerate the change.

Finally, the expansion of the welfare state is a policy par excellence for reducing economic inequalities, for two reasons. First, collective consumption in the form of major social services, such as education, health care, culture, social security, social care, and mechanisms for guaranteeing a minimum income, are generally more efficient than private consumption: It raises people's standard of living more cheaply than when wages are directly increased. Take, for instance, health care expenses in Europe's most developed countries as compared with those of the United States. Whereas in the United States they correspond to 17 per cent of GDP, in the European countries, in which health care coverage is universal, they represent only 11 per cent. Second, collective consumption is financed by taxes;

even if conservative politicians strive to make the tax system more regressive, such taxes will contribute to reducing inequality, because the rich nevertheless pay taxes, and these taxes are used to benefit the poor.

Summary

The dichotomy between a domestic-led strategy and an export-led strategy is, therefore, a bogus one. In a situation of balanced growth, in which the rates of investment and growth are reasonably satisfactory, a country does not need to, nor should it, choose between the two strategies; it needs a balanced strategy. On the assumption of neutral technical progress (a constant output–capital ratio) and an equilibrium exchange rate, there will be equilibrium in the country's foreign accounts and wages will grow at the same rate as productivity, as well as unit labour costs; the wage–profit ratio will remain constant, as will the profit rate that, in the long run, will remain at a satisfactory level for entrepreneurs to invest. It is true that, between the wage rate and the profit rate, there is a profit–wage ratio to which a profit margin or mark-up also corresponds. Given the same level of productivity and reasonably full employment, the higher the profit–wage ratio is, the higher are the profit rate and the rate of investment. But this does not mean that entrepreneurs will always try to increase the ratio, because it makes neither economic nor political sense to do so. Each nation should define a target for the rate of investment and, later, pursue the profit–wage ratio and the profit rate that are necessary to achieve that target.

The nation shall resort to an export-led strategy, and for a brief period, only if the current growth rate is unsatisfactory – if this rate is growing below the rate needed for catching up. It will be growing below its potential because its exchange rate is over-appreciated and, consequently, enterprises using world state-of-the-art technology are not internationally competitive. It will then be necessary to devalue the exchange rate to the competitive equilibrium level, as this will imply an increase in the profit rate and a temporary fall in wages. If the country achieves this change and, at the same time, is able, through progressive taxation, to transfer the sacrifice to rentier capitalists, there will be no increase in the inequality between profits and wages. The alternative of the temporary adoption of a domestic-led strategy would be justified only if we assume that entrepreneurs (not rent-seekers) are gaining excessive profits. But in this case it would be hard to explain why the rate of investment remains at an insufficient level and there is unemployment and low growth.

To achieve its extraordinary growth rate, China depreciated its exchange rate during the 1980s. However, this export-led strategy was temporary. As soon as the country achieved a growth rate of around 9 per cent per annum, its growth became balanced. In the 2000s, however, growth exceeded 10 per cent per annum. This fact and the social problems involved led the Chinese government to modify the policy and to prioritize the domestic market by adopting a domestic-led strategy. The 2008 global financial crisis forced it to undertake dramatic expansive measures, but once they succeeded, the government went back to a balanced growth policy. It now experiences growth rates of around 7.5 per cent, given the long near-stagnation of the rich countries and the substantial appreciation of the yuan since 2010.

Finally, the way of achieving a less unequal distribution of income without jeopardizing the profit margins that encourage entrepreneurs to invest is to reduce the post-tax revenues of rentier capitalists and top professionals, while increasing social expenditure, which is usually an efficient form of indirect wages.

Notes

1 This would be possible only if there were an increase in capital productivity.
2 This occurred in Brazil, for instance. Under the second Lula government (2007–10) the increase in the minimum wage made the domestic market grow and industrial enterprises prospered, despite the continuous exchange rate appreciation. But soon the appreciated exchange rate increased imports of manufactured goods, and the country's deindustrialization accelerated.

13 Neutralizing the Dutch disease

A basic cause of the tendency to the cyclical and chronic overvaluation of the exchange rate is the Dutch disease. In Chapter 7 we discussed in theoretical terms this major and chronic economic failure; in this chapter we discuss how to neutralize it and which developmental approach is required to equalize the current and the industrial equilibriums, thus rendering competitive all competent business enterprises in the country.

The Ricardian rents that derive from cheap natural (and human) resources are a significant source of growth for the poorer developing countries. Usually they are the way these countries can achieve their original or primitive accumulation and, thus, to create the conditions for the subsequent industrial revolution. At this stage it is not essential to neutralize the Dutch disease, because the minimal conditions for industrialization still do not exist. But as soon as these conditions start to appear, neutralization becomes a condition for industrialization, since an overvalued exchange rate makes industrialization impossible.

In the past, when these countries sought to industrialize, they resorted to the "infant manufacturing industry" argument to legitimize tariff protection, whereas the rich countries, beginning with England, argued against protection by appealing to the law of comparative advantage. The developing countries did not argue for the tariff by invoking the concept of the Dutch disease, since they were unaware of it. However, by imposing duties on the imports of manufactured goods they were, in practice, devaluing their currency with respect to imports of the goods subject to the tariff. In this case, the duty was playing two roles: offsetting the infant nature of industrial enterprises and protecting them from foreign competition, and neutralizing the Dutch disease. Thus, the import tax did not just provide protection, as is usually thought, but was also a way of neutralizing the Dutch disease on the import side. How much would be protection and how much would be neutralization? This varies from one good to another. Assume that the import tariff on one good is 40 percent. And suppose that we estimate the severity of the Dutch disease to be 25 percent of the export price, but the government hasn't imposed a 25 percent export tax to neutralize it but instead has imposed a 40 percent import tariff. In this case, of the 40 percent tariff, 25 percent represents neutralization of the Dutch disease and 15 percent effective protection. Therefore, when we study the market exchange rate in a country with the Dutch disease, we should distinguish between the market *effective* exchange rate (which is defined taking into consideration a basket of currencies instead of a sole reserve currency) and what we propose to call the market *net effective* exchange rate. The net effective exchange rate is understood as the average exchange rate that results from taking into account not only the effective exchange rate but also the average import taxes and export subsidies to which goods are subject. Therefore, in the case of a good that attracts an average import duty of 30 percent, the net effective exchange rate for those who import it will be 30 percent higher than the market effective exchange rate.

The country always earns Ricardian rents – this is why they are a blessing – but the problem is to know how these rents will be distributed. If no export tax is imposed, or the export tax is insufficient to neutralize the Dutch disease, theoretically they will be shared immediately by the whole population, as an overvalued exchange rate lowers the costs of all tradable goods, but there will be no industrialization. In practice, as there is in such countries an unlimited supply of labour, wages will remain at subsistence level, and the economic rents will be seized by the middle and upper classes, if not simply captured by politicians of the authoritarian regime that is usually in place.

In this chapter, we discuss how to neutralize the Dutch disease. In the first section we show that the specific instrument to achieve this neutralization is a tax or retainer on the exports of the commodity generating the Dutch disease; if this tax is equal to the severity of the disease, it will raise the value of the exchange rate for the corresponding commodity and will equalize the current and the industrial equilibriums. Second, we show that it is not the exporter of the commodity that effectively pays the tax, but the population of the exporting country. Third, we discuss second-best forms of neutralization that economic authorities adopt when they have just an intuition of what the Dutch disease is and how to neutralize it. Finally, we discuss difficulties in imposing the tax.

Neutralization

The way to neutralize the Dutch disease is to impose an export tax on the commodities benefiting from Ricardian rents.[1] This tax must correspond to the severity of the disease – that is, to the difference between the current equilibrium exchange rate and the industrial equilibrium exchange rate, or, in other words, between the current necessary price and the industrial necessary price, so that the country ceases to present two equilibrium exchange rates. The tax must be variable, so that the government is able to raise or lower it as the international price of the commodity changes (the disease becomes more serious when prices rise, and less serious when prices fall). If there are several commodities generating the Dutch disease, the tax should differ from commodity to commodity. If the country is small, it will be a price taker, and the tax will not affect the international price of the commodity; if that is not the case and the country is the price maker, the increase of the international price will have to be considered in setting the tax.

When the tax is imposed (at the correct rate), the cost that the exporter bears increases. This means, on the one hand, that the value of the exchange rate (cost plus a reasonable profit) increases, and, on the other hand, that the supply curve of the product in relation to the exchange rate (not in relation to the price, which here we treat as given) shifts upwards and to the left, up to the level of the industrial equilibrium rate. Given that foreign demand for the commodity is fully inelastic in relation to changes in the exchange rate, the equilibrium will move up by the amount of the tax. As this tax is equal to the difference between the two equilibriums, these will coincide and the Dutch disease will have been neutralized.

Economists – and in this case not only orthodox economists but structuralist and Keynesian economists as well – have difficulty understanding that an export tax is able to devalue the exchange rate, because they often assume that the rate is determined only by the supply of and demand for foreign money. This misguided assumption, which does not distinguish the market price or the market exchange rate from the necessary price or from the value of the exchange rate, makes it impossible for them to understand why a tax that has no direct effect on the supply of and demand for money is able to neutralize the Dutch disease. Or else they think that an export tax would have this effect if the revenue collected by the government was invested outside the country in a sovereign fund, which, therefore, would not entail an increase in the supply of foreign currency in the domestic market. This is a mistake: what neutralizes the Dutch disease is the tax, not the sovereign fund. It is advisable to use the revenue from the tax to finance a sovereign fund. But since the two concepts that define the Dutch disease – the current exchange rate and the industrial equilibrium exchange rate – are equilibriums in value terms, they are determined not by the demand for and supply of foreign money, but by changes in the cost of production. The tax, not the sovereign fund, does exactly that: It increases the cost to the exporter, and, in this way, increases the value of the export around which the price – the market exchange rate – will float. The exchange rate price follows the increase in the value because the value (cost plus reasonable profit) is the long-term determinant of the supply curve of the commodity. When government authorities impose an export tax, this tax causes the supply curve of the commodity to shift upwards and to the left by an amount equal to the tax rate, and the exchange rate depreciates.

Thus, we must think about the exchange rate in terms of value in the long run to understand why the tax neutralizes the Dutch disease. If the tax corresponds to the severity of the disease (to the per cent difference of the industrial and the current equilibrium in terms of the former), the exchange rate will move from the current equilibrium towards the industrial equilibrium. In other words, the current necessary price and the industrial necessary price will equalize and the Dutch disease will be neutralized – not because there has been a change either in the supply of or in the demand for foreign currency, but because the value of the commodity has increased and its supply curve has shifted. The shift has occurred in the value of the foreign money, and from this moment on the market price of the exchange rate will float around this new value.

The neutralization of the Dutch disease with the help of an export tax can be easily understood from Figure 13.1. We have the value of the exchange rate (not the price) in the vertical line, and the quantities in the horizontal line. The

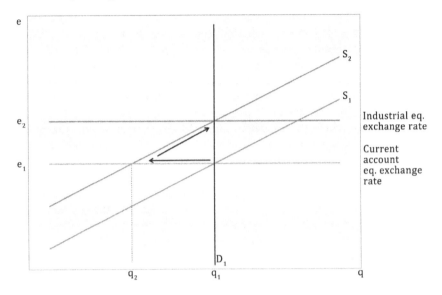

Figure 13.1 Neutralization of the Dutch disease by means of an export tax

difference between e_1 (the current equilibrium exchange rate) and e_2 (the industrial equilibrium exchange rate) represents the severity of the Dutch disease in the national currency. D_1 is the demand curve in relation to the exchange rate; it is fully inelastic since the exchange rate of the country does not affect it. On the assumption that the country is small, world demand and international prices are given. If the country is big enough to affect the total supply of the commodity and its international price, it would be necessary to consider that the short-run reduction in supply caused by the tax will cause the international price to rise. In this case, given that the demand for the good is relatively elastic to the international price, the demand curve in the figure would not be inelastic but moderately elastic and would present a negative slope. This would complicate the figure, but it would not change the analysis. Given the demand and the exchange rate, the quantity exported is q_1.

The supply curves S_1 and S_2 represent, respectively, the supply of the commodity before the export tax and the supply after the export tax, which is equal to the severity of the Dutch disease (e_1–e_2). These supply curves are defined in terms of the prices required to make business enterprises cover their costs plus a reasonable profit. As elementary microeconomics teaches, the tax causes the shift of the supply curve. The quantity offered at this exchange rate falls to q_2, because less efficient producers will consider ceasing production. But since demand is inelastic in relation to the exchange rate, and, thus, constant, the exchange rate will depreciate from e_1 to e_2, so as to re-establish the equilibrium between existing supply and demand. And the depreciation of the exchange rate will be equal to the tax paid by the exporters – that is, to the severity of the Dutch disease.

Assume, for instance, that the industrial equilibrium exchange rate is $2.70 per dollar and the current equilibrium exchange rate R$2.20 per dollar. If the market exchange rate is floating around the current equilibrium, because it is not being devalued further by excessive capital inflows (in the case of Dutch disease, due to a boom in primary exports), a tax of $0.50 per dollar will move the exchange rate to R$2.70 per dollar.

The neutralization is completed by the creation of an international fund with the revenues derived from this tax; the fund will prevent the inflow of tax revenues from causing the re-appreciation of the exchange rate through the supply effect. The creation of the fund and the investment in it of all the revenues from the tax will have the same effect as controlling capital inflows; it will make it easier for the government to adopt a policy of equating the country's net capital outflows with its current account surplus.

Imposing a high tax on exports of oil was essentially what Norway did after it discovered and started to export oil in the North Sea. Britain, which discovered oil in the North Sea at the same time, did not neutralize the Dutch disease and its economy suffered the consequences (Chatterji and Price, 1988). Chile also neutralizes the Dutch disease by heavily taxing copper exports, but it is a partial neutralization because the tax is not equal to the difference between the two equilibriums. All oil-producing countries tax their exports, but usually at a level that falls short of neutralizing the Dutch disease.

Who pays for the neutralization?

As we have just seen, once an export tax has been imposed, the supply curve of the commodity will shift upwards and to the left with regard to the exchange rate, a single equilibrium is established instead of two, and the market price of the exchange rate will fluctuate around the new equilibrium. But who pays for this devaluation? It is important to stress that the commodity exporters who formally pay the tax will not eventually pay it, because the exchange rate will fall by the amount of the tax. Thus, even after paying the tax, commodity producers will continue to earn the same profits. Who will pay, then? The country's population as a whole will pay for it in the short term through the relative increase in the local price of tradable goods resulting from the devaluation.

We are assuming that the change in the local price will immediately follow the change in the value of the exchange rate. If, more realistically, we drop this assumption, exporters will face a transition cost in the time it takes for the local price to increase in proportion to the tax – which explains why commodity exporters are so hostile to the tax. Labour will also have to pay a transition cost, because wages will fall for a period. But whereas exporters would return to their original positions quite soon, depending on the time it takes for price and value to converge, workers would have to wait for the predicted increase in the growth rate and in the demand for labour to see their wages rise; but once this has happened they would soon be better off than they were because their wages would be tracking a much faster increase of the rate of productivity.

This suggests that the government will have difficulty with exporters, and would probably offer them some guarantees, such as (*a*) making a special effort in increasing capital controls or buying more dollars to hasten the transition to the new equilibrium, and (*b*) using part of the tax revenue as a guarantee fund for the price of the commodity – which would be attractive if the overvaluation is not too great (that is, if the Dutch disease is not too severe), because, in this circumstance, there is the risk that, for other reasons, the international price of the commodity might fall by more than is necessary to make the Dutch disease disappear. In this case, even if the government reduced the tax rate to zero, production of the commodity would be unprofitable; but then producers would receive compensation from the fund in the form of a negative tax.

Finally, we must know what the government would do with the revenue it collects from the tax. Ideally, it would set up an international investment fund, as Norway did. In this case, neutralization would be perfect because no foreign currency would flow into the country. As an alternative, the government may spend the revenues from the tax (*a*) on necessary public investment and on increased social expenditure, as Argentina or Chile do, and Brazil plans to do from its exports from the Pre-Salt layer; or (*b*) in reducing or keeping low the tax burden, as it happens in Mexico; or (*c*) in setting up a stabilization fund that guarantees agricultural producers against violent fluctuations in international commodity prices; or, finally, (*d*) allowing them to be captured by a small group of corrupt politicians, bureaucrats, and local capitalists associated with rich countries' multinational enterprises, as usually happens in poor oil-exporting countries. In any of those four cases, expenditure of the tax revenues will lead to an increase in the demand for imports, which will increase demand for foreign money, and the exchange rate price will depreciate.

Second-best forms of neutralization

The Dutch disease has existed since the times of mercantilism. The backwardness of Spain and Portugal from the seventeenth century on was certainly caused by the gold that both countries extracted from their colonies, which appreciated their exchange rates and made industrial development practically impossible. In 1703, the Treaty of Methuen between England and Portugal, which established that Portugal would export wine to England and import manufactured goods, is often used to explain the backwardness of Portugal, but it was rather its consequence than its cause. Given the long-term overvaluation of exchange rate Portugal couldn't develop a manufacturing industry. But the Dutch disease, or the natural resource curse, was only identified in the 1960s, and only in 1982 was a model framed for it. Thereafter, some papers discussed it, but most were interested in discussing its political consequences in poor countries (rent seeking). Only after Bresser-Pereira's paper on the subject was published in 2008 did it became clear that what defines the Dutch disease is the existence of two exchange rate equilibriums and that the appropriate way of neutralizing it is to impose an export tax equal to the severity of the disease. Thus, it is understandable that economic historians who sought to explain why some countries lagged behind should rarely refer to the obstacle represented by the chronic overvaluation of the exchange rate caused principally by the Dutch disease. On the other hand, we know that several countries affected by the Dutch disease were able to industrialize. How can we explain that, given that the policymakers of these countries didn't have a model of the Dutch disease and of its neutralization at their disposal?

To answer this question we must first distinguish three stages of a country's economic development. In a first stage – the stage of primitive accumulation, which precedes the industrial revolution in this country – exploitation of natural resources is a blessing rather than a curse, because it enables the country to take part in international trade and to invest in minimal economic infrastructure, or in other words to achieve the original capital accumulation required for the emergence of a capitalist entrepreneurial class. It is the existence of such resources that makes it possible for a pre-capitalist economy, where only the beginnings of mercantile capitalism exist, to be admitted to world markets. The country still lacks the minimal supply-side conditions to industrialize, economic growth depends solely on commodity exports, and the fact that the Dutch disease has not been duly neutralized does not appear as a clear obstacle to economic development. Yet even in that period the government should tax the exports of the commodity produced by these abundant and cheap natural resources, and use the revenues either to set up a fund or, what is more realistic, to finance education, health care, and infrastructure. But, since the country does not have a middle class to create a vigorous civil society and a capable state, this tax will usually be insufficient to neutralize the Dutch disease, but will be more than enough to stimulate rent seeking by the corrupt oligarchy that most likely runs the country. Given that the exchange rate remains overvalued, in a middle-income country – and even more so in a rich country – the revenues of all households will in the short term be higher than they would be if the tax were sufficient to neutralize the Dutch disease. But this is not the case with a poor country. Wages will remain at subsistence level independently of the exchange rate, and the only beneficiaries of the non-neutralization of the Dutch disease will be the oligarchy.

As the country develops and the conditions for industrialization are realized, the Dutch disease becomes a fundamental obstacle to development. The conditions for industrialization include a certain level of education, infrastructure of a certain standard, an improved state bureaucracy, the emergence of a middle class and of a nationalist elite, and the gradual formation of the key institution for economic development, namely a national development strategy that stimulates investment. At this second stage, the country faces the challenge of industrialization, which is met by the production of non-sophisticated or low per capita value-added manufactured goods. The transfer of labour from agriculture and mining to manufacturing industry automatically implies productivity gains, particularly because the returns to scale in this sector tend to be greater. At this stage, the neutralization of the Dutch disease becomes crucial for industrialization to occur. However, since governments ignore the theory of the Dutch disease, this neutralization usually occurs only in an incomplete and disorganized way with the use of second-best strategies, either by the adoption of multiple exchange rates or by the adoption of high import tariffs on all goods and export subsidies to manufactured goods – strategies that today are forbidden by the WTO's rules.

The system of multiple exchange rates was the usual way of neutralizing the Dutch disease. The simplest systems involved the adoption of two fixed rates, the more appreciated one for commodity exports and imports of goods considered as necessary or basic, and another, more depreciated one, restricted to the exports of manufactured goods and the import of luxury or inessential goods. In the 1950s Brazil adopted a system of five exchange rates; goods were classified into five categories ranging from basic to superfluous and in the interest of protecting local manufacturing industry, and the exchange rate for each category was set in auctions conducted by the local stock exchange where the government offered dollars and importers acquired rights to import. The system worked reasonably well for some time, duly neutralizing the Dutch disease.

Another second-best way of neutralizing the Dutch disease is by imposing high import duties on manufactured goods. Import duties were adopted by the countries based on the Hamilton–List theory of infant manufacturing industry protection and also on the Prebisch–Singer–Furtado theory of the tendency towards deterioration in the terms of trade.[2] In fact, an import duty is a partial but effective way of neutralizing the Dutch disease: it only protects manufacturing industry from foreign imports, that is to say, it neutralizes the Dutch disease for the purposes of the domestic market but does not stimulate manufactured exports. When a country suffers from the Dutch disease, the import duty can be considered only as a manifestation of the country's protectionism if the rate is higher than the rate necessary to neutralize this market failure; otherwise, the duty does no more than partially correct this failure.

A third form of neutralizing the Dutch disease is through a system of import tariffs and export subsidies. When the country reaches the stage at which it starts to acquire the capacity to export manufactured goods, it becomes clear that import duties alone are not enough, because the neutralization takes place, in this case, only on the import side: domestic manufacturing business enterprises, even though their costs are competitive, are still unable to export due to the exchange rate appreciation, worsened by import restrictions of inputs. This is why, sooner or later, the country recognizes the partial nature of this measure, and even if it does not clearly understand the problem of the Dutch disease, it creates a system of subsidies for exports of manufactured goods. In this case, neutralization is completed, although in a poorly conceived way because it would be much more simple and logical to neutralize the Dutch disease with an export tax. In any case, it is important to note that by using import tariffs the country is not just adopting a "protectionist" strategy; it is not only protecting infant industries but neutralizing the Dutch disease on the import side, whereas, when the country extends subsidies to exports of manufactured goods, it is not necessarily granting privileges to these industries but is neutralizing the Dutch disease on the export side.

One example of the application of this way of neutralizing the Dutch disease is the tariff policy adopted by Brazil between 1968 and 1990. The government established an average import tax of 50 percent and an average subsidy for the export of manufactured goods also of 50 percent, whereas commodity exports were remunerated only by the nominal exchange rate. Consequently, if the market exchange rate was #2.00 per dollar, the net effective exchange rate was actually #3.00 per dollar, except for commodity exporters, which in practice paid a tax of #1.00 or 33.3 per cent per dollar exported.

In any case, from the second stage on (the stage of the industrial revolution) and certainly during the third stage (the stage of exporting manufactured goods) the developing country must be actively neutralizing its Dutch disease through the firm management of its exchange rate. When the country begins to industrialize, economic growth will depend on the neutralization of the disease. This is what happened with all Latin American and Asian countries that industrialized in the twentieth century. Latin American countries, for instance, have abundant natural resources, both mineral and agricultural, which allowed them to develop sectors to produce and export primary goods. However, from the 1930s on, when this growth strategy based on exports of commodities with low value added per capita exhausted its possibilities and the challenge was to industrialize, these countries were able to cope with the challenge. Between 1930 and 1980, Mexico and Brazil in particular industrialized and grew extraordinarily fast, because they adopted policies that neutralized the Dutch disease.[3] Their politicians and economists ignored the existence of the Dutch disease but, in the context of the developmental strategy that they adopted, they have often resorted to multiple exchange rates or complex systems of import duties combined with export subsidies that, basically, addressed the problem by devaluing the currency for producers of manufactured goods. Since the early 1990s, however, after a major financial crisis, countries like Brazil and Mexico, which had industrialized, opened their economies under the influence of the Washington consensus, and lost their ability to neutralize the Dutch disease. In consequence, they gradually deindustrialized. In contrast, Argentina was able to impose an export tax in 2002, which neutralized its Dutch disease. For several years, it experienced current account surpluses, fiscal surpluses, and high rates of growth. Yet after 2007, when inflation rose somewhat (which was inevitable), the administration, instead of controlling it with interest rates and fiscal policy, adopted the classical strategy of using the exchange rate as an anchor; the exchange rate then appreciated, despite the tax, and the era of high growth rates was over.

Difficulties

According to the above account, the neutralization of the Dutch disease seems to be a simple task, but in practice it may be very difficult, particularly because the government will have to face resistance from exporters of the commodities that give rise to the Dutch disease. This resistance is usually strong and irrational, because the producer who pays the tax is compensated by the corresponding exchange rate devaluation. In reality, the purpose of the tax is not to reduce the profitability of the commodity-exporting sector, but to maintain it and eventually to make it even more stable. But it is not easy to persuade this sector, especially agribusiness, which is always politically powerful given its presence throughout the country, is able to control local policies, and usually commands an important group of members of Congress. It will be thus necessary to offer to commodity exporters some guarantees that the exchange rate will shift to the new equilibrium. Therefore, the government must follow the imposition of the tax with a reduction in the interest rate and an increase in the control of capital inflows, so as to move the exchange rate in the desired direction. And, with the revenues from the tax, in addition to an international fund to prevent capital inflows into the country putting pressure on the exchange rate, it should create a domestic stabilization fund for commodities, so that, if their international price drops greatly, the government, apart from lowering the tax rate to zero, will have the resources to bail out producers.

If the country has a significant share of the international supply of the good, the tax may also have the effect of increasing its international price. This effect would probably be small but cannot be neglected, because the increase in international prices due to the tax worsens the Dutch disease that the tax is intended to neutralize.

A second and fundamental issue for the resistance to the commodity export tax is the reduction in wages caused by the devaluation of the local currency. Effective depreciation minus inflation, or real depreciation, by definition effects a change in relative prices in favour of tradables, whose prices increase against those of non-tradables. While the currency is overvalued as a consequence of the Dutch disease, wages are artificially high because people benefit directly from Ricardian rents.[4] The imposition of a tax that neutralizes the Dutch disease by appreciating the domestic currency implies, therefore, a decrease in real labour income and in real property rents, even adjusted for inflation. It also implies a relative reduction in the revenues of the importers of price-elastic goods and of the producers of non-tradables, such as the hotel industry and the construction industry, which earn smaller shares of the national income. In other words, as long as the Dutch disease was operating, the country's Ricardian rents were not being captured exclusively by commodity producers, but were benefiting (*a*) all local consumers, who were buying tradables at lower prices, (*b*) importers of both final and intermediary goods, the demand for which was elastic, and (*c*) the producers of non-tradables, the demand for which was growing due to the increase in the population's available income. When the tax is imposed, the Ricardian rents remain in the country, but now become state revenue.

However, as we stressed in Chapter 12 and demonstrated in Figure 12.1 regarding wages, the reduction in real wages is temporary. There will be an immediate loss at the moment of devaluation, but later, given the increase in the rates of investment, growth, and productivity, unemployment will decrease, and the wage rate will start to grow at a higher rate than before the devaluation that neutralized the Dutch disease; and therefore the workers will soon enjoy higher wages and greater job security.

In light of these problems, it is understandable that countries seriously affected by the Dutch disease, such as Saudi Arabia or Venezuela or Bolivia, have difficulty neutralizing it. All the oil-exporting countries impose taxes on oil exports but usually the tax has a merely fiscal purpose and its rate is unable to offset the currency overvaluation caused by the disease. The state lacks power to impose a higher tax because (*a*) the concept and the theory of the Dutch disease are ignored even by those responsible for the government's economic policy, (*b*) even business enterprises exporting the taxed commodities resist it, and (*c*) government leaders are afraid of the consequences of the neutralization of the Dutch disease on wages and on inflation. But even in countries such as Brazil, where the Dutch disease is less serious, neutralizing the disease is very difficult, especially due to the political power of agribusiness.

Financial consequences of neutralization

What is the effect of the neutralization of the Dutch disease? If neutralization is complete, the country will present a current account surplus and perhaps also a budget surplus.[5] The reason for the current account surplus can be inferred from the definitions of the current account equilibrium and the industrial equilibrium exchange rates. The commodity exports giving rise to the Dutch disease determine the level of the exchange rate, placing it at the current equilibrium, because this is the level that makes the commodity-exporting enterprises profitable. Demand for imports will adjust to export revenues. The exchange rate will vary, naturally, around this level. Neutralizing the Dutch disease means shifting the current equilibrium exchange rate towards the industrial exchange rate; it means, therefore, shifting from a current account equilibrium (if net capital inflows are equal to zero) to a current account surplus. The capital-poor country transferring capital to the capital-rich countries is a situation that defies against common sense, but this is the way to stimulate savings, investment, and growth in the developing country. How large should the surplus be? This will depend on the severity of the Dutch disease – that is, of the distance between the current equilibrium exchange rate and the industrial equilibrium exchange rate. The greater the difference between the two equilibriums, the larger the current account surplus should be.

As for the public budget, it too should show a modest surplus when the country neutralizes its Dutch disease. The twin deficits model offers a preliminary explanation for this. If a country achieves a current account surplus, this means that it has built up savings in relation to the rest of the world. If the exchange rate is in current equilibrium, the public and private sectors will be both in equilibrium, and the government accounts should also show a surplus, as predicted by the twin deficits model (which holds only when the exchange rate is in equilibrium). If the exchange rate is overvalued and the public sector is relatively balanced, the country will present a current account deficit associated with the increase in the indebtedness of the private sector. This is common in middle-income countries (and also in rich countries, as we saw in the euro crisis), where government control of the budget tends to be tighter, whereas there is little control over private indebtedness. The inverse (a current account surplus and a budget deficit) may also occur when the exchange rate is overvalued, but this will tend to happen in poor countries where fiscal populism is endemic.

If the government sets up a sovereign fund and applies all the revenues of the export tax, as Norway does, this would be a factor making for a budget surplus in addition to the country's current account surplus. Besides, if it sets up a sovereign fund, the government will not undertake sterilization operations in order to reduce the money supply and, therefore, will not come under pressure from the foreign sector to increase its public debt. However, in developing countries politicians will hardly agree to use all the revenues from the tax in this way. They will use some or even all of the revenues from the export tax to finance public expenditures demanded by society. But this does not mean that the government should run a budget deficit: It could choose to finance public expenditures with export tax revenues rather than resorting to other sources of revenue.

To return to the foreign accounts, the current account surplus is a condition for the neutralization of the Dutch disease. The lack of a current account surplus in a country with the Dutch disease is a sure indication that the country is not neutralizing the permanent overvaluation of its exchange rate and, therefore, is tolerating a major obstacle to its economic development.

However, a fundamental problem with international imbalance emerges from the developing countries' need to neutralize the Dutch disease. If all or many such countries manage to neutralize the Dutch disease, their combined current account surpluses would have to be balanced by the equivalent combined current account deficits of the countries (predominantly rich countries) that do not suffer from the Dutch disease. Does this mean that the rich countries would have no option but to transfer wealth to residents in the countries that have neutralized the Dutch disease? Not necessarily. Given that most of these rich countries – certainly the larger ones – have reserve currencies, they are able to become indebted in their own currencies and repay debt by printing money. Printing money was, until recently, regarded as a sin, but the experience of "quantitative easing" by rich countries after the 2008 global financial crisis has made this practice less objectionable; it has been effective in devaluing their currencies, but has not caused inflation.

In any circumstance, current account deficits in rich countries do not represent a major problem for them. They will continue to be rich and will continue to grow, but *catching up* will be happening. In consequence, not only income but also wealth will flow between countries, thus reducing the disequilibrium of the stock of wealth existing in the world. Naturally, the rich countries' political resistance to this outcome is already considerable, and it will continue to be so. The indifference of their economists to Dutch disease theory, the confusion they create by interpreting the natural resources curse as an institutional and moral problem rather than an economic problem, and, more broadly, their reluctance to take into account the exchange rate in economic development are indications of this resistance.

In poor countries that do not suffer from the Dutch disease, the problem of current account deficits is more serious; but few countries are in this condition, because if such a country lacks abundant and cheap natural resources to export, it will have cheap labour and a wide wage dispersion – and it will, therefore, as we defined it above, suffer from the Dutch disease in its broad sense, which it will be able to neutralize by managing the exchange rate (as Asian countries usually do) and, thus, also achieve a current account surplus or, at least, an equilibrium.

Countries suffering from the Dutch disease appear to be gradually paying attention to the problem and the necessary solution, which involves taxing the commodities that give rise to the disease. As a result, already they are ceasing to run current account deficits and are starting to move into surplus. Yet, for the moment, the disease is only partially neutralized in many commodity-exporting countries. If they ignore the disease and adopt the export tax only for fiscal reasons, they also thereby reduce their currency overvaluation, since the exporting business enterprises that pay the tax start to need a more devalued exchange rate in order to be able to export at a profit. So we are already seeing, in oil-producing countries, large current account surpluses and the formation of large sovereign investment funds.

Summary

We can now bring together the model of the Dutch disease that we presented in Chapter 7 and the discussion of its neutralization in the present chapter.

1 The Dutch disease is a fundamental component of the tendency to the cyclical and chronic overvaluation of the exchange rate that characterizes developing countries.
2 The Dutch disease is a relatively permanent overvaluation of the exchange rate resulting from the export of commodities that use abundant and cheap natural resources; it is a market failure that is characterized by two equilibrium exchange rates: the current equilibrium, which is satisfactory for the commodities benefiting from Ricardian rents, and the industrial equilibrium, the value of the exchange rate that other tradable industries utilizing world state-of-the-art technology require to be competitive or profitable.
3 These two equilibriums are determined in *value* terms; they are the *necessary price* around which the market or nominal price of the exchange rate floats according to the demand for and supply of foreign money; the value of the exchange rate or of foreign money remunerates adequately competent business enterprises producing tradable goods and services, and balances intertemporally the current account of the country. By adequate remuneration we understand the revenue that covers cost plus a reasonable profit rate. When a country suffers from Dutch disease, we should define the value of the industrial equilibrium exchange rate, the rate that covers cost plus a reasonable profit margin of manufacturing enterprises that use world state-of-the-art technology.
4 The gravity or severity of the Dutch disease is equal to the difference between the values of the two equilibrium exchange rates.
5 A non-neutralized Dutch disease represents a major obstacle to a country's industrialization. If the country is already industrialized and ceases to neutralize the Dutch disease, it will face deindustrialization.

6   There is a basic incompatibility between a non-neutralized Dutch disease and economic growth, because economic growth always depends on the possibility of transferring labour to sectors with higher value added per capita, since the most sophisticated manufactured goods necessarily use more highly skilled workers (whose salaries exceed those of unskilled workers to a much higher degree than in the rich countries). Such a transfer of labour is impossible when the Dutch disease occurs because investment in the manufacturing is insufficient.

7   The neutralization of the Dutch disease is effected through an export tax that adequately reflects the severity of the disease, which increases the cost plus a reasonable profit of the commodities that generate the disease: in other words, it shifts the supply curve of the commodity in relation to the exchange rate to the left.

8   Although developing countries have always suffered from the Dutch disease without realizing it, many of them have industrialized; the reason is that, in practice, they have neutralized the Dutch disease by using multiple exchange rates, in addition to import duties and export subsidies that amounted to a disguised tax on the commodities. They justified these policies by reference to the theories of the infant manufacturing industry protection and of the deterioration in the terms of trade; however, there is no protectionism when the tariffs do no more than offset the appreciation caused by the Dutch disease.

9   The more serious the Dutch disease in a country, the more difficult its neutralization will be, and the lower the probability that the country will industrialize and grow.

10 The revenues from the tax imposed to neutralize the Dutch disease should, in principle, be used to set up a fund for foreign investment.

11 Neutralization does not impose a net cost on commodity exporters, who recoup the cost of the export tax from the subsequent exchange rate depreciation. But it represents a short-term cost to the whole population of the country insofar as all tradable goods become more expensive.

12 It is not easy to neutralize the Dutch disease due to resistance of commodity exporters to the export tax and the resistance of the whole population to exchange rate depreciation, because in the short term it causes temporary inflation and temporarily reduces wages.

13 The Dutch disease exists even if the commodities that give rise to it have high technological content, as it happens nowadays with the oil production and with agriculture, which is increasingly sophisticated from a technological point of view. It is an obstacle to growth because mining and agricultural activities are not able to employ the whole workforce and because it implies that the country should give up opportunities to invest and innovate in sectors with potentially higher technological content and, therefore, with higher value added per capita.

14 The Dutch disease can also arise simply from cheap labour; in this *extended concept* of the Dutch disease, the condition for its occurrence is that the gap between wages and salaries in the developing country that exports

manufactured goods using cheap labour is substantially wider than the equivalent gap in the rich countries to which the manufactured goods are exported. This kind of Dutch disease, which characterizes Asian countries, will usually be milder, and its neutralization easier, than the Dutch disease that is caused by Ricardian rents.

Notes

1 The tax should not, in principle, be imposed on exports alone but also on domestic sales, so as to avoid distortion of relative prices. Yet in Argentina, after 2002 the Dutch disease was neutralized by "retenciones", which fall only on exports. This makes the tax more acceptable to the population when the commodity is also a consumer good, as is the case with the soy beans, meat, and wheat that Argentina exports. In 2009 the Argentinean administration tried to make the retenciones variable, but was unable to secure the approval of Parliament.

2 This theory maintained that there was a tendency of increasing prices of manufacturing goods (due to relative higher world demand and wage pressures in developed countries) and of decreasing prices of primary goods (due to relative lower world demand), and the solution lay in industrialization for primary exporter countries. So import substitution was one of the strategies adopted for industrializing and trying to catch up with richer countries.

3 In his excellent paper on the Dutch disease in Latin America, Gabriel Palma (2005) does not discuss the forms of its neutralization, but he clearly assumes that it was neutralized by the industrial policies of the old developmentalism, which involved multiple exchange rates and other forms of exchange rate management.

4 It is obviously possible to argue that, by keeping the exchange rate depreciated, the country is domestically producing sophisticated goods that could be imported at a lower price, so that the consumer surplus is appropriated by their producers; but this does not happen. The country is producing all the high-tech goods, and there is no protection. Wage-earners or consumers, however, lose in the short run in terms of well-being, because this is the condition for neutralizing the Dutch disease.

5 The country will present a corresponding budget surplus when there is a current account surplus and also if the private sector's accounts are balanced – that is, if private investment equals private savings. The surplus is generated by the revenue of the export tax; also, when the country creates a fund for investment abroad it ceases to sterilize the capital inflow, and the pressure from this source to increase the public debt is removed.

14 Exchange rate policy

In this book we claim that fast economic growth and catching up require the neutralization of the tendency to the cyclical and chronic overvaluation of the exchange rate. This overvaluation has a structural cause associated with the value of the exchange rate (the Dutch disease) and policy causes related to the price of the exchange rate (excessive capital inflows resulting from the opening of the capital account and the use of the exchange rate to anchor inflation). In Chapter 13 we discussed the neutralization of the Dutch disease; in this chapter we discuss the exchange rate policy required to avoid the appreciation of the national currency (or of the exchange rate), then go on to discuss the development and macroeconomic policies of which the managed exchange rate is a component.

The objective of such an exchange rate policy is to keep the market exchange rate fluctuating around the industrial or competitive equilibrium. This means that the objective is to achieve a current account surplus, because the exchange rate that is consistent with the industrial equilibrium is more depreciated than the rate that assures the intertemporal equilibrium of a country's current account. This is counterintuitive, because developing countries have a smaller stock of capital than rich countries; but the way to increase this stock of capital is not with an overvalued currency but with a competitive currency, which a high rate of investment requires. In order to achieve this current account surplus, the country must neutralize the Dutch disease using an export tax, and must reject policies that appreciate the exchange rate and cause current account deficits, the policies of attempting to grow with foreign indebtedness and using the exchange rate as a monetary anchor. If a country adopts a tax rate proportional to the severity of the Dutch disease and neutralizes it, but does not reject policies that are associated with immediate consumption or exchange rate populism, the exchange rate will not be competitive and the country's competent business enterprises will not be able to compete.

In discussing exchange rate policy, we proceed from two assumptions: first, that exports and imports are elastic in relation to the exchange rate – that is, the Marshall–Lerner condition is fulfilled – and second, that the exchange rate regime is neither fixed nor fully floating, but is subject to a managed regime. Orthodox economists reject the idea of managing the exchange rate because, against all evidence, they believe that the market regulates it satisfactorily, and because they use

Mundell's "triangle of impossibilities" to conclude that an exchange rate policy is not possible or should not be adopted. But in fact, rich countries as well as developing countries manage their exchange rates.

In relation to the elasticity of imports and exports to the exchange rate in the short term, our assumption is that the Marshall–Lerner condition is satisfied. In other words, we assume that the demand for exports is not inelastic – that if the domestic currency devalues (that is, the cost of foreign goods increases relative to the cost of domestic goods), there will be a positive quantity effect on the current account, but offsetting this is a negative cost effect on the balance of trade, since the cost of imports will be higher; whether the net effect on the trade balance is positive or negative depends on whether the quantity effect outweighs the cost effect. Our assumption is that the quantity effect outweighs the cost effect in the medium term. Exporters are not able to increase immediately their sales abroad in response to a devaluation of the national currency, particularly in the case of manufactured goods. There is always a gap of around three years – the time required for exporters and importers to organize themselves to export or import. Besides, in the case of an exchange rate appreciation, exporters will resist for some time laying off workers, while they attempt to redirect production to the domestic market. But this tactic is short-lived because importers will end up capturing the domestic market, first the market for intermediate goods, and later the market for final goods – the opposite of an import-substitution process. In the case of both a revaluation and a devaluation, the quantums exported or imported takes some time to respond. In the case of exports, this is the so-called hysteresis hypothesis, or the J-curve. Imports take less time than exporters to respond because they don't have to conquer new foreign markets; what they usually do is change their business enterprises into distributors of imports of the goods they used to manufacture, or in other words to transform their firms into maquilas.

In this chapter we discuss, first, the triangle of impossibilities; second, the ensuing and false "fix or float" polar alternative; third, "non-policies", or the rejection of policies that cause the appreciation of the exchange rate; and finally exchange rate policy, distinguishing negative policies (that prescribe avoiding certain actions) from the positive policies that governments and their central banks use to manage the exchange rate in the framework of a floating regime.

The triangle of impossibilities

Can a country have an exchange rate policy? Neoclassical economics denies such possibility, citing Robert Mundell's triangle of impossibilities. According to this economic reasoning or economic syllogism, which is also called the policy trilemma, it is impossible successfully to pursue simultaneously an exchange rate policy, an interest rate or monetary policy, and (perfect) capital mobility. Countries may pursue a combination of two of these policies, never of all three. Thus, so Mundell and the liberal orthodoxy conclude, given that monetary or interest rate policy is necessary, and (perfect) capital mobility is required for developing countries since they do not have the requisite domestic savings for high GDP growth, governments should renounce exchange rate policy. Mundell's trilemma is a perfect example of what we call an "economic syllogism". It is not a historical model, but just a logical demonstration that it is impossible to have the three things in full at once. If, for example, a country that adopts a free-floating exchange rate regime increases the interest rate, this will attract capital, which will necessarily appreciate the national currency. But, first, contrary to historical models, it is not legitimate to derive policy from an economic syllogism; this would lead the country to incur Schumpeter's "Ricardian vice".[1] Second, there is no reason why countries cannot make compromises among the three policies. One cannot say that, if a country makes compromises among the three policies, its stability and growth objectives will not be achieved, because this conclusion does not hold empirically. Countries combine capital controls, exchange rate policy, and interest rate policy because by doing so they achieve higher growth and greater stability.

Fix or float?

When we observe the actual behaviour of practically all countries, we see that they formally float their exchange rates, but in fact they manage them to some degree. This was already true before the 2008 Global Financial Crisis, and even truer after it, when the IMF finally sanctioned some capital controls. For small countries, and sometimes for the major ones, the more obvious option was to tie the national currency to a stronger currency, as France did in relation to Germany in the 1980s. This was a policy. Another alternative, which has been common among developing countries in the recent past, was to peg the exchange rate to inflation. This was a way of keeping the exchange rate fixed or constant in real terms, but it was an inflationary way of doing so since it involved indexation that could end up transforming conventional inflation into inertial inflation, as it happened to Brazil in the 1980s.

Since managing the exchange rate is viewed as a "sin" by the high priests of conventional wisdom, and viewed as aggression, as a case of "beggar thy neighbour" by the governments of the rich countries, no country acknowledged that it was doing so. Before the 2008 crisis, Malaysia's formal decision to control capital flows after the 1997 financial crisis was an exception. According to liberal-orthodox economists, the exchange rate should not and cannot be managed. If a country tries to manage it, they argue, it will commit a succession of policy mistakes. It will be involved in competitive devaluations that provoke inflation while entrenching low productivity. This may happen; exchange rate policy is not infallible. But it is generally correct, while leaving the exchange rate to float freely will surely lead a country to disaster – to the long-term overvaluation of the exchange rate and, eventually, to financial crisis. If we want to understand the enormous success of the East Asian countries since World War II, if we want to know their economic policy *secret*, we may come up with many answers, but the central one is that they used, and continue to use, their exchange rate strategically as a tool for economic growth. For developing countries, the exchange rate, when combined with fiscal austerity, is essentially a tool for economic growth, first, because, by neutralizing the tendency to the overvaluation of the exchange rate it assures stability to the balance of payments of a country, and second, because it assures that competent business enterprises have access to demand, and the opportunity to invest.

This is not the usual view of the matter, and certainly it is not what the liberal orthodoxy preached in the early 1990s. Before that the IMF was uncomfortable with current account deficits. Yet, starting in the early 1990s, when the neoliberal hegemony achieved its apogee, the liberal orthodoxy, which included, by definition, the IMF, started proposing that developing countries should pursue growth with foreign savings, that is, growth *cum* debt. Thus, the IMF became comfortable with the idea of balance-of-payments crises caused by excessive international indebtedness. Before the 1990s, the standard procedure adopted by the IMF when a country faced a balance-of-payments crisis was to impose fiscal adjustment and to demand exchange-rate devaluation. Since the 1990s, the second part of this standard procedure has been abandoned, either because depreciation would cause inflation if the exchange rate was fixed, or because the market would automatically take care of the problem if the exchange rate was flexible. The fact that the market had not taken care of the problem, that, on the contrary, it had caused the problem through an artificial overvaluation of the exchange rate, was not considered.

In reality, the conventional wisdom downplays the fact that large and unstable capital flows became extremely dangerous for developing countries and, in consequence, also for rich countries. Examining this phenomenon, Rogério Studart (2004) argues that this kind of instability was triggered by the abrupt and careless integration of financial markets, which caused the macroeconomic and financial imbalances of the 1990s, particularly in Latin America – a region that wholeheartedly embraced the strategy of growth with foreign savings. Excessive capital inflows create pressure to revalue the domestic currency. On the other hand, Studart, although at the time when he wrote he was not informed of our model on the high rate of substitution of foreign for domestic savings, remarked that consumption, not investment, was increasing in Latin America following the opening of capital accounts and the surge of foreign direct investment.

What options are left for the developing countries, given the huge flows of capital that characterize the global system today? In his discussion of this question, Barry Eichengreen (2004) remarks that the 1997 Asian crisis and its effects on Latin America and Eastern Europe convinced many observers that soft currency pegs are crisis-prone and that emerging markets should embrace greater exchange rate flexibility. Yet he is not satisfied with these two options, and seeks a third: to accept greater flexibility for the exchange rate, and to adopt an inflation-targeting policy as a substitute for the exchange rate anchor that is inherent in a fixed exchange-rate regime. In a footnote, Eichengreen recognizes that a further option, the adjustable peg, may be viable for countries with capital controls, as the experience of China and Malaysia has shown.

Exchange rate policy

An obvious exchange rate policy is for the central bank to buy or to sell foreign reserves in order to, respectively, depreciate (or limit depreciation) or to appreciate the national currency. Another obvious but less frequent policy is to control capital inflows (in order to avoid appreciation) or capital outflows (aiming to constrain depreciation). Capital controls are not fully effective; economic agents always find ways to partially sidestep them. But it is wrong to claim that they are ineffective. At least for a time, they are able to limit the appreciation of the exchange rate.

When the central bank makes monetary policy, when it increases or it reduces the interest rate, it is also making exchange rate policy: It is causing the appreciation or the depreciation of the exchange rate. The same applies to fiscal policy. The more expansionary fiscal policy is, the higher interest rates should be to finance the public debt, and the exchange rate will appreciate. Thus, if the country is committed to neutralizing the tendency to the cyclical and chronic overvaluation of the exchange rate, it will be supposed to have a prudent or conservative fiscal policy. When policymakers define as a target a given primary budget surplus that keeps under control the ratio of public debt to GDP, besides controlling public indebtedness they are determining the exchange rate. In the absence of such a surplus, this ratio will exhibit a rising trajectory. The resulting budget deficits will require the interest rate to increase in order to sustain the demand for treasury bills – which will cause the appreciation of the exchange rate, besides requiring sterilization of the money supply to keep it under control.

The relation between fiscal policy and exchange rate policy is expressed in the twin deficits hypothesis: budget deficits or surpluses would appear together with current account deficits or surpluses. If the government is spending more than it receives, the country as a whole should be also spending more than it receives. But this simple correlation is false. We often see countries that have balanced public budgets and sizable current account deficits, and this combination is explained by the fact that the countries have an overvalued currency. The twin deficits hypothesis assumes that exchange rates are balanced – something that we well know they are not.

The key policies that a developing country must adopt to reasonably manage its exchange rate are negative policies: decisions not to adopt the usual or conventional policies that countries adopt with the support of liberal as well as many developmental economists. These are perverse policies that have a direct impact on the exchange rate. We discussed them when we analyzed the policies behind the tendency to the cyclical and chronic overvaluation of the exchange rate: (*a*) the policy of growth with foreign savings, which ignores the high rate of substitution of foreign for domestic savings; (*b*) the adoption of a high level for the interest rate (around which the actual exchange rate will fluctuate according to monetary policy), justified by the "need" to control inflation, or by the objective of attracting foreign capital, or by the objective of avoiding "financial repression"; (*c*) the use of the exchange rate as an anchor to keep the inflation rate on target;

and (*d*) exchange rate populism – the acquiescence of politicians in the tendency to the cyclical and chronic overvaluation of the exchange rate. The first thing that a developmental administration should do is to suspend such policies, so as (*a*) to end up with the policy of growth with domestic savings, (*b*) to prevent a decrease in the level of the exchange rate, and to avoid it the administration should "keep the interest rate at a moderate level, just a little above to the international level of the interest rate", and frame monetary policy by augmenting or reducing the basic exchange rate around this notional level; (*c*) not to use the exchange rate as an anchor against inflation; and (*d*) not to practice exchange rate populism or not to reveal a preference for immediate consumption.

Summary

Briefly, we argued in this book that the exchange rate and the current account deficit are the two key variables for development macroeconomics. Thus, besides fiscal and monetary policy, a developing country must have an active exchange rate policy. Understanding it in broad terms, it encompasses the neutralization of the Dutch disease; in more narrow terms, it involves strategic capital controls and purchase and sale of foreign reserves. An export tax is required to shift the value of the exchange rate from the current to the industrial equilibrium, whereas the exchange rate policy in narrow terms will take care that the exchange rate price keeps floating around the industrial equilibrium. This role will not be easy, because, besides the endogenous factors that we discussed at length in this book, there are exogenous factors – crises and policy changes in the rich countries – which often deviates the exchange rate price from the equilibrium.

Note

1 Schumpeter believed that to derive policy from theory would be a vice. He didn't restrict the vice to economic syllogisms; we are doing that.

15 The transition to a high-development regime

In this chapter we use the Keynesian–structuralist model of growth developed in Chapter 11 to see how, through the neutralization of the Dutch disease and the exchange rate policy discussed in the succeeding chapters, the economy evolves from a low-growth into a high-growth trajectory, or *catching-up*. Therefore, we take into account a middle-income economy that operates initially with an exchange rate that is highly overvalued due to the failure to neutralize the Dutch disease and to excessive capital inflows. At some point, the government of this economy decides to eliminate the problem of exchange rate overvaluation through an export tax, the purchase of reserves, and the control of capital inflows. The initial (short-term) impact of those measures will be (*a*) a decrease in real wages (and in consumption), (*b*) a decrease in the degree of productive capacity utilization, (*c*) an acceleration of inflation, and (*d*) an increase in the unemployment rate. In the medium term, however, the resulting increase in exports and in investment will lead to an acceleration of the economy's pace of growth, thus leading to a decrease in the unemployment rate. Due to the acceleration in the pace of growth and to the increase in the rate of capital accumulation – which always incorporates new technologies – the pace of growth of labour productivity accelerates, which makes room for a non-inflationary increase in real wages. At the end of the process, the middle-income economy will present a higher growth rate of GDP and of per capita income, gradually reducing the gap between it and the rich countries; investment and savings as a proportion of GDP will be higher than before, inflation will remain stable, and real wages will be higher than they would be had the economy continued on the low-growth trajectory.

Breaking the low-growth equilibrium

Consider a middle-income economy that is in the situation illustrated in Figure 15.1. We will assume that, in the initial situation, aggregate demand and productive capacity were both growing at the same rate (g_*), and the sectorial composition of demand did not alter over time.[1]

After this initial situation, the real exchange rate became chronically overvalued at level θ_{cc} due only to the failure to neutralize the Dutch disease.[2] Hypothetically, this level of real exchange rate leads to a rate of capital accumulation that is

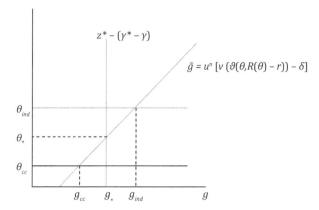

Figure 15.1 Falling behind due to Dutch disease

not enough to stabilize the gap of per capita income between the middle-income economy and the developed countries. Consequently, the economy in question is not catching up. In the initial position, the degree of productive capacity utilization was constant and equal to normal. Therefore, productive capacity and aggregate demand was growing at the same rate. In addition, the investment rate was constant, which means that investment was growing at the same pace as GDP. The functional distribution of income between wages and profits was also constant, so that wages were growing at the same pace as labour productivity. Given the distribution of income, consumption expenditure as a proportion of GDP was also constant, which implies that aggregate consumption was growing at the same rate as the GDP. Finally, the equilibrium in the current account guaranteed that exports were growing at the same rate as imports.

It follows from the above that, in the initial trajectory of growth, we can observe the following ratio:

$$g_* = \hat{Y} = \hat{I} = \hat{C} \quad \text{and} \quad \hat{M} = \hat{E} = \varepsilon . Z^* \tag{15.1}$$

in which: $\hat{Y}$ is the GDP growth rate, $\hat{I}$ is the investment growth rate, $\hat{C}$ is the consumption growth rate, $\hat{M}$ is the imports growth rate, $\hat{E}$ is the exports growth rate, ε is the income elasticity of exports, and Z^* is the income growth rate of the rest of the world.

In equation (15.1) the only exogenous variable is the income growth rate of the rest of the world. The income elasticity of exports is an exogenous variable in the short term, but is endogenous in the long term. The reason is that the divergences between the real exchange rate and its level of equilibrium give rise to changes in the economy's structure, modifying its level of productive specialization, which eventually modifies the income elasticity of both exports and imports.

Therefore, we will assume that the productive structure is temporarily constant, so that the income elasticity of exports could be considered an exogenous

variable. In this context, the growth rate of exports will be exogenously determined, and the growth rate of output will adjust to it.

But considering that the exchange rate became overvalued, let us assume that
the government decides, at a given moment, to eliminate this problem by imposing an export tax on the commodities giving rise to the Dutch disease. The costs
incurred by exporters of the commodities will increase in proportion to the tax.
On the assumption that the tax was well calculated to correspond to the difference
between the industrial and the current equilibrium, the two values will be equalized and the Dutch disease neutralized, as the real exchange rate shifts from θ_{cc} to
θ_{ind}. In fact, there is an *overshoot* before the exchange rate reaches the industrial
equilibrium level at θ_{ind} (Figure 15.2). This derives from the fact that the real
exchange rate adjusts faster than the growth rate of output, due to the advances
made by the financial markets.[3]

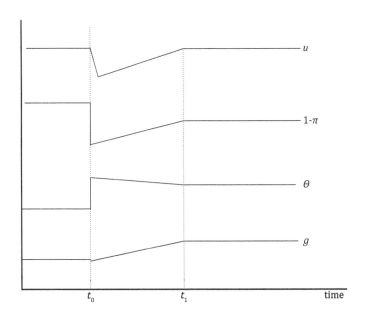

Figure 15.2 Dynamics of capital accumulation, profit share, and capacity utilization after
a depreciation of real exchange rate

Reindustrialization

The strong depreciation of the real exchange rate (which may be accomplished
gradually or in stages) will have two effects. On the productive side, it will give
rise to a process of reindustrialization of the economy, thus making for a gradual
increase in the income elasticity of exports and a gradual decrease in the income
elasticity of imports. Consequently, there will be an increase in the growth rate
of output that is compatible balance-of-payments equilibrium. On the aggregate

demand side, there will be two effects. First, the depreciation of the real exchange rate will give rise to a decrease in real wages, thus transferring the workers' income to the capitalists. Consumption expenditure will suffer a reduction, leading to a contraction in domestic demand. As a result of this contractionary effect, the economy will operate at a level of productive capacity utilization that is below normal, as we can see in Figure 15.2.

Second, the devaluation of the exchange rate, by leading to an increase in the income elasticity of exports due to the process of structural change, will speed up the pace of export growth, thus enabling an increase in demand arising from the foreign sector. In the short run, the effect on consumption tends to outweigh the effect on exports, so that the initial impact of the exchange rate devaluation will be a contraction in the level of productive capacity utilization and, consequently, an increase in unemployment. Over time, however, the gradual acceleration in export growth made possible by the change in the productive structure of the economy will make the growth in demand arising from the foreign sector outweigh the contraction in domestic demand, thus leading to a continuous increase in productive capacity utilization. The combined effects of the increases in profit margins and in the productive capacity utilization will lead business enterprises to increase the investment rate, therefore enabling an acceleration of the rate of economic growth.

During the adjustment of the economy to its position of long-term equilibrium, the real exchange rate, after having depreciated from θ_{cc} to θ_*, will show a small appreciation, which is necessary to reach the level compatible with the industrial equilibrium. Therefore, the dynamics of transition points to an *exchange rate overshoot* as a result of implementing the policy of neutralizing the Dutch disease.

The small exchange rate appreciation that follows the exchange rate devaluation resulting from the neutralization of the Dutch disease will return some of the wages the workers lost at the beginning of the process. The recovery of the real wage, although partial, will stimulate the demand for consumption, thus contributing to an increase in the degree of productive capacity utilization and a decrease in the unemployment rate.

The dynamics of the profit rate, of wages' share of the national income, of the degree of capacity utilization, of the real exchange rate, and of the rate of output growth (and of the stock of capital) during the transition to the long-term equilibrium can be seen in Figure 15.3,[4] where u is the level of capacity utilization, $1-\pi$ is the wage share, Θ is the real exchange rate, and g is the growth rate of capital and output.

During the process of adjustment towards long-term equilibrium, the rate of export growth will be accelerating due to the continuous increase in the income elasticity of exports, made possible by the reindustrialization of the economy, which will allow for the export of higher value added goods. At this stage, the acceleration in the pace of export growth is essential to create the demand necessary to increase the investment rate and, consequently, to accelerate the pace of economic growth. It follows, therefore, that the acceleration in the pace of economic growth is *export-led*, but it will be so only during the period of transition

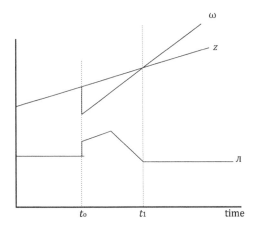

Figure 15.3 Dynamics of real wage rate and profit share after a depreciation of real
          exchange rate

to a new level of exchange rate equilibrium, to a new level or stage of investment,
and to a new level of growth.

Recovery of real wages

What about inflation? How does it behave during the transition? The devaluation of the real exchange rate has an obvious inflationary effect, as long as it
makes it possible to increase the profit margins of business enterprises and leads
to an increase in the prices of the imported inputs in domestic currency. This way,
inflation should increase as a result of a "negative supply shock". The magnitude
and the persistence of the acceleration of inflation will depend on the degree of
indexation of contracts, particularly employment contracts, and the frequency of
adjustments. In a context in which the relevant contracts fully index prices and
wages to past inflation, the "supply shock" will produce a constant increase in the
inflation rate. In this case, the initial acceleration of the inflation rate caused by
the exchange rate devaluation will be automatically transferred to nominal wages,
forcing enterprises to increase the prices of their products so as to keep their profit
margins unchanged. Due to the *exchange rate overshoot*, the real exchange rate
presents a small appreciation after the initial devaluation. Therefore, the economy
will face a sequence of "positive supply shocks", which will lead to a reduction
in the inflation rate. Since the real exchange rate is more depreciated in the final
equilibrium position than in the initial position, it follows that, in a context of full
indexation of prices and wages, the inflation rate at the end of the process will be
higher than at the beginning.

   If the contractual indexation is partial or nonexistent, after the "supply
shock" effect inflation will return to the initial level. Since the real exchange
rate presents a small appreciation during the dynamics of adjustment to the

final equilibrium position, it follows that the inflation rate will be lower at the end of this process. What about wages? We have already said that the initial effect of the exchange rate devaluation will be a reduction in real wages. However, this reduction will be partially reversed during the process of adjustment to the final equilibrium position due to the small exchange rate appreciation that follows the exchange rate devaluation at the beginning of the process. As the economy reindustrializes and growth accelerates, employment and the growth rate of labour productivity increase, due not only to the efficiency gains resulting from static and dynamic economies of scale (the so-called Kaldor–Verdoorn effect) but also to technological innovations incorporated into new machines and equipment resulting from the increase in the investment rate. Since the middle-income economy that we are analyzing has already hit the "Lewis point" and no longer has an "industrial reserve army", the acceleration in the pace of growth of the labour productivity will inexorably lead to an acceleration of the pace of growth of real wages. Consequently, after some time, real wages will recover because now productivity, per capita income, and real wages will be growing faster than they would have if the economy remained in a low-growth trajectory.

The trajectory of inflation and the drop and recovery in real wages are illustrated in Figure 15.3, where ω is the path of the real wage rate considering a depreciation of real exchange rate, z is the path of the real wage rate in the absence of that depreciation and is the path of the rate of inflation. As we can see, real wages are growing at the same pace according to ω and z until time t_o. Then, as a result of real exchange rate depreciation, real wages suddenly fall but start growing at a higher rate than before due to the increase in employment and in the growth rate of productivity. After some time real wages are higher than they would be if the exchange rate had not depreciated. Until time t_o inflation was constant. Then, as a result of the real exchange rate depreciation inflation accelerates. But, due to the absence of indexation, after some time inflation begins to fall and stabilizes at a level lower than before due to the small exchange rate appreciation required to achieve industrial equilibrium after the exchange rate overshoot.

Investment and domestic savings

During the transition to the final equilibrium position there will be, as already seen, an increase in the investment rate. Due to the accounting identity between savings and investment, it follows that there will be a consequent increase in the savings rate. However, the neutralization of the Dutch disease will lead the economy, at the end of the process, to operate in current account surplus, which means that foreign savings will not only decrease but also become negative. It follows that, in the final equilibrium position, domestic savings will be higher than investment, and the country will become a "savings exporter".

The exchange rate devaluation will therefore produce two effects on aggregate savings. First, there will be an increase in the savings rate as a result of the increase in the investment rate. Second, there will be a change in the composition of aggregate savings: The share of domestic savings in the aggregate savings rate will rise, thus reducing the share (which will become negative) of foreign savings.

The change in the composition of aggregate savings results from the effect of the exchange rate devaluation on the functional distribution of income, as we discussed in Chapter 8. As seen in Figure 15.3, the share of wages (of profits) in national income will be lower (higher) at the end of the process of transition of the economy to its long-term equilibrium position (if capital productivity is stable). Since the propensity to consume from wages is greater than the propensity to consume from profits, this redistribution of income in favour of the profits will serve to reduce consumption as a proportion of the national income, thus increasing the domestic savings rate.

Summary

Throughout this chapter, we have used the Keynesian–structuralist model of growth to analyze the economy's transition from a low-growth trajectory, in which the gap between its per capita income and that of the developed countries remains constant over time, to a trajectory of accelerated growth, in which *catching-up* takes place. This transition requires the neutralization of the Dutch disease (and of excessive speculative capital inflows) and a managed devaluation of the exchange rate. The exchange rate devaluation will initially produce a contraction in domestic demand (due to the drop in consumption expenditure) and, consequently, a reduction in the degree of productive capacity utilization and an increase in the unemployment rate. Soon, however, the exchange rate devaluation will lead to a gradual process of structural change with the economy's reindustrialization, which will allow an increase in the income elasticity of exports and a reduction in the income elasticity of imports. In this context, the rate of export growth will accelerate, and the growth in demand arising from the foreign sector will more than compensate for the drop in domestic demand. This way, the degree of productive capacity utilization will gradually increase and, added to the rise in profit margins caused by the exchange rate devaluation, will result in an increase in the investment rate and, therefore, in the pace of growth of real output. The acceleration resulting from the growth rate will be eminently *export-led*.

The transition to accelerated growth is associated with the phenomenon of *exchange rate overshooting*, since the real exchange rate is devalued beyond the level necessary to reach the industrial equilibrium. Consequently, the devaluation of the real exchange rate will be partially reversed during the process of adjustment towards the long-term equilibrium, thus reversing part of the wage loss that took place during the process. At the end of the process of adjustment, real wages will be growing at a higher rate than they would be had the economy remained in the low-growth trajectory. Finally, during the transition to the accelerated growth path, there will be both an increase in the aggregate savings rate and a change in its composition, since the share of domestic savings in total savings will increase, whereas the share of foreign savings will become negative.

Notes

1 This initial situation does not, however, represent a balanced growth path, since the exchange rate overvaluation resulting from the misalignment between the current equilibrium exchange rate and the industrial equilibrium exchange rate causes the productive structure to modify over time, imposing a continuous change in the income elasticities of exports and imports. The initial situation described in Figure 15.1 is just a "temporary equilibrium".

2 This hypothesis is necessary to ensure that, in the initial position of the economy, the current account of the balance of payments is in equilibrium. In this setting, the deficit in the current account – if one exists – will be small and constant as a proportion of GDP. This way, exports and imports of goods and services will be growing at the same rate. Given the income elasticity of imports, this means that, in the initial growth trajectory, imports and exports will be growing at the same pace as GDP.

3 On *overshooting*, see Rudiger Dornbusch (1976).

4 We are supposing, in this case, that capital productivity is stable.

16 Political economy of the once-and-for-all devaluation

The exchange rate plays a fundamental role in economic development because it is the price that coordinates the growth rate of productive capacity (resulting from entrepreneurs' investment decisions) and the growth rate of exports, thus ensuring a long-term growth trajectory in which the external constraint and the productive capacity constraint are satisfied. But, if the economy suffers from the Dutch disease, and if the government adopts a growth with foreign savings policy, or uses the exchange rate to meet inflation targets, or uses exchange rate populism to be re-elected, as usually happens in developing countries, the exchange rate will be chronically overvalued relative to the equilibrium or competitive exchange rate, which is the industrial equilibrium exchange rate, thus resulting in a permanent decrease in the long-term growth rate.

It follows that, in order to ensure the continuity of economic development of a middle-income country, it is essential for the real exchange rate to be kept at a competitive level, that is, at the industrial equilibrium level – the exchange rate level that makes domestic companies that use world state-of-the-art technology competitive. This requires the formation of a developmental political coalition that supports the framing of a national development strategy and, in the context of this strategy, makes it politically possible to adjust the exchange rate towards the equilibrium. This is necessary because the exchange rate has certain effects (discussed in previous chapters) on the real wage that can make it politically infeasible to devalue the exchange rate so as to achieve the industrial equilibrium.

In fact, a devaluation of the real exchange rate will entail, in the short term, a reduction in the real wage, unless capitalists are willing to accept a reduction in mark-ups and, consequently, in their profit margins, and thus not increase their profit rate. Now, the purpose of the exchange rate adjustment is to increase the profit rate, given that, mainly due to the exchange rate overvaluation, the profit rate is depressed and so fails to stimulate investment. But, from this perspective, the phenomenon of real wage stickiness may appear, that is, resistance to the decline of real wages, on account of the indexation of the nominal wages to observed variations in the price level. In this case, the workers are able to prevent devaluations of the nominal exchange rate from causing a devaluation of the real exchange rate and a consequent reduction in the real wage rate. Where real wage resistance occurs, devaluations of the nominal exchange rate will result in a process of acceleration of inflation rather than in actual depreciation, thus blocking the necessary change in the economic policy regime.

The political coalition supporting a competitive exchange rate can be formed as the workers realize that the overvaluation of the real exchange rate is untenable in the long term, so that a drop in the real wage at some point in the future is inevitable, and as they realize that an exchange rate adjustment would enable the economy to grow at a higher rate, thus leading to a greater increase in labour productivity and, therefore, in real wages. Thus, the workers must choose between a higher real wage in the present and, consequently, a lower rate of real wage growth in the future; however, they must accept a lower real wage in the present in exchange for a higher rate of wage growth rate over time.

Why would workers accept a reduction in wages?

Why would the trade unions be willing to accept a reduction in the real wage in order to enable a non-inflationary adjustment in the real exchange rate? The first answer to this question is that the level of the real wage deriving from the exchange rate overvaluation is artificially high and cannot be sustained in the long term. In fact, the exchange rate overvaluation derived from the Dutch disease and from excessive capital inflows will result in a process of increasing deindustrialization of the economy; this will lead to a drop in employment in the industrial sector, which usually offers the best jobs and wages in the economy (along with the modern services sector, whose growth is linked to industrial growth). Ultimately, the economy will fully deindustrialize, becoming a mere producer of natural resource-intensive *commodities* and low-productivity services. This outcome is certainly not in the interests of the working class.

Besides, depending on the degree of exchange rate overvaluation, the economy may also present growing deficits in its current account, which may be untenable in the medium term and give rise to a balance-of-payment crisis. The crisis produces a sudden and violent devaluation of the real exchange rate, generating an instant reduction in the real wage level, which tends to be traumatic for the working class and for all business enterprises whose debts are denominated in a reserve currency. The adjustment of the balance of payments also implies a reduction of domestic demand and consequently, in the short-term, more unemployment and lower real wages. Thus, if the real wage level is not sustainable in the long run, whether due to the risks of deindustrialization of the economy or to the risk of a balance-of-payment crisis, a gradual adjustment in the real wage level (and in the real exchange rate) is certainly in the interest of the working class. Only if trade union leaders were very shortsighted would they oppose the adjustment in the real exchange rate.

There is, however, a second reason why the working class might support a devaluation of the real exchange rate, even with a reduction in the real wage level. The adjustment in the real exchange rate through the neutralization of the Dutch disease makes it possible to increase the growth rate of manufactured exports, which will lead entrepreneurs to increase the rate of capital accumulation and thus to contribute to accelerated economic growth. Due to the incorporation of technical progress into recently produced machines and equipment, and to the existence of static and dynamic economies of scale, the acceleration of economic growth and of capital accumulation will lead to an increase in the pace of growth of labour productivity and employment. As the economy passes the "Lewis point" and, therefore, the tendency for real wages to grow more slowly than productivity is neutralized, the acceleration in the growth rate of labour productivity will be accompanied by faster growth of the real wage. Consequently, the workers will be able to enjoy a higher real wage level in the future if they are willing to accept a reduction in the real wage in the present, in order to enable a non-inflationary adjustment in the real exchange rate.

This reasoning is illustrated in Figure 16.1.

In Figure 16.1 we observe that, up to the moment t_0, the real wage followed a trajectory given by the solid line. On the assumption that the economy in question has already passed the "Lewis point" (so that we can no longer assume an unlimited supply of labour), the growth rate of the real wage up to the moment t_0 will be equal to the rate of labour productivity growth. Due to the exchange rate overvaluation, the economy is growing at a relatively low rate, and therefore the growth of labour productivity and of real wages is also reduced. As an example, let us assume that up to t_0 labour productivity and the real wage grow at the rate of 1 per cent per annum.

At that moment, assume that the government has begun a policy of gradual adjustment in the real exchange rate, in order to eliminate the exchange rate

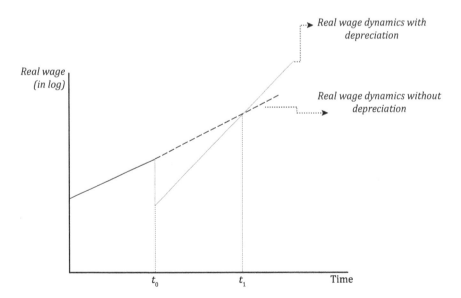

Figure 16.1 Real wage dynamics with and without a depreciation of real exchange rate

overvaluation. Assume, as an example, that this exchange rate overvaluation is 30 per cent. In this context, the real wage will initially be reduced and remain below the trajectory that it would have maintained if the exchange rate had remained at the previous level. Over time, however, the acceleration of economic growth and of the rate of capital accumulation made possible by the exchange rate adjustment will enable labour productivity to grow faster. Since the economy has already passed the "Lewis point", the industrial reserve army will have been exhausted, and the faster growth of productivity will induce an acceleration of the growth of the real wage. Assume that, with the adjustment in the real exchange rate, labour productivity and the real wage may grow at a rate of 3 per cent per annum. Consequently, after some time (between t_0 and t_1 in Figure 16.1), the real wage will be higher than it would have been without the real exchange rate adjustment. In the long term, the workers will benefit from the exchange rate devaluation, because they will be able to enjoy a higher real wage level than if the exchange rate had not been adjusted.

How long would it take for the workers to recover the wage loss due to the devaluation of the real exchange rate? The answer to this question depends on the elasticity of the real wage to the variations in the real exchange rate, on the magnitude of the exchange rate overvaluation, and on the difference between the rate of labour productivity growth before and after the exchange rate. The lower the elasticity of the real wage to the variations in the real exchange rate, the smaller the exchange rate overvaluation will be, and the greater the difference between the rate of labour productivity growth before and after the exchange rate adjustment, the sooner will the workers recover the wage losses due to the devaluation of the real exchange rate.

As an example, assume that the elasticity of the real wage to the exchange rate is equal to -0.2[1] and that the exchange rate overvaluation amounts to 30 per cent. Assume also that the real wage in the year t_0 is equal to 100 and that the growth rate of productivity and of the real wage, in the event that the exchange rate is not adjusted, is equal to 1 per cent per annum. Finally, assume that the exchange rate overvaluation is fully eliminated in t_0 and that subsequently the growth rate of labour productivity and of the real wage increases to 3 per cent per annum.[2] In this setting, the real wage suffers a 6 per cent drop in year t_0, which is fully reversed in two years. Four years after the adjustment in the real exchange rate, the real wage in the scenario with the real exchange rate adjustment is higher than real wage without the real exchange rate adjustment.

If the elasticity of the real wage to the real exchange rate is equal to -0.3, three years would be needed for the workers to recover the wage losses resulting from the exchange rate devaluation, and five years for the real wage with the exchange rate adjustment to be higher than the real wage without the exchange rate adjustment. Yet this is not a long period of time in view of the long-term benefits to the working class.

The numerical example presented above shows that both the wage losses resulting from the exchange rate adjustment and the time horizon involved in the recovery of those losses are reasonable and acceptable to the working class.

A political coalition involving workers, entrepreneurs, and government in favour of an exchange rate policy that promotes a competitive exchange rate is perfectly possible.

Preference for immediate consumption

It is clear by now that a temporary fall in wages, like a temporary rise in inflation, is not an insurmountable obstacle to the neutralization of tendency to the cyclical and chronic overvaluation of the exchange rate. Nevertheless, most developing countries, including the middle-income countries, are often unable to move to a competitive exchange rate. Why do politicians and liberal as well as developmental economists often acquiesce in a chronically overvalued exchange rate?

An extensive economic literature on the political cycle maintains that in all countries, including therefore the rich ones, the heads of government reduce public expenditure at the beginning of their terms of office and increase them at the end, in order to facilitate their re-election. There is also an extensive political literature on political populism, which is generally understood as a direct relationship between the government leader and the masses without the intermediation of ideologically organized political parties and, therefore, as an initial manifestation of popular participation in the government. There are, therefore, two concepts of populism: political populism and economic populism. The concept of economic populism is more recent, and is subdivided into fiscal populism and exchange rate populism. The concept appeared in the 1980s to critically identify the fiscal irresponsibility of several government leaders in the developing countries. However, in addition to this fiscal populism, there is exchange rate populism that is usually ignored by the economic literature: It amounts to promoting or accepting an exchange rate appreciation so that inflation drops and real wages increase. As long as this policy does not cause a financial crisis during the government's term, it will contribute to the re-election of the head of government and of his or her associates.

The usual response of economists to exchange rate populism is not what we might expect. Since a devaluation of the real exchange rate generates a reduction in the real wage, developmental economists often maintain that it is not in the best interest of the working class to join a political coalition in favour of exchange rate devaluation. Besides, they argue that the elasticity of exports to the exchange rate is low. On these grounds, they accept and even legitimize an overvalued exchange rate and chronic current account deficits. The first argument involves the issue of the strength of the preference for immediate consumption; the second argument – that exports are inelastic to the exchange rate – ultimately implies suspending the law of supply and demand. As for the preference for immediate consumption, as we argued in this and previous chapters, the reduction of real wages should be viewed from an appropriate perspective: It is purely temporary because, in the medium and long term, the higher economic growth made possible by the exchange rate devaluation and the ensuing increase of investment opportunities will enable a more pronounced pace of labour productivity growth, due to the existence of static and dynamic economies of scale, thus favouring a faster growth in real wages. Consequently, after some time, the trajectory of the real wage deriving from the exchange rate devaluation would be higher than the trajectory it would follow if the exchange rate remained overvalued.

Liberal economists likewise reject a once-and-for-all devaluation of the exchange rate. Despite their conservative approach, they don't hesitate to cite the reduction of wages, but they object mainly to the inflation that the devaluation will cause. While developmental economists overemphasize the fall in real wages, liberal economists overemphasize the rise of inflation. But, besides these arguments, such economists are ideologically aligned with a liberal class coalition consisting of rentier capitalists and the financiers who manage their wealth, the top executives of multinational enterprises, and foreign interests. This class coalition is interested, on the one hand, in a high real interest rate, which reflects jointly the nominal interest rate and the rate of inflation (the lower the better), and, on the other, in an appreciated local currency and the corresponding current account deficits, which legitimize the loans and direct investments through which rich countries occupy the domestic markets of developing countries.

In thus acquiescing in an overvalued currency, economists manifest a clear preference for immediate consumption. We have already seen that an overvalued exchange rate is associated with a high level of consumption and a low investment rate. Therefore, non-policies, such as the non-neutralization of the Dutch disease, or policies like the growth with foreign savings policy and the use of an exchange rate anchor to control inflation, which we have discussed in this book, reveal a policy-determined preference for immediate consumption. These economists accept as natural a level of consumption that reduces the country's capacity for investment and savings. In addition to this exchange rate populism, there is the fiscal populism manifested in a low rate of savings in the public sector. Public investment should represent between 20 and 25 per cent of total investment, but excessive current expenditures constrain the state to reduce its investments. Some such expenditures, particularly in health care, education, basic income support, and social security, represent relatively efficient (not costly) indirect wages. But other expenditures, particularly those that service the public debt and reflect personnel costs, should be more severely curtailed so as to increase the state's investment capacity.

This policy-determined preference for immediate consumption should not be confused with the marginal propensity to consume that defines the behaviour of economic agents. The preference for immediate consumption is a preference that we deduce from the policies that governments adopt or fail to adopt to depreciate once and for all the exchange rate and, after that, make it float around the industrial equilibrium.

As for current account deficits and the overvalued exchange rate, these economists accept and legitimize them by invoking the foreign constraint argument and the growth with foreign savings policy. Keynesian and developmental economists are more emphatic in their opposition to the temporary fall in wages that a once-and-for-all devaluation would cause, while liberal economists see no problem with current account deficits. Liberal economists associated with the interests of the rentier capitalists are far more emphatic in opposing the temporary increase in inflation. The fundamental concern of the rentier–financier class coalition is high interest rates, and so their absolute priority is the control of inflation: for them, no compromise is admissible between inflation and exchange rate level or between inflation and employment, mainly because, given the nominal rate of interest, a lower inflation rate means a higher real rate of interest.

Summary

Throughout this chapter, we have argued that the formation of a political coalition supporting the adoption of a competitive exchange rate, that is, an exchange rate equal to the industrial equilibrium rate, is entirely feasible. To that end, trade union leaders should realize that (*a*) the real wage level resulting from the exchange rate overvaluation is "artificially" high and untenable in the long term, so that a future drop in the real wage is inevitable in this context; and (*b*) a managed adjustment of the real exchange rate will enable higher economic growth in the long term, thus leading to faster growth of capital accumulation, employment, and labour productivity. As the economy passes the "Lewis point", the faster growth of labour productivity will produce faster growth of the real wage, thus making it possible for the working class to quickly recover the wage losses due to the depreciation of the real exchange rate.

We have shown that the non-neutralization of the tendency to the cyclical and chronic overvaluation of the exchange rate, current account deficits, low inflation rates, and the relatively higher wages that accompany an overvalued currency are consistent with a policy-determined preference for immediate consumption that many economists share, liberal and developmental alike. The alternative policies that we proposed in this book are derived from new developmentalism – the national development strategy that developmental-Keynesian economists have been framing since the beginning of the twenty-first century, and whose theoretical foundation is the developmental macroeconomics that we have sought to present systematically in this book.

Notes

1 According to Oreiro and Marconi (2011), this elasticity held for the Brazilian economy in the period between March 2003 and January 2011.
2 In the example, the wage would be 100.00 in the zero year, whereas the wage with adjustment would to 94.0, but in the following years the latter would increase at a higher rate than the former; already in the fourth year, the wage with adjustment would be higher (105.80) than the wage without adjustment (104.06); and in the tenth year, much higher (110.46 x 126.33).

17 Comparing and summing up

In the time of national developmentalism, countries were poor, and the government was supposed to play a leading role in achieving forced savings and in investing not only in monopolistic industries but also in industries characterized by large economies of scale and so requiring huge amounts of capital. More than half a century later, middle-income countries have already completed, or are in the course of completing, their own capitalist revolutions, which means that the private sector is equipped with a stock of capital and with entrepreneurial, professional, and working-class skills that makes it unnecessary for the state to perform an active role in production. Thus, new developmentalism casts the government in a leading role in terms of ensuring the proper operation of the market and in providing the *general conditions* for capital accumulation, which requires investment in the major social and scientific services (education, health care, and social security) and on the monopolistic industries: transport, communications, and energy infrastructure.

The central difference between the liberal orthodoxy and new developmentalism is the fact that whereas the liberal orthodoxy believes that the market is an institution that coordinates production optimally if it is free of interference, new developmentalism views the market as an efficient institution to coordinate competitive industries, not non-competitive ones, nor the macroeconomic system as a whole. In the macroeconomic realm markets fail to neutralize the tendency to the cyclical and chronic overvaluation of the exchange rate. In this chapter we will compare new developmentalism with liberal orthodoxy. We will discuss, first, the development policies, and second, the macroeconomic policies. Together they form the new developmental strategy, whose theoretical foundation is, broadly, developmental economics and Keynesian macroeconomics, and, specifically, developmental macroeconomics. The two tables and the brief comments to each one are a kind of summary of the main models and policies that we discussed in this book. The number of the comments corresponds to the number of the slots in the tables.

Development strategy

In this section we compare the development strategy of liberal orthodoxy and new developmentalism.

1 Liberal orthodoxy has no room for the nation (the society that shares a sense of common destiny, has a state, and displays a reasonable solidarity when competing internationally), whereas for new developmentalism it plays a major role in economic development. The government is the main institutional instrument of the nation. It is true that, under globalization, nations have become more interdependent, but they have also become more strategic because this interdependence derives from the increased competition among nation-states that characterize globalization.

2 Whereas the liberal orthodoxy envisages all sectors or industries of an economy as well coordinated by the market, new developmentalism divides the economic system into three spheres: (*a*) the competitive sphere formed by an immense number of small and medium-size enterprises, (*b*) the quasi-monopolistic sphere of large infrastructure corporations where economic planning is required, and (*c*) the macroeconomic policy sphere. Whereas liberal orthodoxy acknowledges market failures but asserts that state failures are worse, new developmentalism rejects such pessimism about the possibilities of collective action. It knows that developmental policies may sometime be just wrong, but it is sure that competent policymakers, who know the ability of markets to coordinate the competitive industries, will do better than the market when the industries are non-competitive, or when the problem is to set the macroeconomic prices. Thus, new developmentalism favours the coordination of investments in the non-competitive sector of the economy, and understands that an active macroeconomic policy is required, because, definitively, markets are unable to maintain the macroeconomic prices right. Keynes showed this mainly in relation to the interest rate; developmental macroeconomics tries to do the same thing in relation to the exchange rate. New developmentalism definitely does not believe that it is enough for government to balance its fiscal accounts and to guarantee property rights and contracts; it rejects the neoclassical assumption that once these two things are assured, macroeconomic prices will be right, and stability and growth will follow. Instead, it claims that a steady and self-sustained economic pathway is an illusion, and that government must permanently govern national economies by sound fiscal and financial organization, and by permanently managing and correcting its own policies, while also permanently regulating markets which are not evolving nicely around the equilibrium, as neoclassical economics supposes, but are all the time deviating from equilibrium.

3 Whereas liberal orthodoxy argues for a small state and a strong market, new developmentalism favours a *capable* state – not as a trade-off for a weak market, but as a partner of a *strong* market. If human beings are able to build institutions to regulate human actions, including the market itself, there is no reason why they should not be able to strengthen the government as a normative institution endowed with a sovereign legal system, and as a policymaking organization able to respond to the coordination requirements of the increasingly complex societies of our time. Politics and democracy exist precisely for that purpose – for strengthening the nation and the government, so that

they become effective instruments for achieving the political goals of modern societies. Whereas the liberal orthodoxy supports institutional reforms that reduce the *size* of the state, and ascribes a minimal *role* to it in industrial policy and in investing in infrastructure, new developmentalism supports only those reforms that effectively strengthen not only the market but also the state.

4 Whereas liberal orthodoxy continues to believe that to decide which industries contribute more to economic growth makes no difference in the development process, new developmentalism views that the increase in productivity that characterizes growth is associated with the transference of labour from industries with low value added per capita to industries with higher value added, which use more sophisticated labour, and pay higher wages and salaries. This is the reason why it identifies growth with industrialization, or, in our times of highly sophisticated services, with *productive sophistication*.

5 New developmentalism is not for generalized planning, but strongly favours planning or economic coordination of the *non-competitive*, quasi-monopolistic industries. In this condition (monopoly) the market is obviously unable to exert coordination, and regulatory agencies are not able to act as a proxy for the market.

Table 17.1 Development strategy

	Liberal orthodoxy	New developmentalism/Developmental macroeconomics
1	No role for the nation	Nations are still more strategic in the time of globalization
2	The state is supposed to be small, just to guarantee property rights	The state is supposed to create investment opportunities and invest in infrastructure
3	The state should be small and the market, strong	The market should be strong, the state should be capable and big enough to be a welfare state
4	Economic growth does not require industrialization	Economic growth requires industrialization or productive sophistication
5	No economic planning	Planning limited to the non-competitive industries
6	The government should not invest in any productive activity	The state is supposed to take charge of part of the investment in monopolist projects
7	No industrial policy	Active industrial policy, but separate from the neutralization of the Dutch disease
8	To export commodities (comparative advantages)	To export also manufactured goods. Not export-led, nor wage-led, but balanced strategy
9	For trade and financial liberalization	Only for trade liberalization, provided that the exchange rate is in the industrial equilibrium
10	The key institution is the protection of property rights and contracts	The key institution is a national development strategy including developmental class coalition
11	Inequality favours growth	Growth must be combined with distribution. New developmentalism is a social developmentalism

6 New developmentalism rejects the neoliberal thesis that "the state no longer has resources to invest in infrastructure". It certainly should take charge of part of the required investments. Whether or not the government has resources depends on how much its citizens are ready to pay taxes, and on how much they are ready to sacrifice immediate consumption and accept that the government expends part of the taxes that it collects in productive investments instead of using them to finance the delivery of social services.

7 Whereas the liberal orthodoxy does not identify the industries that should develop and the specific business enterprises the government should strategically support, new developmentalism identifies strongly with industrial policy. It is not, however, thought of as a form of compensating an overvalued currency, as it often was in the past, when industrial policy also involved the neutralization of the Dutch disease. Today, this is not possible.

8 Whereas the liberal orthodoxy asks for "free markets" – in particular for "respect" for the so-called "law" of comparative advantage in international trade – new developmentalism asks for a *capable* government that is able to implement an *active* development policy to change static comparative advantages. It does not reject the existence of comparative advantages, which expresses a smart static syllogism, but since it is not a historical model – since we cannot say that the countries that followed it developed more – new developmentalism rejects its simplistic application to developing countries. Whereas liberal orthodoxy sees no problem in the primarization of countries that cease to neutralize the Dutch disease and implement a competent exchange rate policy, new developmentalism understands that exports are essential to growth, but wants exports of increasingly sophisticated goods, with increasing value added per capita. New developmentalism welcomes the advantage that many developing countries have in exporting commodities, but it bets on the ability of developing countries to export manufactured goods. New developmentalism is not export-led or wage-led. In the short period of transition from the current to the industrial equilibrium, exports will necessarily increase more than wages and consumption. But once a country reaches the industrial equilibrium and, after sometime, we can say that it achieved a reasonable equilibrium in its openness coefficient, the right growth strategy for it is a balanced strategy, which keeps this coefficient constant.

9 New developmentalism is for trade liberalization for middle-income countries provided that the tendency to the cyclical and chronic overvaluation of the exchange rate is neutralized and the exchange rate is floating around the industrial equilibrium. In general, the infant industry argument is not applicable to countries that already have a mature manufacturing industry. But it is strongly against financial liberalization, insofar as accepting it means to renounce capital controls, and, so, to lose control of the exchange rate.

10 Whereas the liberal orthodoxy sees property rights and contracts as the key institutions for growth, new developmentalism asserts that a national development strategy plays this role insofar as it is a cluster of laws, policies, understandings, and values that create investment opportunities for business entrepreneurs.

11 Markets are a clearly unsatisfactory mechanism for distributing income, since they favour the stronger and more capable members. New developmentalism asks for a progressive tax system and an active social policy, which gradually changes the developmental into a social developmental or welfare state. While the liberal orthodoxy seeks to reduce poverty, not to redistribute income, new developmentalism is committed to reducing inequalities. It is true that in the short term the basic policy that it proposes – to move the exchange rate to the industrial equilibrium – implies a reduction in wages and an increase in the profit rate, which is required to motivate business entrepreneurs to invest. In the medium term, however, wages will increase much faster than before the devaluation, and, in addition, the government will have an opportunity to tax rentier capitalists and the high salaries and bonuses of financiers and the top executives of the large multinational corporations – three groups whose incomes cannot be explained by their contribution to the economy.

12 New developmentalism rejects the policy-determined preference for immediate consumption, which is revealed in policymakers' acquiescence in an overvalued currency to avoid temporarily reducing wages, or temporarily increasing inflation.

Macroeconomic policy

Let us now compare liberal-orthodoxy with new developmental macroeconomic policies. Comments corresponding to slots 8 to 12 explain what are the possibly more innovative issues in developmental macroeconomics.

1 For neoclassical economics, savings depend on private frugality. Developmental macroeconomics welcomes frugality, but, according to the key, counterintuitive principle discovered by Keynes, understands that savings depend on private investments and the availability of credit. They depend also on public savings, which open room for public investments without budget deficits.

2 Inflation must be kept under control. Yes, but not by all means; not by transforming the exchange rate into an "anchor" against inflation. This is perverse. Not also by using the prices of state-owned enterprises to hold down inflation; this is equally perverse. Governments must make trade-offs between inflation and growth; central banks must control inflation with interest rate policy, fiscal policy, and macroprudential control of credit. And accept a rate of inflation a little higher than the 3 per cent today aimed by rich countries. After all, inflation is also a means to balance disequilibrium in relative prices, and such imbalance is more frequent in developing countries including middle-income countries.

3 Whereas for liberal orthodoxy the real interest rate should be relatively high (a high nominal rate and a low inflation rate) to avoid "financial repression", or, in other words, to achieve "financial deepening", developmental macroeconomics understands that the real interest rate should vary according to the

central bank's monetary policy around a relatively low level. In rich countries the real interest rate varies around 1 per cent positive; in middle-income countries it should vary around, let us say, 2 per cent.

4 Whereas liberal orthodoxy asserts that central banks should have just one objective (the control of inflation) because it recognizes just one instrument, the interest rate, new developmentalism proposes two objectives: the control of inflation and the maintenance of the exchange rate around the competitive or industrial equilibrium. The one instrument – one goal policy may be "logical" but it is not realistic. The central bank has other instruments besides the interest rate.

5 Whereas liberal orthodoxy acknowledges only two macroeconomic policies – monetary and fiscal policies – new developmentalism affirms emphatically the need of a third macroeconomic policy: exchange rate policy. Whereas for liberal orthodoxy the choice of exchange rate regimes is important, new developmentalism views the radical opposition "fix, or float" as unrealistic. Whereas liberal orthodoxy defends the floating exchange rate regime and calls its management, "dirty floating", developmental macroeconomics defends a *managed floating* regime, which implies (*a*) to neutralize the Dutch disease (which implies the shift of the equilibrium exchange rate from the current to the industrial equilibrium) and (*b*) to conduct an active exchange rate policy aiming to keep the exchange rate floating around the industrial or competitive equilibrium. For less developed countries the alternative of the crawling peg system should not be dismissed.

6 Whereas liberal orthodoxy rejected hastily capital controls in the neoliberal years, but moderated this view after the 2008 Global Financial Crisis, new developmentalism views them as tools of the exchange rate policy. But its objective is *not* to block capital flight, but to avoid excessive capital inflows, which, besides being the origin of balance-of-payment crises, "frequently finance consumption or unsustainable real-estate booms".[1] Capital flights are a problem of financially fragile countries which adopt the growth cum foreign savings policy: their currency gets overvalued, the current account shows a high deficit, and the foreign debt is relatively high.

7 Whereas liberal orthodoxy views some volatility or frequent misalignments as the problem with the exchange rate, the core model of developmental macroeconomics is the tendency to the cyclical and chronic overvaluation of the exchange rate. Misalignments are frequent, but they have a direction.

8 Whereas liberal orthodoxy usually ignores the Dutch disease and explains the lack of growth of natural resource–rich countries with the "natural resource curse", which they identify with rent-seeking or corruption, thus deviating the problem from exchange rate overvaluation, developmental macroeconomics views the Dutch disease as a major benefit when dully neutralized and a real curse when it isn't, and, not denying rent-seeking, takes as synonyms the expressions Dutch disease and natural resource curse in order to avoid the disavowal of the exchange rate overvaluation. The Dutch disease is a major market failure which impedes the transference of labour from low

Table 17.2 Macroeconomic policies compared

Liberal orthodoxy	New developmentalism/Developmental macroeconomics
1 Savings depend on private austerity.	Savings depend on private investments, which depend on the exchange rate and on public savings.
2 Inflation must be kept under control.	Yes, but not with the help of the exchange rate; only with interest rate policy and fiscal policy.
3 The real interest rate should be relatively high to avoid "financial repression".	The level around which the real interest rate will vary should be small.
4 Central banks should have only one objective: the control of inflation.	Central bank should have two objectives: control inflation and competitive exchange.
5 Defends the floating exchange rate regime and rejects exchange rate policy.	Defends a managed floating regime and requires an active exchange rate policy.
6 Rejects capital controls (after the 2008 crisis, opened some room for them).	Capital controls are required, but to avoid capital inflows, not capital flight.
7 The problem with the exchange rate is some volatility.	Its core model is the tendency towards cyclical and chronic overvaluation.
8 The Dutch disease is ignored, and the natural resource curse is associated with corruption.	Its neutralization is required; the natural resource curse is a synonym to it.
9 Sees current account deficits as natural and desirable.	Sees current account surpluses as desirable; they result from neutralizing the Dutch disease.
10 Recommends the growth with current account deficits (foreign savings).	Rejects them; foreign savings don't add to domestic savings, but to consumption.
11 Fiscal responsibility is required.	Yes, fiscal responsibility is required, but also counter-cyclical fiscal policy is required.
12 Explains balance-of-payment crises mainly with budget deficits.	Explains them mainly with current account deficits.

value added to high valued added sophisticated industries, not only the existing ones, but also the potential ones.

9 Whereas liberal orthodoxy views current account deficits as desirable insofar that recommends the growth cum foreign savings policy, which would add to domestic savings, developmental macroeconomics views current *surpluses* as usually desirable, because they necessarily result from the required neutralization of the Dutch disease, and also, as stated in slots 10 and 11, because foreign savings add to consumption rather than to domestic savings, and because they are the cause of balance-of-payment crises. The claim that "capital rich countries should transfer their capitals to capital poor countries" is intuitive, but in this case the counterintuitive claim is true.

10 Whereas liberal orthodoxy recommends growth cum foreign savings policy (current account deficit), because foreign savings would add to domestic savings, developmental macroeconomics rejects this claim because the rate of substitution of foreign for domestic savings is usually high, and, in consequence, foreign savings usually add to consumption and, always, to the foreign debt.

11 Whereas liberal orthodoxy sees fiscal responsibility as its main objective, new developmentalism see it as an important objective, but combined with exchange rate responsibility, which involves a current account surplus when the country has the Dutch disease. Fiscal responsibility means that the country's primary surplus is enough to keep the public debt ratio constant in a satisfactory level and to finance the required public investments. Liberal orthodoxy has only a remedy to macroeconomic disequilibrium – fiscal austerity – whereas new developmentalism acknowledges that fiscal adjustment is required, but combined with a once-and-for-all depreciation of the national currency. Actually, exchange rate responsibility and fiscal responsibility should go hand in hand. The country that neutralizes its Dutch disease, besides portraying a current account surplus (which shows that the private and the state sector together are in the black) should have a budget surplus or, more reasonably, a balanced budget, because when the macroeconomic prices are right, the twin deficits hypothesis holds. There is no reason why the private sector should show a surplus in its financial accounts, while the government, a deficit, if the country portrays a current accounts surplus, which corresponds to the sum of both. Besides, new developmentalism starts from the assumption that the state is the nation's instrument for collective action par excellence. If the government is so strategic, its apparatus must be strong or capable; and for this very reason, its finances must be in balance, i.e., its public debt to GDP ratio must be relatively small and its maturity, long. New developmentalism rejects the misleading notion that growth should be based chiefly on chronic budget deficits – an equivocal but widespread conception wrongly associated with Keynes's thought. It does not view fiscal discipline as a panacea, but strongly favours a balanced budget in normal times. Only when a clear problem of insufficiency of demand is present is an expansive fiscal policy legitimate. In this case, additional expenditures should finance additional investment, not additional consumption. Keynes pointed out the importance of aggregate demand and legitimized resorting to public deficits in recessions, but he never advocated chronic public deficits. He always assumed that a fiscally balanced national economy might, for a brief time, move away from this balance to re-establish employment levels. Notable Latin-American developmental economists as Raúl Prebisch, Ignacio Rangel, and Celso Furtado were Keynesians, and regarded aggregate demand management as an important tool for promoting development. But they never defended chronic budget deficits or fiscal populism, which was always a problem for the countries of that region.

12 Whereas liberal orthodoxy explains financial fragility and financial crisis with budget deficits, developmental macroeconomics explains them with over-valued currency and high current account deficits. Liberal orthodoxy argues that it does not need to focus in the current account because budget deficits imply current account deficits, but the twin deficits hypothesis does not hold when the exchange rate is overvalued. It only holds when the exchange rate is balanced, and that is the reason why exchange rate responsibility and fiscal responsibility must come hand in hand when the economy is balanced and growing satisfactorily.

Note

1 This phrase is from Adair Turner (2014), former Chairman of the United Kingdom Financial Services Authority, in a Project Syndicate column.

References

Acosta, Pablo A., K. K. Emmanuel Lartey and Federico S. Mandelman (2009) "Remittances and the Dutch disease", *Journal of International Economics* 79 (1): 102–116.

Alejandro, Carlos Diaz (1981) "Southern Cone stabilization plans", in W. Cline and S. Weintraub, eds. *Economic Stabilization in Developing Countries*, Washington DC: Brookings Institution.

Aliber, Robert Z. (1987) "Exchange rates", *Palgrave Dictionary of Economics*, London: Macmillan.

Amsden, Alice H. (1989) *Asia's Next Giant*, New York: Oxford University Press.

Bhaduri, Amit and Stephen Marglin (1990) "Unemployment and the real wages: the economic basis for contesting political ideologies", *Cambridge Journal of Economics* 14 (December): 375–393.

Bhalla, Surjit S. (2012) *Devaluing to Prosperity. Misaligned Currencies and Their Growth Consequences,* Washington, DC: Peterson Institute for International Economics.

Blanchard, Olivier (2013, November 27) "Monetary policy will never be the same", *Vox,* available at www.voxeu.org/article/monetary-policy-will-never-be-same.

Bresser-Pereira, Luiz Carlos (1986) *Lucro, Acumulação e Crise [Profit, Accumulation and Crisis].* São Paulo: Editora Brasiliense. English version available at www.bresserpereira.org.br.

Bresser-Pereira, Luiz Carlos (2002) "Financiamento para o subdesenvolvimento: o Brasil e o Segundo Consenso de Washington" [Finance for underdevelopment: Brazil and the second Washington consensus], in Ana Célia Castro, org. Desenvolvimento em Debate: Painéis do Desenvolvimento Brasileiro, vol. 2. Rio de Janeiro: Mauad/BNDES: 359–398.

Bresser-Pereira, Luiz Carlos (2006) "New developmentalism and conventional orthodoxy", *Economie Appliquée* 59 (3): 61–94.

Bresser-Pereira, Luiz Carlos (2007 [2009]) *Developing Brazil: Overcoming the Failure of the Washington Consensus*, Boulder, CO: Lynne Rienner Publishers, 2009. Original publication in Brazil, 2007.

Bresser-Pereira, Luiz Carlos (2008) "The Dutch disease and its neutralization: a Ricardian approach", *Brazilian Journal of Political Economy* 28 (1): 47–71.

Bresser-Pereira, Luiz Carlos (2009 [2010]) *Globalization and Competition*, Cambridge, UK: Cambridge University Press, 2010. Originally published in French, 2009.

Bresser-Pereira, Luiz Carlos (2013) "The value of the exchange rate and the Dutch disease", *Brazilian Journal of Political Economy* 33 (3): 371–387.

Bresser-Pereira, Luiz Carlos and Yoshiaki Nakano (2003) "Economic growth cum foreign savings?", *Brazilian Journal of Political Economy* 22 (2): 3–27. In Portuguese, in the printed edition; in English, in the journal's website: www.rep.org.br.

Calvo, Guillermo, Leonard Leiderman and Carmen Reinhart (1995) "Capital Inflows to Latin America with Reference to the Asian Experience", in Edwards, Sebastian

Capital Controls, Exchange Rates, and Monetary Policy in the World Economy, Cambridge, UK: Cambridge University Press, 1995: 339–380.

Carvalho, Fernando Cardim de (1992) *Mr. Keynes and the Post Keynesians*. Cheltenham: Elgar Press.

Chang, Ha-Joon (2002) *Kicking Away the Ladder*, London: Anthem Press.

Chatterji, Monojit and Simon Price (1988) "Unions, Dutch disease and unemployment". *Oxford Economic Papers* 40 (2): 302–321.

Chenery, Hollis B. and Michael Bruno (1962) "Development alternatives in an open economy: The case of Israel", *Economic Journal*: 79–103.

Collier, Paul (2007) *The Bottom Billion: Why the Poorest Countries Are Failing and What Can Be Done About It*, Oxford: Oxford University Press.

Collier, Paul and Anke Hoeffler (2004) "Greed and grievance in civil war", *Oxford Economic Papers* 54: 563–595.

Corden, W. M. (1984) "Booming sector and Dutch disease economics: survey and consolidation", *Oxford Economic Papers* 36 (3): 359–380.

Corden, W. M. (1994) *Economic Policy, Exchange Rates and the World Economy*, 2nd edition, Oxford: Clarendon Press.

Corden, W. M. and J. P. Neary (1982) "Booming sector and de-industrialization in a small open economy", *Economic Journal* 92 (368): 825–848.

Davidson, Paul (1986) "Finance, funding, saving and investment", *Journal of Post-Keynesian Economics* 9 (1): 101–110.

Dornbusch, Rudiger (1976) "Expectations and exchange rate dynamics", *Journal of Political Economy* 84 (6): 1161–1176.

Dutt, Amitava Krishna and Jaime Ros eds. (2003) *Development Economics and Structuralist Macroeconomics*, Cheltenham: Edward Elgar.

Dutt, Amitava Krishna and Jaime Ros (2007) "Aggregate demand shocks and economic growth", *Structural Change and Economic Dynamics* 18 (1): 75–99.

Edwards, Sebastian (1988) *Exchange Rate Misalignments in Developing Countries*, Baltimore: John Hopkins University Press.

Eichengreen, Barry (2004) "Can emerging markets float? Should they adopt inflation targeting?", in Mathias Vernengo, ed. (2004) *Financial Integration and Dollarization: No Panacea*, Cheltenham: Edward Elgar.

Eichengreen, Barry and David Leblang (2003) "Capital account liberalization and growth: Was Mr. Mahathir right?", *The International Journal of Finance and Economics* 8 (3): 205–224.

Flood, Robert P. and Peter M. Garber (1984) "Collapsing exchange-rate regimes: some linear examples", *Journal of International Economics* 17: 1–13.

Franco, Gustavo H. B. (1999) O Desafio Brasileiro, São Paulo: Editora 34.

Furtado, Celso (1963) *Plano Trienal de Desenvolvimento Econômico e Social (1963–1965) [The Three Years Plan of Economic and Social Development (1963–1965)]*. Rio de Janeiro: Síntese.

Furtado, Celso (1966 [1970]) *Obstacles to development in Latin America*. New York: Anchor Books-Doubleday. Original Brazilian publication, 1966.

Gala, Paulo (2006) Política cambial e macroeconomia do desenvolvimento [Exchange rate policy and development macroeconomics], São Paulo: São Paulo School of Economics of Getulio Vargas Foundation, PhD dissertation, May 2006.

Galbraith, John Kenneth (1954) *The Great Crash, 1929,* Boston: Houghton Mifflin.

Gerschenkron, Alexander (1962) *Economic Backwardness in Historical Perspective: A Book of Essays*. New York: Praeger.

Harcourt, G. C. (1972) *Some Cambridge Controversies in the Theory of Capital*. Cambridge, UK: Cambridge University Press.

Harrod, Roy F. (1939) "An essay in dynamic theory", *Economic Journal*: 14–33.

Hirschman, Albert O. (1981) *Essays in Trespassing*, Cambridge, UK: Cambridge University Press: 1–24.

Johnson, Chalmers (1982) *MITI and the Japanese Miracle*, Stanford: Stanford University Press.

Kaldor, Nicholas (1956) "Alternative theories of distribution", *Review of Economic Studies* 23 (2): 83–100.

Kaldor, Nicholas (1957) "A model of economic growth", *Economic Journal* 67 (268): 591–624.

Kaldor, Nicholas (1978) *Further Essays on Economic Theory,* London: Duckworth: 100–138.

Karl, Terry Lynn (1997) *The Paradox of Plenty*, Berkeley: The University of California Press.

Keynes, John Maynard (1936) *The General Theory of Employment, Interest and Money,* London: Macmillan.

Kindleberger, Charles P. (1978) *Manias, Panics, and Crashes*, New York: Basic Books.

Kohli, Atul (2004) *State-Directed Development*, Cambridge, UK: Cambridge University Press.

Krugman, Paul (1979) "A model of balance of payment crises", *Journal of Money, Credit, and Banking* 11: 311–325.

Krugman, Paul (1998) "What happened to Asia?", available at http://web.mit.edu/krugman/www/DISINTER.html.

Larsen, E. R. (2004) "Escaping the resource curse and the Dutch disease? When and why Norway caught up with and forged ahead of its neighbors", Discussion paper 377, Statistics Norway, Research Department, May 2004.

Lederman, Daniel and William F. Maloney, eds. (2007) *Natural Resources: Neither Curse nor Destiny*. Washington and Stanford: World Bank and Stanford University Press.

León-Ledesma, M. A. (2002), "Accumulation, innovation and catching–up: an extended cumulative growth model". *Cambridge Journal of Economics* 26 (2): 201–216.

Lewis, Arthur W. (1954) "Economic development with unlimited supply of labour", *The Manchester School* 22: 139–91.

Libânio, Gilberto A. (2009) "Aggregate demand and the endogeneity of the natural rate of growth: evidence from Latin American economies", *Cambridge Journal of Economics* 33 (5): 967–984.

List, Friedrich (1846 [1999]) *National System of Political Economy*. Roseville, CA: Dry Bones Press, 1999. Originally published in German, 1846.

McCombie, J.S.L. and M. Roberts (2002) "The role of the balance of payments in economic growth" in Setterfield, M., ed. *The Economics of Demand-Led Growth*. Cheltenham: Edward Elgar: Aldershot.

McKinnon, Ronald (1973) *Money and Capital in Economic Development.* Washington, DC: Brookings Institution.

Marconi, Nelson and Marcos Rocha (2012) "Taxa de câmbio, comércio exterior e desindustrialização precoce – o caso brasileiro", *Economia e Sociedade* 21 (número especial): 853–888.

Minsky, Hyman P. (1972 [1982]) "Financial instability revisited", in Hyman P. Minsky (1982) *Inflation, Recession and Economic Policy*, Armonk: Whetsheaf Books: 117–161. Originally published in 1972.

Minsky, Hyman P. (1975) *John Maynard Keynes*, New York: Columbia University Press.

Minsky, Hyman P. (1986) *Stabilizing an Unstable Economy*. New Haven, CT: Yale University Press.

Miranda, Mauro Costa (2006) "Crises cambiais e ataques especulativos no Brasil", *Economia Aplicada* 10 (2): 287–301.

Montiel, Peter J. (2003) *Macroeconomics in Emerging Markets*, Cambridge, UK: Cambridge University Press.

Moreno-Brid, J. C. (1998–99) "On capital flows and the balance-of-payments-constrained growth model", *Journal of Post Keynesian Economics* 21 (2): 283–298.

Neftci, Salih (2002) "Excessive variation in risk factor correlation and volatilities", Computing in Economics and Finance, Working Paper 254, Society for Computational Economics.

Obstfeld, M. (1986), 'Rational and Self-Fulfilling Balance of Payments Crises', *American Economic Review* 76: 72–81.

Obstfeld, M. (1994), 'The Logic of Currency Crises', *Cahiers Economiques et Monetaires* 43, Bank of France: 189–213.

Oreiro, J. L. (2000) "O debate entre Keynes e os 'clássico' sobre os determinantes da taxa de juros: uma grande perda de tempo?" [The debate between Keynes and the 'classic' on the determinants of interest rates: a big waste of time?], *Brazilian Journal of Political Economy* 20 (2): 95–119.

Oreiro, J. L. (2004) "Accumulation regimes, endogenous desired rate of capacity utilization and income distribution", *Investigación Económica*, Vol. LXIII (248).

Oreiro, J. L. and N. Marconi (2011) "Câmbio: adiar o ajuste pode sair caro". Valor Econômico, São Paulo: A15, 13 mai.

Oreiro, J. L., G. J. Silva and W. Fortunato (2008) "Gasto publico com infraestrutura, acumulação privada de capital e crescimento de longo prazo: uma avaliação teórica e empírica para o Brasil (1985–2003)", XIII Encontro Nacional de Economia Política, João Pessoa.

Oreiro, José Luís and Luiz Fernando de Paula (2009) "O novo desenvolvimentismo e a agenda de reformas macroeconômicas para crescimento sustentado com estabilidade de preços e equidade social" [New developmentalism and the agenda of macroeconomic reforms for sustained development with prices stability and social equity], copy, version dated October 19, 2009.

Ötker, Inci and Ceyla Pazarbasioglu (1995) "Speculative attacks and currency crises: the Mexican experience", IMF Working Paper 95/112, Washington: Fundo Monetário Internacional.

Palma, Gabriel (2005) "Four sources of 'de-industrialization' and a new concept of Dutch Disease", in José Antonio Ocampo, ed. (2005) *Beyond reforms: structural dynamics and macroeconomic vulnerability*, Stanford, CA: Stanford University Press and World Bank.

Palma, Gabriel (2013) "Desindustrialización, desindustrialización 'prematura' y un Nuevo concepto del 'sindrome holandés'", Cambridge, UK: School of Economics of the University of Cambridge, copy.

Park, M. S. (2000). "Autonomous demand and the warranted rate of growth", *Contributions to Political Economy* 19 (1): 1–18.

Paula, Luiz Fernando de (2006) "Repensando o desenvolvimentismo" [Rethinking developmentalism], *São Paulo em Perspectiva* 20 (3): 47–58.

Prado Jr., Caio (1945 [1956]) *História Econômica do Brasil [Economic History of Brazil]*. São Paulo: Editora Brasiliense, fourth impression. First impression, 1945.

Przeworski, A. (2001) "How many ways can be third?", in A. Glyn, ed., *Social Democracy in Neoliberal Times: The Left and Economic Policy Since 1980*, Oxford: Oxford University Press: 312–33.

Robischek, W. (1981) "Some reflections about public debt management". Santiago do Chile: Banco Central del Chile, Estudios Monetários VII.

Rodrik, Dani (1998) "Who needs capital-account convertibility?", in Stanley Fischer et al. *Should IMF Pursue Capital-Account Convertibility?* Princeton, NJ: Princeton University Press: Essays in International Finance no. 207, May 1998: 55–65.

Rodrik, Dani, Arvind Subramanian and Francesco Trebbi (2004) "Institutions rule: the primacy of institutions over geography and integration in economic development", *Journal of Economic Growth* 9 (6): 131–165.

Rosenstein-Rodan, Paul (1943) "Problems of industrialization in Eastern Europe and South-Eastern Europe", *Economic Journal* 53, June 1943, 202–211.

Sachs, Jeffrey D. and Andrew M. Warner (1999) "The big push, natural resource booms and growth", *Journal of Development Economics* 59 (1): 43–76.

Sachs, Jeffrey D. and Andrew M. Warner (2001) "The curse of natural resources", *European Economic Review* 45: 827–838.

Sala-i-Martin, Xavier and Arvind Subramanian (2003) "Addressing the natural resource curse: an illustration from Nigeria", Working Paper 9084, Cambridge, MA: National Bureau of Economic Research.

Sargent, Thomas J. (1987). *Macroeconomic Theory*. New York: Academic Press.

Setterfield, M. (1997) *Rapid Growth and Relative Decline*. Oxford: St. Martin Press.

Shaw, Edward (1973) *Financial Deepening in Economic Development*, Oxford: Oxford University Press.

Solow, Robert M. (1956) "A contribution to the theory of economic growth", *Quarterly Journal of Economics* 70: 65–94.

Solow, Robert M. (1957) "Technical Change and the Aggregate Production Function", *Review of Economy and Statistics* 70: 65–94.

Studart, Rogério (2004) "Integrating uneven partners: the destabilizing effects of financial liberalization and internationalization of Latin American economies", in Mathias Vernengo, ed. (2004) *Financial Integration and Dollarization: No Panacea*, Cheltenham: Edward Elgar.

Tavares, Maria da Conceição (1963 [1972]) "Auge e declínio do processo de substituição de importações no Brasil". [Peak and decline of the process of import substitution] In M. C. Tavares *Da Substituição de Importações ao Capitalismo Financeiro [From import substitution to financial capitalism]*, Rio de Janeiro: Zahar Editores. Original publication in Spanish, 1963.

Taylor, John B. (1993) "Discretion versus Policy Rules in Practice", *Carnegie-Rochester Series on Public Policies* 39: 195–214.

Taylor, Lance (1983) *Structuralist Macroeconomics*. New York: Basic Books.

Taylor, Lance (1988) *Varieties of Stabilization Experience*. Oxford: Oxford University Press.

Taylor, Lance (1991) *Income Distribution, Inflation, and Growth*. Cambridge, MA: The MIT Press.

Taylor, Lance (2004) *Reconstructing Macroeconomics*. Cambridge, UK: Cambridge University Press.

Thirlwall, A. (1979) "The balance of payments constraint as an explanation of international growth rates differences", *Banca Nazionale del Lavoro Quarterly Review* 32 (128): 45–53.

Thirlwall, A. (1997). "Reflections on the concept of balance-of-payments-constrained growth rates", *Journal of Post Keynesian Economics* 19 (3): 377–385.

Thirlwall, A. (2001). "The relation between the warranted growth rate, the natural growth rate and the balance of payments equilibrium growth rates", *Journal of Post Keynesian Economics* 24 (1): 81–88.

Thirlwall, A. P. (2002). *The Nature of Economic Growth*. Cheltenham: Edward Elgar: Aldershot.

Torvik, Ragnar (2001) "Learning by doing and the Dutch disease", *European Economic Review* 45 (2001): 285–306.

Wade, Robert (1990) *Governing the Market*, Princeton, NJ: Princeton University Press.

Weiss, Linda (1998) *The Myth of the Powerless State*, Ithaca. NY: Cornell University Press.

Williamson, John (1990) "The progress of policy reform in Latin America", in John Williamson, ed. *Latin American Adjustment: How Much Has Happened?* Washington, DC: Institute for International Economics: 353–420.

Index